A MAN ABROAD

Angus Rich

Published in Australia in 2018 by Angus Rich

Email: angus_rich@yahoo.com

ISBN 9780648445500 (paperback)

A catalogue record for this book is available from the National Library of Australia

To my mother, Flick

Contents

Acknowledgements

Thank you to my mother, Flick, for your constant feedback and encouragement to believe in myself enough to put these words on the page. It was from you that I inherited my love of travel.

Thank you to my editor, Scott Forbes, and book designer, Kirsty Ogden, for your practically and guidance through what was, at first, a daunting process for me.

Introduction

I first travelled when I was eighteen months old, my parents taking my sisters and me all the way from New Zealand to England for three months to stay with my grandparents and other relatives. The fact that I had parents who roamed so widely and family so globally spread suggests that the desire to travel runs in my blood; whatever the case, I've been inclined to wander ever since: family trips during school and university holidays, group tours and solo adventures, ski trips with friends.

Travel is intoxicating and something I love, a chance to escape the humdrum of everyday life and expand my horizons; savour the anticipation of the unknown; see things that are straight out of the movies or the Bible, places where epic wars and battles once raged and mighty empires ruled. Experiencing different climates, extraordinary natural wonders and exotic cultures that make me question my beliefs and outlook in turn teaches me about myself. Travel is exciting and fun, a priceless education offering challenges that a day job could never provide, and it deepens one's appreciation of life. The inspirational travel writer Bill Bryson sums it up well: "To my mind, the greatest reward and luxury of travel is to be able to experience everyday things as if for the first time, to be in a position in which almost nothing is so familiar it is taken for granted."

Thus was born *A Man Abroad*. After a business I began failed to work out, my life became an ongoing series of short-term jobs, and I was repeatedly in and out of work. So I decided to turn this lack of continuity into an opportunity and made the decision to spend two months in Europe. I'd travel to places that I hadn't managed to see during an earlier two-year sojourn in London and which, in the five years since my return to Australia, I had been yearning to visit.

Relishing the prospect, I planned an ambitious itinerary for a solo adventure: nineteen cities in ten countries. After a stopover in Singapore, I'd visit some old haunts in London while spending time with my beloved Londoner aunt, then cross the English Channel to traverse Continental Europe on high-speed trains with a Eurail Pass.

A Man Abroad is a memoir of those two months on the Continent, a journey that also allowed me to realise my long-held ambition to be an author. This is the book I always felt destined to write. I want to take you, the reader, with me as I try to capture the spirit of this personal journey, my curiosities, the ups and downs of solo travel, exotic locations, fascinating history, world-beating art, architectural wonders, important religious sites and relics. But my story is also about the people I meet along the way, including fellow Aussies, and the completely unexpected and random encounters just waiting round almost any street corner in an unfamiliar place.

It's a journey that takes in Paris's famous Moulin Rouge, Flamenco dancing in Andalusia and that region's fascinating Moorish history, theatre in London, bustling and frenetic markets, Spain's charming Jewish quarters, Monte Carlo's casino, Budapest's famous public baths and "ruin pubs", scenic city squares, Switzerland's serene lakes and the mighty Alps – the list goes on and on.

My motivation for writing this travel memoir is for you to enjoy visiting these places in my company and experience what I saw and felt. So I urge you to read on – and enjoy the ride!

One

Singapore Slings

I thank the taxi driver as he drops me off at Brisbane International Airport. Two days prior, I was staring at my work computer, doing spreadsheets, journal entries, financial reports, tax returns – dry stuff indeed! Forty years old, unmarried, no kids, my career affected by the "global financial crisis", and living back at home while renting out my apartment to pay the mortgage, I'd become officially a "free man", or so my work colleagues were telling me.

For the next two uninterrupted months, however, this man of leisure is going to travel Europe, free of the daily grind of work. The "bucket list" will get extensively ticked off in cities in ten different countries: Singapore, England, France, Belgium, Germany, Switzerland, Austria, Hungary, Spain and Portugal – quite a list! Not surprisingly for an obsessive accountant-planner, every hotel has been pre-booked, except for the last couple of days in Spain before flying home.

As a result of the weak Euro economy, there have been plenty of good deals available on hotels, especially in Portugal and Spain, members of the so-called "PIIGS" (Portugal, Italy, Ireland, Greece and Spain) nations in the European Union. My NAB Traveller card is loaded with funds transferred at the handsome exchange rate of 80 Euro cents to the Aussie dollar. When last in Europe six years ago, the rate was 50 Euro cents. The plan is to eat, drink and shop well.

In excited anticipation, I reread parts of Lonely Planet's *Western Europe* guide in the departure lounge, before posting the obligatory Facebook update: "In the Brisbane Airport departure lounge. Two months in Europe awaits!" The post is followed by a barrage of well-wishing comments and "likes". I plan to share photos galore with these friends while taking time off life's treadmill.

Though hesitant about travelling alone for two months, I know civilised Europe well, having previously visited the Continent on coach tours (which I found to be restrictive at times) as well as weekend breaks while living in London. I'm an experienced traveller in general, having been born in New Zealand before moving to Australia as a child, with most of my relatives living in England. My family is an intrepid clan, and we spent plenty of Christmases with relatives in England while I was growing up. I've also been lucky enough to visit Africa, much of Asia, Europe (especially the UK), India, east and west-coast USA and Egypt. However, each of these trips was only a few weeks at most, so a continuous two months in Europe will be a bit of a luxury.

For the first time, I have opened a Skype account, and I have installed the software on my new iPad, a gift for my fortieth birthday. Skype calls made using hotel Wi-Fi will help me keep in touch with home, and thereby prevent too much solitary introspection.

I browse the duty-free stores, wondering as always why anyone would spend three hundred dollars on a pair of sunglasses? There is an R.M. Williams Outfitter store, selling the company's world-famous, high-quality "craftsmen" boots, which are popular with Brits returning home from holidays Down Under. I buy a bottle of Wild Turkey bourbon, as I know the highly taxed alcohol in Singapore is very expensive.

It is soon time to board Qantas flight QF51 to Singapore's Changi International Airport. I don't enjoy long flights. My generous, stocky build finds little comfort in Economy class seats and my insomniac tendencies make it near-impossible for me to sleep en route. Fortunately, this flight departs at lunchtime and arrives mid-evening in Singapore.

It's not long before the Boeing 747 is at 40,000 feet above the arid centre of Australia. I vividly remember returning five years ago from living in London, flying over this region and being gobsmacked at the sheer emptiness of it all. Having just spent two years in leafy England, the comparison was stark indeed. The desert seems to go on for ever and ever.

It makes me think of school history lessons about famous explorers like Burke and Wills, setting off into the outback with naïve courage to explore for king and country, or maybe just personal glory, then getting lost and perishing. With its extraordinary range of flora and fauna, much of it adapted to survive the dryness and heat, Australia must have fascinated Charles Darwin. That stark outback environment has been used as the perfect backdrop for films set on the planet Mars, as well as many classic Australian films, including *Gallipoli* and *Mad Max*. Farmers must have a real calling to operate in these conditions. The irony of course is that Australia is one of the most urbanised countries on the planet.

Breaking away from the mainland, the plane begins flying over the politically contentious waters of the Timor Sea, plied by the boats of people smugglers. After a B-grade movie and a typically bland meal, followed by a dip into the Tim Winton novel *Cloudstreet*, Singapore soon beckons on the TV flight monitor. It's 7 pm but the sun is far from setting. Singapore is geographically a small place, and as yet there are no signs of civilisation from the air as we fly over plenty of Indonesia's seventeen thousand islands.

Then I begin to see the ships. Soon more and more ships, seemingly all lined up, up to 50 kilometres from our destination. Dozens become hundreds, maybe even thousands! They advance like clockwork on the sea below, directed by unseen ship traffic controllers and smart computers. What do they contain? Some seem to be LNG carriers, with their massive storage tanks resembling enormous bubbles. Others are super-tankers containing thousands of tightly packed and sealed crates. In our globalised economy, the average middle-class Western home is adorned with cheap furniture and other foreign-made goods, thanks to cost-effective twenty-first-century shipping practices and technology. Their efficiency ensures that the shipping price seldom makes up more than one per cent of the final price. Half of the planet's annual supply of crude oil is transhipped through Singapore, which explains why the Singapore Tapis index is so commonly quoted in stock market news.

Yet other vessels, I imagine, are filled to the brink with cars on transit to the ever-expanding Chinese middle class. Singapore was the world's busiest port in terms of total cargo tonnage until 2005 and has utilised this to help create its high living standards. It is a truly great trading nation, as evidenced by what I can now see below. The Port of Shanghai has since taken the mantle of the world's busiest port, though, as a result of the insatiable Chinese economic growth.

The plane lands at Changi, which has won the title of "world's best airport" many times in recent years. I make my way through passport control to the luggage pickup area. I love Asia and am fortunate to have visited the great far-eastern metropolises of Hong Kong, Bangkok and Ho Chi Minh City. However, when I was last in Bangkok, it struck me as somewhat dirty, loud and sleazy. I have the opposite expectation for Singapore.

Approaching the taxi rank, I take comfort that no taxi driver here is likely to rip me off, as can happen to tourists in some cities. What also hits me as I exit the terminal is the humidity. Even having lived in Brisbane most of my life, I've still never become accustomed to the humidity of a subtropical summer. Unfortunately, the hotel I've booked doesn't have a pool, but then it didn't cost me much, and you get what you pay for in life.

I am soon greeted by a friendly taxi driver with a wide smile on his face, the kind that says "welcome to my home". Looking back on my Asian travels, I have memories of mostly kind, friendly interactions with locals. Perhaps the prevalence of Buddhism encourages Asian people to take the good and the bad in life and just "roll with it". Most are also very respectful towards Westerners.

I tend to mind my own business in taxis, so I'm pleasantly surprised when the cabbie follows his smile with a spontaneous welcome-to-Singapore promotional speech. As we set off, I see that the roads are efficient and uncluttered, and he explains that in Singapore just to be permitted the privilege of buying a car you have to pay an upfront cost of around fifty thousand Singapore dollars every ten years for a Certificate of Entitlement – hence the lack of traffic and a preference for luxury cars. I also learn that 80 per cent of Singaporeans live in government housing, irrespective of income or ethnic background, in a religiously and ethnically diverse society. In some kind of utopian ideal, recognising and maintaining cultural differences is actively encouraged. Singapore has a distinct and eclectic society, stable government and very low crime levels. It also has some of the most varied menus in the world, and locals like to eat out rather than cook at home.

The driver points out some famous landmarks and popular night spots and then, at the end of that quick lesson in politics, culture, economics and geography, we arrive at my Chinatown hotel. He's a breath of fresh air, so I give him a good tip.

I'm in a very happy mood as I enter the hotel reception. The staff welcome me to the hotel and I feel somewhat important when they inform me I've been upgraded to an executive room. "Great," I say. But next I'm asked whether I would like to pay by credit card or cash. This was the first hotel I booked after purchasing my airfare a few months ago, and I'm certain I've already paid.

Suddenly feeling tired, I ask, "Are you certain about that?" The receptionists' English is slightly patchy. I then recall reading some reviews on hotels.com that said the reception service was poor at this hotel, and I start to wonder. Of course, you almost expect to be ripped off at some point while travelling abroad, but not this early! I ask them to please check their records. They point out to me that it says on my printed booking receipt "full payment on arrival".

The female staff member then phones hotels.com customer service and their information is corroborated. I then hand over my Visa card as they accept my apology, telling me not to worry about the "minor misunderstanding". Thus I relearn one of the first lessons of travel: be patient!

Next morning, while exiting the hotel for my first day of sightseeing, I apologise to reception one last time. No meals are on offer in the hotel, so I exit into the humidity to find somewhere for breakfast. At the corner of the block I discover the Chinatown MRT station. In Singapore, close access to the underground MRT transport system is important, and in my case it's less than 100 metres.

I take the train from Chinatown to Promenade station, en route to the Singapore Flyer. Completed in 2008, the "flyer" is the tallest Ferris wheel in the world at 165 metres, 30 metres higher than the London Eye. It is a similar design to the London landmark, which was built to mark the advent of the new millennium. These giant "eyes" have proved so popular they now appear in cities all over the world. The Singapore wheel's views are supposed to extend to 45 kilometres. However, I'm more interested in seeing from on high the reclaimed land of Marina Bay and the futuristic Gardens by the Bay nature park. Originally the wheel was built to rotate counter-clockwise, but its direction was reversed on the advice of feng shui masters.

I already printed my ticket at home and can see the flyer above, but I soon get lost in the shopping mall below. Eventually, once I make my way into one of its twenty-eight large air-conditioned capsules, there's only me and a couple inside. I think of the Wheel of Brisbane, which is struggling, and wonder if this one is more successful financially. The London Eye may have been a runaway success, but it has the great advantage of views over the Houses of Parliament and London's historic skyline.

All up, it takes half an hour to do a full spin. The original architecture of the Marina Bay Sands resort is striking, with the world's highest "infinity pool" atop, and our perspective on it changes as the Flyer rotates. Opened in 2010, and an amazing architectural achievement, the Sands simply says, "Build it and they will come", to quote the Kevin Costner film *Field of Dreams*. Next to the Sands is the ArtScience Museum, shaped like a lotus flower opening. In the near distance are the skyscrapers of downtown Singapore, plain and tired in comparison.

At the Flyer's peak, the view opens up to the state of the art Gardens by the Bay, which occupy 100 hectares of reclaimed land. The two giant glass structures, side by side, of the Flower Dome and Cloud

Forest wouldn't look out of place in a Star Wars film. Close by the domes stand the "Supertrees", tree-like structures rising between 25 and 50 metres tall. Their designers took inspiration from the film *Avatar.* Costing around $1 billion to construct, the gardens also say, "Build it and they will come." It is also fascinating to look eastwards towards the ocean, where the hundreds of containerships are lined up awaiting entry to the port.

Planning on seeing the Gardens tomorrow, I decide to seek out the famous ethnic neighbourhood of Little India, only a short MRT trip away. As a result of the British Raffles Plan of Singapore, a policy of segregation in the early nineteenth century, competition for land escalated, and Tamils of Indian, Sri Lankan and Malaysian descent moved into what became Little India, located east of the Singapore River.

The Little India area is reported to have developed around a former settlement of Indian Convicts. Its proximity to the Serangoon River originally made it attractive for raising cattle, and trade in livestock thrived. Eventually, other economic activities developed and, by the turn of the twentieth century, it was a busy ethnic Indian neighbourhood. The district is more commonly called "Tekka" by the local Tamil community and has kept its bygone-era character, remaining distinctly un-Singaporean, with an appeal of its own.

Emerging from the MRT into bustling Buffalo Road, I proceed past street facades, produce shops and Hindu shrines and stalls. It resembles any one of hundreds of streets I'd ventured through in India six years before, although India was grittier and more chaotic. Especially familiar are the symbolic flowers on sale, used to make garlands of lotus and jasmine for purity and yellow marigold for peace. Down a narrow side street off Buffalo Road is the well-known Tan House, or Residence of Tan Teng Niah, a colourful and vibrant building. The history of this house goes back to 1900, when Tan Teng Niah, who was one of the few Chinese businessmen in Little India, built it for his wife.

Where Buffalo Road ends, I enter the Tekka Centre wet market, where locals buy fresh produce in the mornings. Now it's mid-afternoon, there is little action, with only a few locals sitting around. Inside the market, however, intense aromas of spices, yoghurts and halal meats linger, as well as, to my personal distaste, the pungent smell of seafood. It is unfortunate that I have come at the quiet time of day. In a few more hours the market's restaurants, with their cheap plastic chairs, will come to life again. The Tekka markets are best experienced early in the morning for the market itself or at night for a cheap and tasty meal in the unique Little India atmosphere.

I continue on south to Serangoon Road, the district's main commercial thoroughfare, lined with stores selling saris, jewellery, Indian sweets, crafts, cheap electronics and all kinds of spices. I enter a large spice supermarket on Dunlop Street, the likes of which I have not experienced before – it's nearly as large as a Coles or Woolworths supermarket back home. This market is the real deal, with an amazing selection of spices. I well know that Indian food is often a complex, nuanced and subtle blend of spices, vegetables and meats.

Ahead of me along Dunlop Street are four travel-worn backpackers, with, no doubt, the bare essentials organised neatly into their backpacks; spare shoes dangle by their laces. On Dunlop Street is a famous mosque, the Masjid Abdul Gaffoor. One of its best-known features is the elaborate sundial at its entrance. Arabic calligraphy adorns each of its twenty-five rays, denoting the names of twenty-five prophets. I take my shoes off as a customary mark of respect before walking inside and then kneeling down to pray with the Muslim worshippers. Outside meanwhile, the shaded areas around the mosque provide respite from the Singaporean sun and humidity for some local men, allowing them a good afternoon kip.

Slipping my shoes back on, I continue to the end of Dunlop Street, then left into the busy street of Jalan Besar. I am looking for a nearby market known for its tasty food and is supposedly worth seeing. However, after 50 metres I run into massive roadworks, horribly loud and virtually rebuilding the road from the ground up. This prompts me to retrace my walk back to the wet market.

Hot and sweaty, I could really do with a beer. There is a dark little sports bar on Dunlop Street and I go in and order a pint. I've never heard of the brand of ale, but it proves very refreshing after the

Singaporean heat. A myriad of sports play on a large TV screen, but no rugby, unfortunately for me. The relaxed backpackers I'd been trailing earlier enter the bar and it turns out they're American. They have long sun-bleached blonde hair – definitely surfing types. The watering hole is clearly also a backpackers' hostel, as the boys ask the bartender if accommodation is available. Unfortunately, it appears to be fully booked. In a very laidback manner, the young men simply turn 180 degrees, exit and carry on to the next hostel.

I never had that classic backpacking experience in my youth. My friends and I were all too busy trying to finish our degrees before maybe doing a quick Contiki tour of Europe and then beginning the corporate-ladder climb. Maybe we missed out?

The beer goes down a treat and I'm soon onto more, while observing a progression of fresh backpackers trying their luck with accommodation. Though I've enjoyed my short time in Little India, thanks to my bad timing for the Tekka wet market and the unexpected roadworks, it's not been anything really special. I decide I could come back for a curry in a hurry at the Tekka markets one evening, though.

After fifteen minutes on the MRT, I enter the hotel foyer back in Chinatown and return to my room. I can't for the life of me find my Apple SD card reader to enable uploading photos to my iPad and then to Facebook. After a thorough look, I am convinced it has disappeared into a black hole, never to return. The markets of Chinatown are only a couple of blocks away, though, so I venture out into the heat once more, without phone or camera, with the sole purpose of finding a replacement.

These are stock standard Asian markets, similar to scores of others I've explored in other parts of Asia. Of course, as this is Singapore, there are plenty of electronic goods on offer and I easily find the frost-white accessory, which costs only twenty Singapore dollars, cheaper than at home. I browse through the crowded alleys, ignoring the aggressive sales pitches of local tailors. Craft stalls and fake Ralph Lauren polo shirts are ubiquitous and there are some nice little food stalls, including a popular German hotdog stand. There are plenty of eateries here to try out over the next few days. I sample a tasty bratwurst hotdog and it reminds me of a weekend in Berlin years ago.

There's no sign of an end to the heat and humidity, and I'm about to call it quits. But then, out of nowhere, I stumble upon a large square lined with tourist crowds watching a hundred or so senior-aged locals line-dancing, of all things. It's just turned 7 pm when the speakers start blaring country and western music. On go the cowboy shirts and pants, hats and boots. These golden oldies are having a marvellous time.

It's not entirely seniors though; a few younger Chinatown locals join in, but they're in a clear minority. There are some pretty young Asian women, though, smiling away while strutting their stuff. Apparently I can pay three Singapore dollars at the corner desk and join in the fun as well, but I'd be too self-conscious to start an impromptu dance on my own. Instead I just look around at my fellow travellers and see everyone getting a kick out of the performance, a real feel-good vibe. Frustratingly, I've left both my iPhone and camera behind and can't capture what would be great video footage. It's yet another case of walking around an unfamiliar corner to find something completely unexpected – truly one of the best things about travel.

After a long, hot and tiring day, I hit the sack early in the oasis that is my hotel room, with the air-conditioning turned on extra cold.

Next morning, the first decision is where to go for breakfast. Asian food provides an ongoing feast, but noodles at 8 am, as with curry in India, does not appeal, so I fall back on my local Chinatown McDonald's. Soon after boarding the MRT at Chinatown, I exit Bayfront station and find the enormous Marina Bay Sands resort looming large above me.

The world-famous building is an impressive landmark, so original and commanding that it could have revitalised Singapore tourism almost on its own. Its unique architectural design was originally inspired by the structure of a house of cards, with flat blocks leaning against each other and one block balanced horizontally on top. Its most distinctive feature is the SkyPark, a 1-hectare park on that top deck, which incorporates the world-famous infinity pool, as well as gardens and jogging paths. The SkyPark spans the three enormous towers and a segment is cantilevered off the north tower.

I would love to have a beer or cocktail in the world's best rooftop pool, but it's for guests only. I'm here mainly to visit the Gardens by the Bay and walk amongst the Supertrees, which are like something straight out of *Avatar*'s science-fiction planet Pandora.

For five dollars, a shuttle bus takes visitors directly to the Gardens ticket booth. However, I decide to walk, which is quite surreal, looking up at the Supertrees and back to the Marina Bay Sands. Getting lost is easy, but before long I'm at the ticket booth, with a combined ticket to the two giant glasshouse conservatories and the Supertree Grove skywalk.

First, I venture into the larger of the two, the Flower Dome. Spread across an area of 1.2 hectares are plants from the Mediterranean and subtropical regions, like Australia, South America and South Africa. The glasshouse's design replicates these mild, dry climates and looks like the prototype for a dome for colonising Mars in the future.

The two conservatories are designed to be energy-efficient showcases of sustainable building technologies. The Flower Dome is divided into seven areas, each showcasing plants from a different part of the world. I particularly enjoy the Australian garden, with its native eucalypts, the continent's most common and distinctive group of trees.

The Flower Dome is impressive and educational, though its colourful floral displays are slightly lost on me, a non-gardener. Through the dome's glass exterior are amazing views of Marina Bay Sands and the Singapore Flyer. I do my best to get an all-inclusive panoramic photo encompassing the Sands, the Flyer and the exoskeleton of the Flower Dome.

The Cloud Forest dome is only slightly smaller and replicates the cool, moist conditions found in tropical regions of Southeast Asia and Central and South America. Coming from tropical Queensland, which is renowned for its rainforests, I'm interested in the dome's pseudo environment. The interior is similar to walking through the rainforest of Lamington National Park in the Gold Coast Hinterland, and it reignites my desire to visit the Daintree rainforest in North Queensland. It is quite surreal to have rainforest so well replicated within this structure.

I do not stop to read about each tree species; I just enjoy them in their peaceful setting, and a welcome break from the humidity outside.

The dome's highlight is 42-metre-high Cloud Mountain, an intricate and organic-looking structure clad with orchids, ferns and stag horns. With a 35-metre waterfall pouring down the side of the structure, it makes for excellent video footage and the refreshing, cool spray has me lingering at its base for quite some time. After sweating like a draft horse for a couple of days, the water spray is a joy and relief.

An elevator hidden behind the waterfall takes visitors up to the Cloudwalk. This aerial walkway allows a fresh and up-close perspective on different types of epiphytes, growing as they would in a natural habitat. As I observe the waterfall from above, one obvious question that occurs is how all of this artificially pumped water could be in keeping with the dome's environmentally friendly mission statement? It must be offset by some other kind of green energy I assume.

After enjoying the refreshing water spray a little longer, I venture out with reluctance into the humidity again. In the Supertree Grove, a lift inside one of the "trees" whisks visitors up to another walkway high above. About 130 metres long, this skywalk is especially photogenic where it changes direction in front of me. Although artificial, the "trees" have a pleasing symmetry and beauty, with consistent red and green colours. Real and exotic ferns, vines and orchids grow up the sides of their trunks, bringing them to life. The trunks supposedly contain technologies that mimic the ecology of living trees. For example, photovoltaic cells throughout the structures harness solar energy in a similar way to natural photosynthesis in plants. The power generated is used for some of the Supertree functions, such as lighting.

Retracing my steps back to the Marina Bay Sands, I'm gobsmacked at the ambition and innovation on display in the Gardens, so perfectly and elegantly executed. The internal foyer of the Marina Bay Sands is built to impress: around a large hollow space, hotel rooms rise up to the rooftop pool like a tall, narrow pyramid. A documentary I'd seen on the Sand's construction explained the intricate engineering behind the mesh-like art sculpture inside the hollow lobby.

The foyer has some unremarkable restaurants and high-end jewellery shops. I search for information about the rooftop pool, with the vaguest of hopes of a swim with views and a beer. It turns out that for twenty dollars I can take the elevator up to the Sand's Skypark observation deck; but, as I'd thought, access to the infinity pool is strictly for hotel guests.

No pool access is a deal-breaker, so I proceed aimlessly into the upmarket Marina Bay shopping mall, reminiscent of the luxury equivalents I've seen in Dubai. It really is shopping for wealthy people in pursuit of Italian and French clothes and Swiss watches. As I peer through windows at the $200,000 Rolexes on display, I ponder how the apparent low turnover of customers must be offset by healthy profits from just a few daily transactions with rich customers.

Next to the mall is the entrance to the busy-looking $8 billion casino, supposedly the most expensive on the planet. I'm not a fan of gambling and the entrance fee is quite steep, so there's no point in me going in. The fee would of course be small change to the heavy gamblers who flock here from all over the world, especially, it seems, from China.

It's now mid-afternoon and I decide to take the MRT to Orchard Road. Shopping is a national obsession for Singaporeans and this wide boulevard represents the centre of its shopping universe. Upon exiting the MRT station I'm overcome by the tasty smells of one of Singapore's mega food courts. Singapore hawker centres were once wet and dirty shelters, but as Singapore modernised, its food spots followed suit and many of the hawker centres moved into air-conditioned food courts.

As a seasoned Asian traveller, I've had my Western constitution put to the test by street foods on a number of occasions. While at home I'm quite unadventurous when it comes to food, I enjoy leaving my food comfort zone when I'm abroad.

In the food court, distinct smells of Chinese, Malay, Indonesian and Indian stalls tantalise the taste buds. I examine them all thoroughly, as I am quite discerning (translation = fussy) and specific when it comes to making such choices. I settle on what seems to be a popular Malaysian barbecue stall, where I order chicken wings with satay sauce, rice and egg. The marinated chicken is succulent, and absolutely delicious with the satay sauce. Although I'm looking forward to sampling many other dishes on my Singapore visit, this one becomes an instant favourite.

An escalator then takes me up to Orchard Road, where I emerge under a large overhanging structure that probably once appeared futuristic but now looks rather dated. What was once a dusty road with spice plantations and orchards is now one of the most renowned shopping streets in the world, a 2-kilometre boulevard of malls, specialty shops and department stores.

Next to the MRT exit is an elegant galleria housing all the big Italian brands: Gucci, Prada, Armani, Dolce and Gabbana and so on. The large Prada store is impressive. The brand's signature large, round sunglasses, the style made famous by Audrey Hepburn in *Breakfast at Tiffany's*, reflect the current trend in women's sunglasses, and start at a mere three hundred Singapore dollars.

I move next door to the Armani store and go up a couple of floors to the men's section, with its stylish, trendy jeans. They're unrealistically expensive and mostly slim-fit, so I'd never stand a chance of actually fitting into them. I hope there's no "designed in Italy, made in China" tag inside these garments. All of a sudden, I feel dressed like a pauper in my Industrie shorts and Billabong T-shirt. With so few customers, it's awkward, as a sales clerk asks if I need any help. "Just browsing mate." It's very obvious he won't make any sales to the likes of me.

Heading further along Orchard Road, I search for more familiar stores, such as Zara and Gap. There are plentiful high-quality garments and jewellery in lower-profile stores on the way. It proves difficult to spot the small, understated Zara sign across the wide, busy boulevard. On the men's floor are a dozen or so varieties of smart-looking jackets. However, these are for smaller-sized Singaporeans, not big burly Australians.

Close by is Gap, but their jackets don't fit either, so a Gap "Singapore" T-shirt becomes a compromise instead: it's comfortable and good value and, importantly, it fits! In an adjacent mall, there's a young

Singaporean fellow smiling away while standing 4 metres above the ground on stilts outside a new store he's clearly being paid to promote. I hope there's proper workplace health and safety cover! He's doing a fine job, giving shoppers a wide grin for their cameras. It becomes a little alarming when some children wrap their arms around his stilt legs while their adoring parents snap away with smartphones. But he still smiles on cue for me when I take a selfie.

Now at the eastern end of Orchard Road, I take the short walk up into Fort Canning Park. The park provides soothing quiet and a refreshing break from Orchard Road's hustle and bustle. In the green surrounds, I'm on the lookout for the Battle Box Historical Museum, which marks the site of the former British-Malayan command headquarters during World War II. The museum has a re-creation of the final hours before the fall of Singapore in 1942 to the Japanese. It's not on many must-see lists, but I've heard that it is worth a visit. However, there's not a soul in sight when I eventually locate the museum and then find signs apologising that Battle Box is temporarily closed for renovations.

Disappointed but enjoying the exercise, I continue through the park's shading trees and well-kept green spaces. Soon after exiting the park at its eastern end, I encounter the unexpected and lovely sight of the Singapore Cricket Club, where a match is underway and players are wearing traditional cricket whites despite the heat and humidity. Its clubhouse is in a charming location at the south end of the Padang, in Singapore's central business district. The sportsmen look to be highly skilled and I rest a while watching the game, doing my best to photograph a bowler mid-delivery or a batsman playing a cut or pull-shot to the boundary.

My hike comes full circle at the popular Singapore Merlion statue, which sprays water from its mouth into the harbour. The Merlion, a mythical creature with a lion's head and the body of a fish, is the national icon and mascot of Singapore. Subconsciously, the fountaining Merlion was the first image I ever associated with Singapore, or Asia for that matter.

More than a hundred tourists crowd the jetty that runs alongside the large statue. People jostle for space for the obligatory photograph: a simulation of the fountain of water landing in a tourist's hands – just like holding up the Tower of Pisa or kissing the face of Egypt's Sphinx. There is no shortage of people to take my fountain photo, but unfortunately the guy I choose lands the fountain somewhere on my forearm. Oh well, no great loss, and I'm soon walking again in a westerly direction about a mile back to my digs in Chinatown, with electrolytes in mind after 15 kilometres or so on foot today in the constant humidity.

Opposite the hotel are a couple of spas, offering reflexology massages for ten Singapore dollars. When I poke my head through the front doors, the attendants spring to attention. After the hours of walking I'm very malleable as I lie back in the reclining seat with a couple of San Miguel beers, enjoying the icy air-conditioning. Reflexologists assert that a system of zones and reflex areas on the feet and hands affect different parts of the body and that massaging these areas can bring benefits. There's no verifiable scientific proof for this and I'm sceptical, but those objections become irrelevant as the masseuse pounds away with pocket-rocket hand-strength. It feels replenishing, and slightly painful at the same time. By the end of the treatment I do feel reinvigorated (and it's not just a placebo effect, I think) and my once weary feet are ready to soldier on.

I head out early evening to the legendary Raffles hotel, a Singapore institution for 120 years. I think of all the mini-series and movies that have used this iconic hotel as a setting, and of the royalty, politicians, movie stars and other VIPs who have stayed here.

Raffles dates back almost two hundred years to the 1830s, when it was built as a private beach house. In September 1887, Armenian hoteliers the Sarkies Brothers leased the property with the intention of turning it into a high-end hotel. Just two months later, on 1 December, they opened the ten-room Raffles Hotel, named after British statesman Sir Stamford Raffles, considered the founder of modern Singapore. The hotel's proximity to the beach (at the time), and its reputation for high standards of service and accommodation, made it popular with a wealthy clientele. Within its first decade, three new buildings were added to the original beach house, expanding the total guest rooms to seventy-five. Further extensive modernisations and a growing reputation for innovative cuisine gradually made it a major tourist attraction.

The hotel's exterior is minimalist, ivory in colour, with wide verandas wrapping round the square-shaped building. It is understated, sophisticated, with an old-world charm sadly lacking in the over-the-top, size-obsessed buildings of more modern times. Epitomising the simplicity of colonial-style architecture, Raffles is a true heritage gem. Nestled inside is a tropical open-air garden courtyard, an oasis of quiet and calm in the middle of this bustling metropolis.

Upon entering, I get directions to the Long Bar, where any appropriately dressed member of the public can go and have a drink and get a glimpse of the refinement experienced by the chosen few. Having done my research, I'm decked out in a Ralph Lauren collared mesh polo shirt and chinos and feel confident as I approach the very tall turbaned Indian doorman.

After a five-minute wait I enter the bar, which actually feels welcoming and relaxed. Well-attired ladies and gentlemen occupy rattan tables, while large ceiling fans spin lazily overhead. People seem happy to sit there enjoying pleasant conversation and perhaps a bit of people watching. Needless to say, the overwhelming drink of choice is the famous Singapore Sling cocktail. Invented in the Long Bar in the early twentieth century, the Singapore Sling recipe was quite an enigma, carried forward through the years in bartenders' memories and hand-written notes. The current recipe – a mix of gin, cherry brandy, Cointreau, Benedictine, grenadine, pineapple juice, lemon juice and a touch of bitters – is supposedly a heavily modified version of the drink from one hundred years ago.

Disappointingly, the cocktail is now premixed and made by an automatic dispenser. On second thoughts, this seems understandable, considering the high volume that would be served on any given night of the week. For a premium price, however, the bartenders will mix and shake the cocktail in front of drinkers. I then remember a couple of people back home telling me that the sling served on Singapore Airlines flights beats this premixed version.

I take a seat at the bar on a stool with the sole focus of gaining the bartender's attention. I'm excited to sample the Sling, but after my long and tiring day almost any kind of alcoholic refreshment would suffice. After the cocktail is placed in front of me, the barman asks if I'd like to create an account. Given the relaxed and comfortable surrounds, I feel I could definitely hang around, so I nod in the affirmative. However, the first sip proves an anticlimax for my taste buds. It really tastes quite ordinary. I can recall half a dozen cocktails that would trump this, and the alcohol content seems quite low – definitely no Long Island Iced Tea! It is reminiscent of the premixed daiquiris at Brisbane's Treasury Casino in both its ordinariness and potency – but about five times the price.

Bowls of raw, unshelled peanuts have been set out in front of the drinkers and I have my own personal bowl. By this time of day, the floor is strewn with discarded shells.

Presently, I notice a couple of fiftyish-looking blokes take the couple of bar stools to my left. When they ask politely if I mind, their Kiwi accents are instantly recognisable. After introducing myself, I find out they are businessmen who visit Singapore regularly for work and that they've started many a good night at the Long Bar. I'm glad to have found company on what could have been a potentially lonely night. When I inform them of my town of birth – New Plymouth, New Zealand – they immediately exude the same friendliness that most Kiwis abroad seem to possess. Our cousins over "the ditch" are very much like Australians, only nicer, I've often thought.

The Kiwis soon begin talking about their business, describing themselves as an odd but complimentary partnership. Dave seems an easy-going and gregarious marketing guy, and John an intelligent, though slightly autistic-like scientist – "not a people person" his partner says. Between the two of them, they hope to make an inroad into the Singapore technology market with their inventions.

Naturally we talk about rugby, specifically the Wallabies and All Blacks and the one-sidedness of the Bledisloe Cup. They are very diplomatic about this, not trying to put the boot into an All Black–weary Wallabies supporter.

The beers start flowing in quick succession and the Kiwis are turning out to be excellent drinking buddies, happily sharing stories and a few laughs with their new antipodean friend. John suggests we ditch the Long Bar for the secluded courtyard bar downstairs. He possesses the prized company credit card. My professional advice as an accountant is that he better get receipts to be on the safe side.

Settling my account at the Long Bar, I find that two Singapore Slings and three draught beers have cost one hundred Singapore dollars, roughly ninety Australian dollars.

"A bit bloody steep, don't you think?", I observe audibly to my Kiwi companions, having not paid much attention to prices on the drinks menu beforehand.

"You Aussies should be happy as 'pugs' in 'shut' overseas these days, with the Aussie dollar exchange rate!" Dave quickly responds in a Kiwi accent. He makes a good point and I settle the account readily, encouraged by the prospect of free drinks next on the company account.

We head downstairs into the courtyard, which has a quieter, more exclusive feel. "Three of your best single malt whiskies for us bartender and keep them coming. Here's my card. Charge away." We jokingly quiz the man to reveal if anyone famous is currently staying at Raffles or tell us about any celebrities he may have served over the years. He evades the question with a polite, professional and discreet response.

After three rounds of Chivas Regal, the guys start telling me their plans for the night. They ask me if I know Orchard Road and I recount my impression of the wide, clean boulevard and its high-end designer chic from the afternoon.

"Well, well, well", says Dave, "We know of an interesting little place you'd never have known existed in such an esteemed location." They tell me about a disused shopping centre at the very end of Orchard Road housing an outrageous establishment where anything goes. They elaborate further that it's a multi-level bar/strip joint/brothel, which caters for all sexual preferences and tastes, "an eye-opener which has to be seen to be believed". The plan for them is to go get a bite of dinner in the vicinity, then head on over the street and up the "elevator to hell".

They seem like pretty harmless blokes, and before I know it the evening night lights of Singapore are flashing by our taxi. However, by the time we arrive, I decide that I'm not really keen on the venture and change my mind. "Dinner sounded good, but I'm not really hungry after three bowls of peanuts" I say.

We get out as I pay the driver – the least I can do – and the boys shake my hand while wishing me a fond, drunken farewell, with the expected parting shot, "Don't worry too much about those Wallabies mate. Have a good one."

Out of curiosity, I look for the intersection with Orchard Road amongst the flashing lights and cars. Sure enough, over the other side of the road is what appears to be the red-light equivalent of the Wild West. It's not immediately obvious, though, so I ride the elevator from the ground floor into the complex, making my way to the lift. There are some odd-looking people around. Following me into the lift are some alternative types who could pass for extras in the futuristic film *Blade Runner*.

The Kiwis have prepped me to be certain I enter the appropriate floor for a straight male. A couple of gay men exit at level three – easy enough to figure out. The fourth floor seems to be for their female counterparts, as a couple of butch women with short, parted hair disembark. I'm now alone in the lift and my powers of deduction suggest that mine is the next floor.

The doors open and I walk a few metres, seeing dresses and bras. However, after a few more trepid steps I realise that these ladies are, in fact, lady-boys! A few disused shop fronts operate as bars, and lady-boys stand out front touting for business. Being a Westerner gets their attention and they proposition me to enter their establishments. I swiftly retreat to the lift, hearing a few expletives directed at me as I do so. The harsh words don't bother me but I'm relieved when the lift doors close.

At the next level, with the experience fresh in my mind, I cautiously take a few steps from the lift and then breathe a sigh of relief at the sight of heterosexual people – no ladies with Adam's apples! The car park behind the lift catches my eye. There appear to be small groups of people hidden in the dark, most likely making small sales of party drugs. It is a good warning to stay alert and buy only capped bottled drinks.

I quickly opt for what appears to be the most popular bar. The swift choice is necessitated by the fact that I'm now fatigued again, with little energy for hanging around. Inside, the bar is very much the kind of place you might see in Bangkok, filled with lonely men being flattered by demure and petite Asian girls, and groups of young men on bucks' parties.

I order a bottle of Heineken at the bar and observe the bartender taking the cap off in front of me. The music playing as I take a stool at a table is fairly generic dance-chart fare. I'm happy to people-watch for a while then head back home after one beer. Before long, two working girls take the stools on either side of mine. They are pretty enough, their skimpy bras and skirts revealing their slim bodies.

"What your name? Where you from?" they ask. I use Matt as an alias. "Nice name for a gentleman," they say. Apparently kangaroos are their favourite animal. When the conversation lags, I feel soft skin move assertively against my own and a hand placed on my thigh. They have clearly done this often and I have to start asserting that I'm not up for a "good time". As an inducement, they suggest that the two of them come back to my hotel room together as a double act. "Good price too."

My ultimatum of "you're both very lovely girls but I am not interested in your offer and I feel unwell" sends them on their way. I pay for my beer and the overpriced drinks they ordered at the outset. A part of my ego urges me to take a sneak peek to see if I am missed, but, unsurprisingly, they have moved on to other potential customers.

After leaving, the safety of Singapore's streets is welcoming. Back in my comfort zone, I hail down a cab to end a strange and oddly memorable night.

The next day, I sleep in with a hangover, eventually appearing for a greasy recovery breakfast. For my last day in Singapore I decide to head over to Sentosa Island, an appealing idea given my seedy and delicate state. Located just a couple of miles south of Singapore's main attractions around the harbour and reached via a short bridge, Sentosa Island is where locals go to have fun.

The number-one attraction here is Universal Studios, but there are many other options, such as indoor skydiving, rollercoasters, a state-of-the-art maritime museum, and Ibiza-inspired beachside bars and clubs. There are also a few five-star hotels and the Marine Life Park, which contains a world-class aquarium. As I flew into Singapore, Sentosa was easily identified from above by its two eighteen-hole golf courses.

I've been to Universal Studios in Los Angeles a couple of times and feel I'm too old for that kind of theme park now. The first thing on my list is the S.E.A. Aquarium, with its more than 100,000 marine animals, including over 800 species, occupying 45 million litres of water. I'll have the opportunity to visit another famous aquarium during the final days of my trip, in Lisbon, but Singapore's facility is the world's largest, and has many good reviews on TripAdvisor.

After queuing for twenty minutes, I descend into the aquarium's core. Behind the world's largest marine-viewing panel, 36 metres long and 8 metres tall, sharks, stingrays and a huge variety of marine life glide above and around me. It is beautiful and peaceful, and takes my mind off my hangover for a while.

The aquarium has ten distinct zones and forty-nine different habitats. Giant tanks display a wide variety of species from all over the world. The memorable ones include a giant (and very ugly) red octopus with long, gangly arms; glowing jellyfish that rock'n'roll in rhythmic motion; and a large centrepiece tank with a coral reef populated by hundreds of *Finding Nemo* fish.

The most fun though are the clever and playful dolphins, which occupy their own special habitat, teasing excited little kids as they place their hands on the glass. I take an excellent video of one particular dolphin as it peers through the glass on its first turn, accelerates into a leap out above the water and then comes back for a second turn – a real show-pony.

Retracing my footsteps back past the viewing panel, I return to land level and continue to explore Sentosa. I enjoy a lengthy and gradual hill climb, via a series of long staircases and escalators, up to the Merlion Plaza. At the end of the stairs is a Merlion statue, far larger and tackier than the icon by the harbour from yesterday. Armed with a bottle of icy water in the humidity, I continue my climb to the Imbiah Lookout. There's a luge track from the lookout which I'm keen to try. But soon after trundling slowly down the hill on a sled on wheels, accompanied by mainly kids and mothers, I realise it's very tame – not the adrenaline rush I anticipated.

On the hill's other side is a large building that houses indoor sky-diving. It's quite expensive and I um and ah about its worth. Standing around the giant wind cage are about fifty people. The turbines below create a huge amount of thrust, lifting punters up to 10 metres into the air. Faces and sky-diving outfits are massively distorted and pounded by some kind of giant Dyson hand-dryer. An experienced guide is inside the cage with the paying customer, doing her very best to send her flying – in this case a teenage girl, who seems to be not only having a ball but is also actually flying, which in turn makes me almost decide to fork out the big bucks.

Next though is a big fella like myself, probably around the 90-kilogram mark. The young, averaged-size girl rocketed up to 10 metres, but this poor bloke can't catch a break. Time and time again, accompanied by the instructor, he attempts to fly, but he just floats through the jet stream from one side of the cage to the other at just 2–3 metres off the ground. He is clearly disappointed as the next customer flies up in the air, providing some great video footage.

Though ultimately of limited interest to me, Sentosa is a good diversion. It's a great place for children to explore or for adults to stay in luxury resorts with all their trappings or play golf. A chairlift carries me back down the hill, providing fine views of the island and its luxury resorts. Outside one are eight Rolls-Royces and a line of other European cars, all in mint condition and sparklingly polished.

A monorail train takes me back across to Marina Bay, where I spend my last few Singapore dollars on things for my late flight to Frankfurt that night. At Uniqlo I buy a pair of the most unattractive but very comfortable tracksuit pants, in the hope they will lead to a better sleep on the night-time journey, for this insomniac anyway.

Two

London Calling

The cab driver who takes me back to Changi Airport is a young man who doesn't talk unless spoken to, quite the opposite of my driver from a few days ago, but I don't need any tourism advice on departure of course. As with most things in Singapore, check-in and security are very efficient. However, the staff at the check-in desk inform me that my plane is running late for take-off, so the transfer at Frankfurt Airport could be a potential issue.

Changi Airport has fast free Wi-Fi, allowing an instant upload of photos from Singapore to Facebook and a catch-up with the news websites. It really is difficult picking a dozen or so highlights from four hundred photos! Also, my 16-gigabyte iPad will quickly run out of disk space going forward without constant and aggressive culling.

Boarding the plane, I find my seat, stuck between two big blokes with shoulders about the same width as mine. They look me up and down probably thinking the exact the same thing I'm thinking. The captain in his welcome announcement informs us that this will be the last flight from Singapore to London via Frankfurt, a result of the new business alliance between Qantas and Emirates, a necessity after Qantas' declining financial fortunes. His final words, "sad days indeed", have the flight attendants eyeing each other forlornly and possibly feeling rather cynical about the new business model. The service on board this flight, however, proves second rate.

Downing a beer and a scotch and dry, I swallow some sleeping pills in the hope of arriving in London not completely jet-lagged. As I doze off, it becomes apparent that being held in my seat by two sets of shoulders on either side is actually quite conducive to a good night's rest. Resting on my human pillows, I drift off into a deep sleep. It is comfortable for me, but I hope I don't snore too much.

I'm pleasantly surprised when I wake up just as breakfast is being served, one hour before landing at Frankfurt. As we descend, Frankfurt Airport seems rather large, a major international air hub, and I begin to really worry about the transfer. When the plane doors open, I rush up the aisle and out the exit door. Fortunately, the departures board indicates that British Airways flight 8731 for London City Airport is at the very next gate.

At 7 am on a Monday morning, the BA plane is full of "suits" on an early business commute to London. It's not long before I see the English Channel below, the white cliffs of Dover and then the mighty Thames Barrier. As we reach the city, I can make out the great arc over Wembley Stadium, the "Gherkin", the Houses of Parliament and the dome of St Pauls Cathedral. A rarity for London, there's not a cloud in the sky!

There are some new additions to the skyline, most notably the controversial but unmistakable glass skyscraper, The Shard, and the Olympic Park, located in an area of urban renewal in East London. According to the weather forecast I consulted in Singapore, it seems that the long English winter has suddenly, and conveniently for me, morphed into spring. The plane soon lands at London City Airport and I'm back on English soil, feeling like I only just left yesterday. Sentimentally, it's great to be back in London after five years.

Going through passport control is still a frustrating business for any international arrival without a British or European passport. Of the dozen or so passport officers, only two have been allocated to those from outside of Europe. While the European businessmen get whisked through passport control and off to their meetings, the rest of us stand in line, the discrimination causing much resentment in my neglected queue.

Then a middle-aged lady with an East London cockney accent starts to call, "Rich. Rich. Anyone 'ere called Rich?"

"Yes, I'm Mr Angus Rich."

"I 'ave to inform you, sir, that your luggage never arrived from Frankfurt. Please make your way over to luggage claim after you get through passport control."

As I fill in the luggage claim form, she is very efficient, which is more than fine by me. This is London after all, and things happen fast in London.

After assurances that my luggage will be back in my safe hands by mid-afternoon, I make my way to the TFL overland train line. It's a pleasant surprise that the Oyster card a relative lent me back home has a healthy twenty-pound balance. I tap the scanner and walk straight onto the train; I'll be in the thick of London's underground network in about twenty minutes flat. If only Heathrow and Gatwick airports were this convenient, never mind distant Luton airport.

As the train makes its way westward, London looks as large and busy as ever. The views through the adjacent windows look northward to the Olympic stadium and village, and south to Canary Wharf and Greenwich. A new point of interest 100 metres above the ground is the Emirates Skyline, a chairlift that transports passengers all the way from the Olympic village across the Thames to Greenwich.

When I transfer to the London Underground at Bank station, the Monday-morning rush hour is in full swing but fairly easy to negotiate with just my carry-on bag. Bank station is on the Northern line, a line that I've travelled many hundreds of times. Coloured black on the Underground map, it is as familiar to me as the trains back home. I remember many commutes to work along this line, with passengers stuffed into the train like sardines.

As I disembark at Tufnell Park, I note that the clunky old lift is still there, taking commuters to street level. The lifts have the exact same stern and maternal recording of an English woman saying, "There is no smoking on the underground. Please mind the gap while boarding trains." I must have heard that same line hundreds of times!

It is but a five-minute walk to my aunt's place, through streets of charming Victorian-era terraced houses. I press the doorbell, looking forward to seeing everyone in my family's favourite aunt, Margaret, my father's older sister. An octogenarian retired psychiatrist, she is always a wonderful host for the many relatives and friends who visit her continuously from all over the globe. As she lives on her own, I'm sure she enjoys the company as it comes and goes. The two of us became quite close during my two years living in London.

The sturdy green door opens, followed by a smile and kiss, and "You look exactly like your father." She's definitely not the first one to say that to me over the years. It's great to be in her presence again and her house always feels very cosy and welcoming. Immediately, she puts a coffee pot on her gas stove and I hope it's going to be strong enough to help my jetlag. She's keen to hear about the adventure I have planned. As we had discussed by email, she's interested in going to the theatre with me too, and she also makes the great suggestion of visiting London's famous Kew gardens tomorrow.

As always, The Guardian entertainment guide is on the kitchen table and we find that it highly recommends *The Winslow Boy* at the Old Vic Theatre. Logging onto lastminute.com, I buy good tickets for the following evening, while Margaret heads off to work at her beloved London allotment. I assure her my luggage will arrive before 6 pm.

After Margaret returns mid-afternoon, I ride the Northern line to Leicester Square and before long I'm at Covent Garden. With its usual array of street performers, it's as vibrant as ever, and always a hit with tourists. Located in a very central and old part of town, the "garden" has an interesting history. Countryside until the sixteenth century, it was briefly settled before being abandoned and walled off in 1200 for use as orchards by Westminster Abbey and referred to as "the garden of the Abbey and Convent". The land was eventually seized by King Henry VIII and granted to the Earl of Bedford in 1552. His family built some fine houses for wealthy tenants and designed the Italianate arcaded square. The new precinct became the benchmark for town planning, a prototype for new estates as London grew.

By 1654, a small open-air market had developed in the square, which gradually fell into disrepute as taverns, theatres, coffee-houses and brothels appeared. The gentry moved away, to be replaced by a bohemian community of rakes, wits and playwrights, and by the eighteenth century Covent Garden had become a well-known red-light district.

An Act of Parliament was drawn up to take back control of the area, and the neo-classical Covent Garden market building was erected in 1830. The sleaze declined as the market grew and further buildings were added. By the end of the 1960s, traffic congestion had become problematic, and the market was relocated in 1974 to New Covent Garden Market, 5 kilometres south-west at Nine Elms. Covent Garden's central building reopened as a shopping centre in 1980 and its cafes, pubs, boutique shops and craft market fast became popular with visitors. The Royal Ballet is based in London's renowned Royal Opera House, smack bang in the centre of Covent Garden.

As I reach Trafalgar Square, the sun is shining and the temperature gauge is in the twenties (Celsius). Londoners are out in enthusiastic full bloom, enjoying the first glimpse of the new spring season. Beyond Leicester Square I reach the long curvature of Regent Street at Piccadilly Circus, dotted with exclusive shops, high-end brands and custom tailors. Hamleys, one of the world's great toy stores, seems to be as popular as ever. I have a long-lasting memory of being taken to Hamleys as a seven-year-old child by my mother and marvelling at the selection of toys, which was unlike anything I'd seen before. My family lived in Sussex with my grandparents for two months in 1980, and I have many great and long-lasting memories from that period of my childhood.

The Oxford Street shopping crowds are as big and fanatical as ever. With the working day ended, people are walking shoulder to shoulder, but many more hours of sunlight are still to come due to summertime daylight saving. I always enjoyed browsing in the Virgin Megastore, so I make a couple of inquiries here and there. To my disappointment, I find out that digital online music has precipitated its demise and the famous flagship store has had to close its doors.

Across the way further along Oxford Street are a Hare Krishna group, dancing and chanting trance-like through the hordes of shoppers. The sound builds while a group of bratty London teenagers dance and sing alongside these mad monks, having a gleeful time in their unsubtle mockery.

It's not long before I'm reminded that I'm in English Premier League territory. Footpath vendors are selling Chelsea, Arsenal, Man-U, Man-C, Liverpool, Everton and West Ham scarves, T-shirts and jerseys, cashing in on tourists and loyal fans. I'm not sure how much of the merchandise is official, though.

Soon after, I approach the impressive façade of my favourite department store, Selfridges, entering through the giant swinging front doors of its corner entrance. Opened by Harry Gordon Selfridge in 1909, the store is the second largest retail premises in the UK, behind Harrods. An American, Mr Selfridge was unimpressed by the quality of British retailers when he visited on a holiday, at a time when London's large stores had not yet adopted the latest selling ideas being used in the United States. He decided to build his own department store on what was then the unfashionable western end of Oxford Street, and slowly bought up a series of Georgian buildings on the desired block.

The Selfridges building is now considered classic architecture and an icon of Oxford Street. Inside are all my favourite brands, which cater perfectly for my demographic. The range of brands in Selfridges is not as elitist as that of Harrods, which is way outside of my budget. I experience a flash of déjà vu on seeing that the internal layout is exactly the same as five years ago – as will be most of London, I know, a city where continuity and tradition are prized.

Across the street is another Zara store, which looks as popular as ever. Time to see if the jackets I nearly split in Singapore are available here in my size. To my disappointment they're still too tight around the shoulders.

I look at my watch and decide I'm done with browsing; I don't actually intend to buy anything today. Oxford St can be energy-sapping, and on this occasion I feel it's not worth the effort and decide to make my way home.

My old favourite number ten bus at Oxford Circus takes me through inner North London, an enjoyably scenic route. I take a seat on the top floor of the double-decker to enjoy the view. Number ten weaves through Camden Town, revealing its gritty charm. Camden High Street is brimming with energy and vibrancy. The area is famous for its alternative culture; there are fewer Punks these days but still plenty of strange-looking Goths, and now the subculture of Emos is obviously prevalent here as well.

Doc Martens were famously first sold in Camden Town at the British Boot Company. The distinctive ruby red exterior of The World's End pub still faces the tube station. The bus continues on through Kentish Town before I disembark near Hampstead Heath.

Back at Tufnell Park, my aunt is a tad cross with me. The luggage has yet to arrive and she's now one hour late for choir practice. After she leaves, my bag arrives within half an hour. Margaret is having friends over later for dinner and jetlag suddenly hits me, so I take a well-earned snooze. I wake to the sound of voices below in the kitchen, some of them familiar, as I have got to know quite a few of Margaret's friends on previous visits.

All but one of the guests are retired mental-health professionals. Highgate, the area around Hampstead Heath, is a bit of a mecca for people in the psychiatric field, and the hospital here is known to be at the cutting edge of mental-health sciences in Britain. An old part of London, it also attracts intellectuals, artists, actors, thinkers and left-wingers. The poet Keats wrote many of his great works in the surrounds of Hampstead Heath. The odd person out at the dinner party, Nick, is a professor of ancient religions. I imagine the average IQ of this table to be quite high.

They are a chatty group, and the discussion begins with the controversial new bedroom tax, which takes effect the next day, brought into law by David Cameron's Tory government. Plenty of dissent ensues. Talk then turns to the funeral of Dame Margaret Thatcher, for which parts of the city centre will be closed to traffic the following day. "Good riddance," they all agree. "There'll be a few parties in the Midlands and north England tomorrow, I imagine", one says. "How dare they allow such a ceremony to close down Central London," says another. I ask their opinions on the celebrations in working-class Croydon the previous week which followed the news. Of course, they're fine with it. It's not all about politics and they're an interesting, very well-read bunch.

After a couple of beers, the jetlag hits hard and I expediently retire, wishing them all well. It has been lovely to catch up with them all again.

It's Tuesday morning when the two of us take the overland train from Hampstead to Richmond. Margaret has generously offered to show me around London's Kew Gardens. During many previous visits and while living here, I never managed to make the journey out to see this world-famous attraction. Some of my family members have been, though, and rave about it. Richmond is a well-off suburb with lovely, and no doubt expensive, real estate. We make our way from the station to the Victoria Gate entrance.

I learn that the gardens are a UNESCO World Heritage Site and date back to the mid-eighteenth century, when botanists began collecting specimens to plant in the original 3-hectare plot. Initially known as the Royal Botanic Gardens, they now cover 120 hectares and contain the most comprehensive biological collection on the planet. The living collections include more than 30,000 different kinds of plants, while the herbarium, which is one of the largest in the world, has over seven million preserved plant specimens.

From Victoria Gate we make our way to the Palm House, a magnificent piece of Victorian-era architecture. The long, thin glasshouse was built in the mid-nineteenth century and is adorned by a central nave rising in the middle to 19 metres. An elegant building and an icon of the gardens, it has a curved and weathered glass exterior that quarantines a steamy interior. The 100-metre-long curved walls are made entirely of beautiful rounded-glass panels. Adding character, the interior of the glass is slightly mouldy. Palms from all over the globe are complemented by large and green lily pads in still ponds. There is also a narrow, elevated walkway which climbs up and around the inside of the glasshouse, offering a different perspective.

Outside, as if protecting the Palm House are ten heraldic statues which look out over the adjacent pond, all made from Portland stone. They're simply known as "The Queen's Beasts" and are replicas of sculptures that stood at the entrance of Westminster Abbey during Queen Elizabeth's coronation in 1953.

A short and pleasant walk away is the Princess of Wales conservatory. A post-modern, multilayered construction, it was commissioned in 1982 and was officially opened five years later by Princess Diana. Housed inside are ten computer-controlled microclimate zones containing mostly dry and wet tropics plants. A great array of orchids, waterlilies, carnivorous plants and cacti thrive here on the sun's energy, maximised by the conservatory's long and exposed roof. The very original and modern architecture is an interesting contrast to the older gardens and rustic glasshouses. Particularly impressive among the plants are a small number of large and magnificent waterlilies, ideal photogenic subjects for my digital photo collection.

The nearby Treetop Walk, which opened in 2008, takes visitors up 18 metres into the tree canopy of a woodland glade of lime, sweet chestnut and oak trees. The thick steel supports for the walkway were designed to rust, resulting in a natural treelike appearance which blends in with its surrounds.

With Margaret being a pensioner, we take the easy option, ascending in the lift rather than climbing the stairs. The view from the top is hemmed by trees but on the very far horizon are a couple of Canary Wharf's skyscrapers, as well as The Shard. There is also a perfect view down to the Temperate House, the signature building of Kew. The Temperate House is in very much the same style as the Palm House but is even larger and has a more conventional design without the curves.

When we wander down there, I'm blown away by the sheer variety of plants and trees from the world's temperate regions. Australian flora is well represented due to its unique and important biological status. The glasshouse, which opened in 1863, is the largest surviving Victorian glasshouse in existence, with double the floor area of the Palm House. It took forty years to construct and costs blew out accordingly. The end result encapsulates the rigour and attention to detail for which the English are well known and respected. The glasshouse interior is nicely complemented by a temporary exhibition of wooden sculptures by UK artist David Nash.

In the surrounds outside are more works by Mr Nash, many of which were created ingeniously out of charcoal wood. The gardens employ a young army of enthusiastic and motivated maintenance workers including many students studying biology at university. Working with dedication, they look genuinely privileged to be in the employ of such a famous, important and historic centre of biological excellence.

By mid-afternoon, the far too common sight of rain clouds appears in the London sky above. With the deteriorating weather and Margaret tired, we decide to pass on the long walk to the popular pagoda, and head home. I tell her on the train that, to my pleasant surprise, Kew Gardens has blown me away, despite the fact I'm no green thumb. The glasshouses and gardens were awe-inspiring and it's easy to appreciate the care, passion and respect for the environment that is the mission of Kew Gardens.

My aunt is a keen gardener, spending much of her time in her prized London allotment. The concept of allotment gardening, whereby small gardening plots are formed by subdividing a piece of land into a few or up to several hundred land parcels, is a strange one for Australians, with our plentiful land and low population density. The individual gardeners are usually organised in an allotment association, which leases or is granted the land from the owner who may be a public, private or church-based entity, who usually stipulates that the land be only used for gardening. Margaret is forever enjoying the fruits of her individually cultivated London plot, in particular the sweet berries in her yoghurt desserts.

I wake the following morning feeling full of energy and free of jetlag. With great enthusiasm, I begin my first day of exploring London, my "home away from home". Leaving the terraced house, I look forward to a good old walk around Hampstead Heath. Heading down terraced streets and then up the long and steady hill of Highgate Road, I enter the famous surrounds of the Heath. Over the decades it has been a favourite place for my family members to roam around on each visit to London, while staying with Margaret. There's the same crowded school en route, with students playing basketball, making the most of a game before the school bell signals the start of the day.

Passing the popular tennis courts, I walk up Parliament Hill to what is one of the best views of the London skyline. The hill, with its old and weathered grass, is windy and exposed to the elements and always a favourite spot for keen kite flyers. The iconic vista remains the same, encompassing the Gherkin, St Pauls and Telecom Tower, with the only recent addition being The Shard, which rises above them all.

I go back down the hill then walk up the winding length of the Heath, with its lovely ponds dotted with geese and ducks. The Heath's ponds become popular swimming pools each summer, with one pool for ladies and one for gentlemen. At night, though, the Heath has a rather dubious reputation as a place for gay men to go "cruising", in search of random and impersonal sex.

The shaded paths run up and down, weaving through paddocks as far as Kenwood House at the very top. The heath is a bit of rural England in the big smoke. I fondly remember many pleasant weekend runs along the leafy, autumn-swept paths before stopping for a breather at Kenwood House. Sloping in front of the house is a large area dotted with some fine permanent outdoor sculptures. The cream-white building is a large traditional English home dating back to the seventeenth century. A popular film set, it has been used in numerous movies and TV series over the years; notably, it appears frequently in the film *Notting Hill*. I then get lost in the "old-money" suburb of Highgate and have to resort to the iPhone to find a bus route to Camden Town.

Hopping off the bus at Camden Town, I join the Goths hanging out in groups at Camden Lock. Shops selling alternative footwear and clothing line the high street. As it's early on a weekday, plenty of customer service comes my way while I'm checking out the Doc Martens on display. Now in my forties, I'm probably a bit too old for the signature footwear, which was oh-so-popular back in my university days. However, there's a great looking style of Docs called the Chelsea Boot, a soft slip-on style boot with no laces. It's a cross between traditional Docs and R.M. Williams boots from back home. Unfortunately, despite moving from shop to shop I don't have much luck finding a pair of size ten Chelsea Boots. And I decide there's no way I'll even consider any of the other styles, which are mainly strange-looking punk or skinhead designs with bright colours, thick soles and long laces.

Thankfully, one shop assistant sends me to the British Boot Company, which is right next to the tube station. It is actually quite a famous store, being the original Doc Marten specialist. In fact, this inconspicuous shop was the first in all of England to sell Doc Martens, which were, ironically, invented by a German.

Klaus Martens was a doctor in the German army during World War II. After injuring himself while skiing on leave in the Bavarian Alps, he found his standard-issue army boots were too uncomfortable for his injured foot. While recuperating, he redesigned his boots with soft leather and air-padded soles made from tyres. After the war, Martens further adapted his design, refining the concept of boots with air-cushioned soles.

His comfortable shoes initially became popular with housewives, and sales grew so quickly that Martens opened a factory in 1952. The shoes first made their way across the English Channel when a British shoe manufacturer bought patent rights to manufacture them in the United Kingdom. Dr Martens' boots proved popular among workers such as postmen, police officers and factory workers, and by the late 1960s were being worn by skinheads. Shunned for a while after my younger years, Doc Martens have recently made a comeback on the fashion scene.

The 'alternative' retail assistant with multiple piercings hears about my bad luck with the Chelsea Boot. She's genuinely passionate about Docs and tells me straight off that many on Camden High Street are likely to be knockoffs. Fortunately, the British Boot Company has all sizes of the genuine Dr Martens Chelsea Boot in stock, and they feel automatically comfortable as I slip them on. I become easily convinced that I need this pair, such is the comfort and quality. Very happy with my impulsive purchase, I exit the store after thanking the young lady for her helpful advice.

Heading back into the bowels of the Tube network next door, I take the Northern Line further south to Charing Cross station. The Underground is very old, of course, and was the world's first subterranean metro. The original Metropolitan Railway was opened in 1863 and is now part of the Hammersmith and City Line. The first line to operate underground "electric traction trains", the City and South London Railway, built in 1890, now forms part of the Northern Line.

After a line switch, I soon exit Hyde Park Corner station and as it's a lovely spring day I walk the length of Hyde Park. Strangely enough, after many London visits and having lived here, I've actually spent very little time exploring Hyde Park at all.

I look for the Lady Diana Memorial and am really disappointed to find it closed for maintenance. I still get a good look at the size and design of the memorial and it's not overly impressive anyway – too modest in my opinion. Poor Diana still remains a bit shunned many years after that fateful day in Paris which shook the world's news channels.

I continue to Kensington Palace, where horse riding is very much the thing to do on "Rotten Row", a wide track along the south side of Hyde Park. Kensington Palace was originally built in 1605 and was used as the main royal residence until George III became King in 1761, when he moved across to Buckingham Palace. In more recent years it has been home to Diana, Charles, William and Harry, and the Queen mother. It was closed to the public for a number of years but reopened recently after costly renovations. Part of the palace is a permanent residence for members of the royal family; members of the public can, however, take a tour through some of the original and beautifully restored royal apartments.

The ground level contains portraits of Prince William and Kate Middleton alongside some younger photos of Princess Diana in happier times. Moving to the first floor, the tour focuses on the theme of historic scandals in the royal family. In one room you can sit in a corner or stand at a window sill and hear whispers of rumours about unsavoury goings-on in the palace, a great little touch that feels very English. The tour guides in each room are kitted out in fantastic traditional costumes, similar to the famous Beefeaters of the Tower of London.

After the palace tour and a bite of lunch in fashionable Kensington, I get back on the Tube and make my way to Tower Bridge station, seeking out one of London's more recent attractions – the viewing platform atop the 300-metre-high Shard skyscraper. The price is a bit off-putting: twenty-five pounds if booked online or thirty pounds at the ticket office. As I pay the latter fee, my photo is taken against a blue background by a photographer in the hope that I will buy a photo souvenir after experiencing the uninterrupted views above.

The Shard is the tallest building in the United Kingdom and the European Union, and the viewing platform is 245 metres above the ground. The views are spectacular, and the hefty entry price soon forgotten. The building's sheer height gives me a new perspective on many of the iconic landmarks of this great city: the dome of St Paul's, Olympic Park, the Gherkin, Canary Wharf, the London Eye, the Houses of Parliament, Waterloo station and the Tate Modern's giant chimney.

Easy to make out in the distance are the giant white arc over Wembley Stadium, and the Thames Barrier. Often unnoticed by first-time London visitors is Arsenal Football Club's Emirates Stadium. Another tall, new skyscraper standing opposite The Shard, called Strata SE1, resembles a giant electric razor.

I zoom my camera and take detailed photos in all directions. I hear the occasional Londoner near me comment that, while the tickets are expensive, it is well worth it to see the city from this height. Fortunately, today's weather is clear, but on a typical cloudy and rainy London day, The Shard is a letdown, according to forums on TripAdvisor.

Back in the ground level foyer forty-five minutes later, my photo awaits, transposed onto an artificial backdrop of London in various sizes. The high price is, however, unjustifiable, especially as I have already taken many great photos myself.

After a beer at a nearby pub on South Bank, I head out to the O2 arena (formerly the Millennium Dome) at Greenwich. My intention is to catch the Emirates Skyline chairlift over the Thames to London Olympic Park. The Dome was built as some kind of statement for the beginning of the Third Millennium, but it proved to be a giant "white elephant" for a number of years as it struggled to establish an identity, relevance or any useful role. When I was living in London in 2006, the structure began to make a comeback, as a concert venue, and proved to be an important facility for the London Olympics and Paralympics.

On a weekday afternoon, though, the Dome interior is empty and forgettable. So far during my visit, the London weather has been great, but this afternoon the wind is howling, so strongly in fact that the chairlift has had to be temporarily closed. After I've gone out of my way to reach the Skyline, this is disappointing, and unfortunately the chairlift is so far from anything else of note that it's unlikely I'll be back.

After passing under the Thames on the Tube, I exit St Paul's station and cross the suspended Millennium footbridge to the Tate Modern gallery. I've always enjoyed looking back across the bridge from here at the imposing bulk of St Paul's Cathedral rising above the river on the horizon. It must have been an extraordinary sight when completed in 1710, following a long period of construction supervised by the acclaimed English architect Sir Christopher Wren.

In fact, many of London's most important structures were built or rebuilt in the period after the Great Fire of 1666, which gave city planners a blank canvas on which to redesign the city, often in the then-fashionable classical style.

My visit to the Tate Modern shows that the collection is still thought-provoking and interesting but that the layout hasn't changed much in six years. Nevertheless, even though I don't linger in the renovated power station, it is still a massive drawcard for tourists, especially those seeing its fascinating contemporary works for the first time.

After a long day I arrive home at my aunt's place, and then the two of us venture out to the Old Vic Theatre to see *The Winslow Boy*. Following a straight run on the Northern Line to Waterloo station, we pick up our tickets at the box office and seek out a good Indian restaurant. As is often the case in London, it's hard to decide which of the many curry houses to choose.

We soon find a popular little family-run Indian restaurant. After pappadams, chutney, naan bread and a couple of spicy dishes complemented by cold Kingfisher beer, we head back to the Old Vic. This used to be the National Theatre of England. When the National Theatre moved to a new complex in the South Bank precinct, the Old Vic became quite rundown for a time. However, it has had a revival in recent years, particularly after Hollywood A-lister Kevin Spacey took on the role of artistic director, spending his time between Hollywood and London while overseeing Old Vic productions.

My first job straight off the plane at Heathrow a few years back was at this beloved old theatre, where I found myself working in the finance team. I met Mr Spacey on a couple of occasions, and he seemed a friendly enough guy. Also appearing in an Old Vic production at the time were other Hollywood actors Matthew Modine and Neve Campbell, who would also come in to see the finance team from time to time.

Before the play we have a quick drink in the downstairs bar, where I actually had my informal job interview with the theatre's finance manager. *The Winslow Boy* turns out to be a solid, if slightly earnest story of a loving father who'll stop at nothing to defend his son of false allegations which have bought shame upon his family. A thing I love about staged theatre in London is how cleverly the entire stage set can be changed between scenes, right under the nose of the audience.

Theatre's not for everyone and the occasional well-trained and domesticated retiree-aged husband can be seen nodding off next to his wife, who is usually wrapped in the unfolding drama and having a wonderful time. At the end, the audience, including some polite and newly awakened husbands, stand to applaud the bowing cast of actors, before quickly dispersing outside.

The following morning, Wednesday, I wish to view one of the latest "must-see" exhibitions. Based on reports in the ever-reliable *Guardian Guide*, the most recent offering at the British Museum is supposed to be excellent. Ice Age Art: Arrival of the Modern Mind is a collection of some of the earliest art ever found, dating from between 40,000 and 10,000 years ago and thought to be some of the first signs of a developing human intellect. To me, it looks like the perfect combination of art and history.

The show has apparently been booked out weeks in advance, but I Google it and find that, as is often the case, a limited number of tickets are being put aside each day for early birds, on a first-come-first-served basis.

I take the tube next morning from Tufnell Park to Tottenham Court Road, and half an hour later find myself at the front of the early-bird queue at the British Museum. I manage to buy a reserved ticket, but my entry to the exhibition isn't until 11 am and, with the permanent collections not opening until 10 am, I sneak a second coffee at a cafe in the Great Court to fill in some time. The court is a remarkable open space under a glass-and-steel roof, which surrounds the old library (the "Reading Room") in the museum's centre. The ceiling creates a beautiful blue sky above, lightening what is actually the largest covered public square in Europe, 2 acres in size. The cafe is a great spot to sit and people-watch visitors from far and wide.

The museum itself is Britain's largest and considered one of the finest in the world. I have also visited the Metropolitan Museum of Art ("The Met") in New York and, based on my personal experience, these two museums seem to be far ahead of the pack, both so diverse and awe-inspiring.

My favourite part of the British Museum is the Egyptian section. For the umpteenth time I find it a wonder, with its well-preserved mummies, stone reliefs from ancient temples carved with hieroglyphics, and other extraordinary treasures, most of which were of course pillaged by the British during their nineteenth and early twentieth-century occupation of Egypt. Indeed, the extent and size of the British Empire helps explain the quantity and wide diversity of the ancient artefacts on display throughout the museum. The Egyptian collection is actually the largest collection of Egyptian artefacts outside Egypt.

The Egyptian museum in Cairo, which I have visited, is larger but has only about twenty per cent of its massive collection on display at any one time. Though the collection in London is smaller, most of it can be viewed and the presentation is superior and more informative. And, moreover, it is free!

One of the key exhibits is the ancient Rosetta Stone, on which a decree issued in Egypt in the second century BC is inscribed in three different scripts: hieroglyphic and demotic Ancient Egyptian, and Ancient Greek. These inscriptions famously helped archaeologists decipher Egyptian hieroglyphics. Hewn from black granodiorite, the stone is believed to have originally been displayed in a temple in the ancient Egyptian town of Sais. Archaeologists think it was probably moved during the early Christian or medieval period and was eventually used as building material in the construction of Fort Julien near the town of Rosetta.

It was rediscovered in 1799 by a French soldier during the Napoleonic campaign in Egypt and aroused widespread public interest for its potential to help decipher previously untranslated hieroglyphic language. Translation of the texts took many decades to accomplish, but ultimately provided a breakthrough in the study of ancient Egyptian texts and culture, and changed the modern view of Egyptian history and its influence on architecture, government and education.

At 11am on the dot I go into the exhibition and it's a unique experience to see these masterpieces of Ice Age sculpture, ceramics, drawings and ornaments from all over Europe, and all over ten thousand years old. Though clearly very delicate, most are in excellent condition and presented as art rather than archaeological finds. The objective of the display is to emphasise that these pieces were created by a species that now had the intellect to use sculptures and drawing to embody and communicate ideas and information.

Delighted to have acquired these last-minute tickets, I head back to Tottenham Court Road before walking the well-worn route down Charing Cross Road, passing Leicester Square and its last-minute ticket booths, to Trafalgar Square, where Nelson's Column towers 50 metres above its four large-chested and outward-facing Barbary lion statues. For 150 years they've stared out next to two enormous fountains. There are still plenty of pigeons here, but not as many as there were before feeding them was banned.

The view from the balcony of the National Gallery over Trafalgar Square, busy and thriving as usual with tourists, never fails to impress me. Today I have a very quick look through the National Gallery, where I have spent many a happy hour on previous visits to London.

The National Gallery was established in 1824 and houses well over two thousand paintings, which date back as far as the thirteenth century. It is one of the most visited art museums in the world, along with the Louvre in Paris, the Met in New York and London's Tate Modern and British Museum. These are officially the five most popular art museums in the world, and three of them being in central London. Now that's impressive! As with the Tate Modern and British Museum, the National Gallery is free, a handy concession in such an expensive city and providing some excellent experiences for any first-time tourist.

The works at the National Gallery are grouped according to the period in which they were created. Many of the earlier paintings have a religious subject and can be a little repetitive; I'm not really a fan of religious art. I do, however, love the gallery's large, beautiful landscape paintings by J.M.W. Turner depicting locations throughout Europe, Venice and England in particular. London's Tate Britain devotes half its space to Turner's magnificent paintings, and he is very much one of my favourite artists. So highly regarded is his work that the annual Turner Prize, the most coveted accolade in British art, is named after him.

Skipping the National Gallery today, I head down Whitehall en route to Westminster Abbey. This is Britain's political nerve centre, the site of 10 Downing Street. In a sign of the times, the entrance to Downing Street is heavily fortified by soldiers with powerful automatic weapons. A highly disciplined British soldier stands guard, staring straight ahead, like the well-known guards of Buckingham Palace. This guy, however, looks the real deal and a complete professional in comparison to the more ceremonial guards outside the palace.

Large, dark clouds appear and it begins raining heavily. As I don't have a raincoat, I lift my London Metro newspaper over my head and run down the rest of Whitehall, ignoring Big Ben and the Houses of Parliament and going straight into the Westminster Abbey ticket queue.

One of London's greatest architectural gems, Westminster Abbey has for centuries been the traditional place of coronation and burial for British monarchs, beginning with William the Conqueror in 1066. Queen Elizabeth II was crowned in the Abbey in 1952, Charles and Diana married in the great Gothic structure in 1982 (she wearing her famously long lace wedding gown), and, more recently, William and Kate exchanged their vows here.

On entering the dark and serene interior, I'm greeted by smartly dressed middle-aged tour guides. They come across as more mature than your average tour guide, proudly welcoming curious visitors from all over the world, and wearing long, flowing traditional English gowns, decorated with detailed British religious and royal symbols.

The Abbey is always popular and crowded. Even so, the stop-start audio tour guide provides an informative and condensed trip through Britain's fascinating history, some of it served up on cold slabs of stone – the final resting places of many of the country's most influential figures. Significant royal family tombs are grouped together in a number of side chapels off the main nave. These tombs are quite similar to those of the popes that I'd seen beneath St Peter's Basilica in Rome. But it's the diversity of people buried here that is so striking.

Poet's Corner is the resting place of many of the greats from British culture, including Geoffrey Chaucer, Charles Dickens, Thomas Hardy, Lord Tennyson, Dr Johnson, Rudyard Kipling and Laurence Olivier, and there are memorials to Shakespeare, Jane Austen, Emily Bronte and many more. I'm a keen fan of the many romantic-drama film adaptations of Jane Austen novels that have been produced over the years and I've been told that way back in my family's English past, we are related to Jane Austen. This adds a certain poignancy to the visit and gives this forty-something man from Down Under a tiny connection to the Abbey's historic centre of the British universe.

Back outside, the rain has gone and the sun is shining again. I walk through St James's Park on my way to Piccadilly Circus, where the iconic neon-flashing curved wall of advertisements looms over the fountain and its famous statue. Although the statue is generally known as Eros, this is actually incorrect, as it is an image of Eros's brother, Anteros. The word "circus", in this context, derives from the Latin word meaning "circle", which refers to a round open space at a street junction. Piccadilly Circus was originally the roundabout connecting Regent Street and Piccadilly, as well as other less famous streets, with Anteros as its centrepiece. But sending heavy traffic around such a central monument became impractical, so after World War II, the statue of Anteros was moved from its original position in the centre to the south-eastern side of Piccadilly Circus.

"See you at Piccadilly" is a common term used by both tourists and Londoners, as Piccadilly Circus is an ideal meeting place, right next to Oxford Street's shopping and the West End's theatre and entertainment venues, or "Theatreland". The neon advertising panels above Piccadilly Circus have been operating since the early 1900s. It would be very interesting to know the price for promotional space on this most prized billboard.

I continue along the wide straight street of Piccadilly, lined with fashionable tailors' shops. Other points of interest here include the Royal Academy of Arts and the famous Ritz Hotel opposite. High tea at the Ritz, with cucumber sandwiches of course, is very popular and bookings need to be made months in advance.

I'm soon passing through Green Park past Buckingham Palace to Constitution Hill and then Hyde Park Corner. Time has gotten the better of me: in just over one hour I'm due at the New London Theatre to see *War Horse*. Having walked at least 15 kilometres, I'm tired and sweaty so I head home to shower and freshen up before the show.

That accomplished, I print my e-ticket and race out of the door, needing to be at Covent Garden in twenty minutes! Margaret is in the house and a little surprised by my total disorganisation, to say the least.

From Leicester Square tube station, I sprint the half mile to the New London Theatre. It's actually closer to Covent Garden station, but, with time of the essence, a switch from the Northern Line to the Piccadilly Line would have been a mistake (as I know from experience; also, Transport for London (TFL) strongly recommends visitors to Covent Garden depart at Leicester Square station on Sundays and walk the extra distance due to crowd numbers). I'm soon jumping triple steps at the theatre's escalator as the last warning sirens advise of the imminent start of the performance. Sucking in deep recovery breaths, I take my pre-allocated seat is in the last row. In the two rows below are a group of approximately twenty teenage English girls.

The play *War Horse* made its debut in 2007 and is based on a novel of the same name by Michael Morpurgo. It has been a huge critical and commercial success ever since. I knew little about it until Steven Spielberg adapted the story for a big budget movie which garnered critical acclaim and Oscar nominations when released in 2011. The story revolves around the love and emotional attachment felt by a young English boy (Albert) for his horse (Joey). During the trials and tribulations of World War I, they are separated and seemingly lost to each other for good, only for Billy to be reunited with his equine friend in the third act behind enemy lines in France. The story is emotionally involving and draining, and accompanied by phenomenally creative and exciting visual and effects.

On the stage, the real star is Joey, who is brought to life in the form of a horse-sized puppet controlled by two expert puppeteers. The incredibly realistic, vivid and detailed movements of the horse are extraordinary; the puppet horse comes across as a living character with a wide range of emotions, just like the human cast members. It is amazing to watch and would be entertaining on its own even without the context of the story.

This production of *War Horse* has been the number-one show in London's West End in recent months, so I feel very lucky to have secured a late ticket – one of the benefits of travelling solo! As I exit the theatre, I imagine that the words "Oh my God, how about that puppet?" must have been repeated thousands of times since the play's first performances many years ago.

My final day in London is spent just taking it easy, and Margaret and I discuss my travel plans further. I've thoroughly enjoyed my stay, reading her *Guardian* newspaper every day and watching great telly (as the English say) on the BBC and other networks.

At Waterstones bookstore in Camden Town, I purchase travel guides for Paris, Budapest and Lisbon – a smart move as it saved on luggage space on the way over and takes advantage of the strong Aussie dollar. Then I decide to go for a run, following my old favourite route through Hampstead Heath and up to Kenwood House. There are the usual keen dog owners walking their dogs and romantic couples lying together on the grass. Next to the ponds, children are playing with geese and ducks. Kites are flying at the top of Parliament Hill. Walkers are talking into their smartphone headphones, having conversations on the move. Moreover, there are plenty of other runners to pace myself against.

On our final evening together, Margaret kindly takes me out to dinner. She's booked a small Greek restaurant hidden away off Camden High Street. After our arrival, we watch it steadily fill with customers, most of whom seem to be Londoners and repeat customers. Unfamiliar with Greek food, we sample a few shared dishes and wash them down with a couple of beers. The waiting staff of the family-run restaurant are quick, friendly and highly personable. It's "a great choice", I tell my dining companion. We make a toast to safe and enjoyable travels ahead.

To finish the evening, we watch the latest edition of *Mock the Week*, a BBC comedy satire TV show enjoyed by us both in the past. As my head hits the pillow, I reflect that while I have enjoyed my few days' dose of London, I am even more excited about heading to Paris tomorrow and the prospect of new destinations in the weeks ahead.

Three

Paris, the City of Light

It has been a pleasure seeing my aunt again. My family all love her dearly and always look forward to her hospitality. Of all the people I've known, she has real integrity, and is not flashy or pretentious like others can be in the medical profession. What you see is what you get.

In a gesture that's a bit of an honour, she offers to drive me down to St Pancras station in her little red Ford Fiesta hatchback. Her economical car has only utilitarian value. The driver's door won't shut properly and is out of alignment, due to being broken into half a dozen times or so. The car has been stolen on a couple of occasions, but somehow eventually was returned to its owner each time.

Margaret zips erratically through Camden Town, avoiding the odd Goth casually walking across the street. After a few backstreets and shortcuts, and halts at occasional road works, we arrive at St Pancras. She jumps out of the car, gives me a quick kiss on the cheek and then she's off again to her next activity on this Saturday, be it pottery or the allotment. She is kind and endearing but maintains her reserve to the very end.

St Pancras station is a classic and iconic building; its 200-metre-long glass roof is the largest of its type in the world. Previously neglected, the station was reopened in 2006 after a billion-pound makeover, carried out with painstaking attention to detail, which restored some of the glamour and romance once associated with travelling to Paris. Travel in Europe has lost its soul somewhat in recent years, with the likes of low-budget airlines like EasyJet and Ryan Air.

Not long after I've checked in and passed through security, I'm hurtling at 300 kilometres an hour towards Paris. As the train descends under the English Channel, my ears pop with the combination of speed and change in air pressure. The tunnel has been a mixed success since opening to great fanfare in the mid-1990s. Its construction threw old enemies France and England together in a precarious engineering project. With separate teams digging from each side of the Channel, the joint venture became a race to the middle. The costs blew out massively, and initially neither country had a clear idea of how to best utilise the 50-kilometre tunnel. These days both countries wouldn't know what to do without it.

As the train advances through the tunnel, I begin to tune in to French voices around me. The language is as elegant, refined and romantic as ever. Soon the train rises out of the tunnel back to sea level and my ears pop again as I'm listening to some music. The terrain is immediately different from the English countryside, consisting mainly of wide, flat, healthy-looking cultivated fields.

The train progresses through the outer suburbs of Paris, which are quite plain compared to the beautiful central districts and a residential patchwork of immigrants, races and religious creeds. With each passing train station though, the urban environment grows more attractive and the journey begins to resemble the final ride into Paris that is seen on millions of television screens during the annual Tour de France.

Before long, the train docks and its doors open onto the Gare du Nord station, historically famous like the St Pancras station of two hours ago. Arriving in Paris by train has far more appeal than travelling via the city's main airport, Charles de Gaulle, generally considered second rate and a long, expensive cab fare from the city centre. And an added bonus with the train journey is that you are not subjected to the many ordeals of plane travel like check-in and security screening.

The high-speed train network throughout Europe has been extensively expanded in recent years and there are now many express routes between cities and countries along which trains travel at up to 350 kilometres an hour. My Eurail Pass was expensive but hopefully will prove to have been a good investment going forward, offering as it does full access to all of Europe's routes.

I tear the city centre map out of my guidebook and start walking, my backpack counter-balanced by a bursting carry-on bag in front and my new Doc Martens providing good foot support. After many years of using digital maps, using a paper map proves a challenge. I think I know where north and south are, and I hope I'm moving in the general direction of my central Paris hotel.

Determinedly holding the large map out in front of me, I start walking south along Boulevard de Magenta in the conviction it will take me directly to the side-streets near the hotel. Twenty minutes later I'm walking up the narrow street of Rue d'Aboukir to number 106, the Comfort Hotel Royal Aboukir. The hotel is tiny and a bit rundown but it's cheap and cheerful and it's all about location, location, location – it's just a twenty-or-so-minute walk from the Louvre, Notre Dame Cathedral and other famous Parisian landmarks.

"Bonjour, monsieur" says the slightly untidy-looking hotel receptionist. Plenty of tourists are hopping in and out of the lift in the popular three-star hotel. After I squeeze my 36-inch waist and bags in and emerge on the fifth floor, the lights to the corridor automatically switch on. In my compact little room, the queen-size bed takes up much of the space. Importantly though, the room is quiet and has a safe, cable TV, a strong Wi-Fi signal and a good bathroom. Perfect!

After checking in, I'm peckish and eager to explore, and I soon discover a great little restaurant street a few hundred metres away. It turns out that Rue Montorgueil is quite well known for its restaurant and cafe culture, cheeses, wine, bakeries and a weekend market. From the river end of the street it is but a five-minute walk to the Louvre and its iconic glass pyramid in the central court. Over the years, I've heard divided opinions on this striking architectural feature, people either seeming to love it or hate it and few sitting on the fence, but I am still of the opinion that this ultramodern glass entrance to the Louvre perfectly complements the classic old-style architecture that envelopes it.

A bar on the square at the Louvre patronised by a trendy Saturday afternoon crowd catches my eye. I walk up its small steps to the entrance, drawing the attention of a waitress. But when I check out the drinks list my jaw drops at the prices, clearly a reflection of the high rent. From my reaction it's obvious that I can't afford this place and the waitress doesn't mind in the slightest when I say, "Maybe another time." As in many tourist spots around Europe, the premium charged for having a drink or a meal while looking out over a famous landmark is prohibitive. St Mark's Square in Venice is another prime example, where prices seem to become more and more reasonable the further you proceed away from the beautiful square (except along the Grand Canal obviously).

To the west of the Louvre are the Tuileries Gardens, with their marvellously wide and roomy paths, fountains and greenery, and then the giant roundabout of Place de la Concorde, which covers a whopping 8.5 hectares in area. Cars and mopeds fly around the massive concourse. One thing I love about European cities, and especially Paris, is that they're smart when it comes to modes of transport, many people using small hatchbacks and mopeds. Australian cities always seem to have a ridiculous number of four-wheel-drives and utes – very American.

At the roundabout's centre is a famous Egyptian obelisk that was given to the French by Egypt. King Louis Philippe had the obelisk raised in the centre of Place de la Concorde in 1836, right where the guillotine stood during the French revolution. Enormous at 23 metres tall, the obelisk is inscribed with ancient Egyptian hieroglyphics. It once marked the entrance to Luxor Temple, which I've been fortunate enough to visit as well.

Today the centre of the roundabout is occupied by a large Chinese wedding party, celebrating with a blushing bride having her fairy-tale wedding in Paris. They've hired a professional-looking photographer for this most romantic of settings. Of course, I take a photo of the family surrounding the blushing bride – all thirty-six of them! Does it go without saying that a country of 1.4 billion people has very large weddings too? Making their way through the sheer volume of hectic traffic at this most central of roundabouts must have been a logistical challenge, and they all look proud and primed for the great photo opportunity.

Having got my bearings, I begin a meandering walk back to my hotel. Along the way are countless beautiful and historic buildings. I find a little cafe-bar that looks out at the grand Paris Opera House. The bar is stylish and very French, and the beer inexpensive.

Feeling refreshed, I seek out Paris's most famous department store, the Galeries Lafayette. After getting a little lost ("Rue du" this, "Rue du" that), I find the store, which is actually spread across three buildings – the main store, one hundred years old; a men's store; and home design store – all facing each other at a three-way intersection.

I make a beeline for the men's store, where I find a selection of all the great fashion labels – Ray Ban, Ralph Lauren, Armani, Prada, Gucci and more. I try on expensive sunglasses and browse the leather jackets, belts, wallets, hats and suits on display for wealthier customers than me.

I'm a long-time fan of Ralph Lauren, so I head up the elevator to the second floor to look at the range there. Anything you could possibly want with the iconic polo pony stitched onto it is available. And of course, being in Paris, the Lacoste range is enormous. Lacoste was *the* brand of shirt to wear growing up in Brisbane's affluent western suburbs. The little crocodile is locked deep into my subconscious as an everlasting icon of French fashion and sophistication.

Growing up I played a lot of tennis, and the Lacoste crocodile originated in tennis circles when a French superstar of the 1920s, René Lacoste, challenged the status quo of restrictive traditional tennis attire, long-sleeved button shirts, long pants and a tie. Monsieur Lacoste began wearing shirts used by British polo players, which he adapted for the tennis courts of the Grand Slams. Lacoste had been nicknamed "the Crocodile" by his fans and the media because of his tenacity on the tennis court. Not only did he embrace the nickname, but he also began embroidering the logo of the reptile onto his blazer, thereby creating an image for his brand.

Most of these big brands are above my price range, besides which would be quite impractical to purchase any fashionable clothes given my lengthy travel plans.

Walking along a couple of busy streets back to the hotel, I find a wine store with a great range of French wines for my taste and budget. I mark it on my map after buying a bottle of Bordeaux red. I'll definitely be back (more than once) in the next five days. Also nearby is a pastry shop with all sorts of sweet treats, all of the superior quality one would expect in Paris. This store will also become part of my ritual of trying something new every day during my stay.

Although I am grateful to be back in Paris, after my walk I realise the city has lost a little of its magic the second time around. It's still as beautiful and sophisticated as last time, but you simply can't replicate the feeling of your first sighting of the Eiffel Tower and Arc de Triomphe or your first experience of Parisian food, wine and fashionable locals. It's a pipe dream of mine to maybe live and work here for a year. However, such a large, sophisticated and foreign place would make fitting in and meeting friends difficult, particularly as I am naturally shy. New York is another awesome city I've visited that I'd like to live and work. I have similar misgivings about that, though having a resumé in finance as a CPA would probably help in the Big Apple and at least I'd speak the language!

On Sunday, I leap out of bed full of anticipation, as this is my first full day in Paris. Twenty minutes after taking a shower and breakfast, with a couple espressos for stimulation, I am walking down the street in search of the local metro; it's a little annoying that Sentier station is on one of the minor metro lines. Margaret has given me twenty metro tickets, left behind by one of her many visitors. I'm unsure if they'll actually work, so it feels like a small win as the ticket validates, allowing me through the turnstile gate to the network below.

The Paris metro is just as I remembered. Not as old and rundown as the London Underground and definitely cleaner. After typing in a reminder to email Margaret a thank you for the tickets, I plug in my earphones and listen to a playlist I've made for walking and tubing around Paris.

One line-transfer later, I'm soon rising up the escalator at Pigalle station. Straight in front of me is the giant windmill of the Moulin Rouge. In the light of the day it makes little impression, but it will come alive at night in the brilliant neon colours it is famous for. I'm planning on taking in the late cabaret show tomorrow evening, so I block out the landmark in anticipation of something more spectacular after dark. Pigalle is also infamously known as something of a red-light district.

It is soon apparent that I'm not the only one heading up to the steady incline towards the Basilica of Sacré-Coeur. As at many popular tourist sites around the world, finding it is just a matter of putting away the map and becoming a sheep in the flock.

The basilica is at the heart of Montmartre, supposedly atop the only hill in the flat expanse of Paris. My new Docs make light work of the cobblestones, reassuring me that they'll become invaluable on hundreds of cobblestone streets ahead in Europe. At the very base of the basilica, five hundred white steps await me.

A number of young African men hover as the droves of tourists arrive. In no time at all one has me in his sights. Flashing a white smile, he grabs my hand, asks me where I'm from and then gives the insincere compliment that I look like a "successful businessman". All the while he proceeds to weave multiple colours of cotton around my wrist. After what seems like only ten dazed seconds, he tells me I look like a "nice man" – this on top of being successful! For good luck on my travels I'm supposed to make a wish, as if it's my birthday.

It is at this point that his smile turns 180 degrees into aggression, the counter side to his cunning plan. Apparently, because I'm "successful", for this shallow gesture I am expected to pay him fifty euros. Now one of his dark friends stands behind him. My passivity is slightly to blame for the hole I've dug for myself, but with plenty of other tourists around in a very public area, I haggle. "I'll give you ten euros."

Insulted, his aggression lifts to a new level. I've now created a scene, and a couple of male tourists have backed up behind me. I glance sideways at them for reassurance, thinking to myself, enough! After slipping ten euros into his hand, from deep down inside me (somewhere) come the words "Please piss off and leave me alone!" After the ultimatum, I turn around with blinkers on and head towards the next set of steps. Having got away with this one and only ten-euro lost, I swear to myself not to be swindled again for the rest of the trip.

The sun is out and the temperature is in the high twenties Celsius. I climb the steps, counting down from five hundred to one. The gleaming white dome of the basilica rises above, under clear blue skies. Wiping the sweat off my brow, I turn around to take in the view. The panorama is wide and spectacular, with the Eiffel Tower, Notre Dame and other famous landmarks easily visible as you look towards the horizon.

I resist the first instinct to take a panoramic photo – better to take some time for contemplation at the top of the steps, seated between groups of teenagers who are socialising and soaking up the Sunday rays. Particularly lovely is a harp player plucking away at his strings. Now this *is* a perfect photo opportunity: harp player in the foreground, Eiffel Tower in the distance behind him.

Now I've cooled down and relaxed, my mind moves on to the prospect of climbing up into the basilica dome for the ultimate view. However, maybe because it's a Sunday, the queue for the steps to the top is long and not moving anytime soon, so I make a quick decision to strike it off my must-see list.

Then proceeding along the shaded side of the cathedral, I go searching for a famous artists' square recommended by a friend after a recent trip to Paris. A fitting instrumental diversion on the side corner of the church is a pretty Frenchwoman in traditional bright purple dress playing the accordion. It's so very Paris! I take a video which I plan on uploading to Facebook to make friends back home a wee bit jealous.

The cobblestone streets continue down from the rear of the cathedral. Countless shops flog mass-produced oil paintings of the Eiffel Tower, Arc de Triomphe and so on, for the bargain price of twenty euros. In one such shop I flick through dozens of paintings before asking for directions to the artists' square, assuring the owner that I'll come back. It's not a lie and I'm genuinely interested in his paintings, but, from the look on his face, he clearly thinks I'm pulling his leg.

Following the directions of the shop owner, I have no trouble locating the Place du Tertre, which turns out to be a tiny yet funky square. Around the edges, on display in the open, are pictures of the Eiffel Tower that are far more avant-garde and contemporary than the stock-standard oil paintings in the tourist shops. Naturally, the high prices for this genuine art reflect this.

Montmartre has attracted artists and bohemian writers for much of the last two hundred years, and the square of today is actually a bit of a throwback to the time when the area was the mecca of modern art in Paris. In the early twentieth century, many penniless painters lived here, among them a certain Pablo Picasso, who was little known at the time. Picasso, my absolute favourite painter, lived and worked for a number of years in the heart of Montmartre. Pablo moved here to be in the art capital of Europe and his early time in Paris was spent living in poverty; he even burned some of his works just to keep his small room in the shared apartment warm.

There are quite a few portrait artists busy with eager customers. I watch a couple ply their trade, impressed by their attention to detail and the likeness of the works in progress to the subject. These guys are taking their time, unlike the dime-a-dozen portrait drawers you see in tourist-heavy areas the world over.

After taking in the square, I'm soon retracing my steps back down the hundreds of steps I climbed an hour ago – no need to count this time. The African men are still being a nuisance.

There are so many charming streets and lanes to wander through. It is easy to imagine how living here would be a breath of fresh air, even for a short stint. Paris may have a large city's pace of life, but the atmosphere in Montmartre is relaxed and quiet, just the way I like it, and to regularly take in the view of the Eiffel Tower at night, with its light doing circles in the evening like a beacon, would be amazing.

It has been a memorable and fulfilling morning. Now I make my way back down into the Metro, en route to south of the River Seine to experience one of Paris's largest open-air street markets. The Marché Bastille market is only open on Thursdays and Sundays from 7 am in the morning till 2.30 pm.

Shopping in street markets is a way of life for Parisians and the French as a whole. Parisians will be found with their shopping trolleys at the markets, rather than at supermarkets, searching for the best produce. Locals will usually sample produce before committing to buy, be it fruit, meat, vegetables or cheese. "Allez-y, goûtez!" is a common phrase, meaning "Go on, have a taste!" Unlike in most regular flea markets there is no haggling over prices; it's just not the done thing.

For 800 metres from the roundabout outside the Bastille metro station, the hustle and bustle of the market runs all the way to Richard-Lenoir station. Everything imaginable at a Paris market is here. There's stall after stall, with cheeses, fresh raspberries, stacked baguettes, spit-roasted chickens, olives and olive oils, various kinds of eggs, mushrooms, truffles, large fresh oranges, pig carcasses, and *saucissons* (French salami sausages). It also offers a seafood-lover's paradise of lobsters, crabs and fresh fish on beds of crushed ice. It's foodie heaven! There are also plenty of belts, books, trinkets, wallets, hats, T-shirts, colourful scarfs, baskets, wind-up toys, and fresh buckets of flowers which radiate a spring-like glow.

There are two distinct lines of stalls to meander between, back and forth, just how I had imagined. The food produce is generally arranged in groups of perhaps three or four competing sellers of, for example, fresh fruit. A wonderful loud banter goes on back and forth between the competitors. They are charismatically French, over the top, and confident that their produce is the best.

Unfortunately, I'm not a fish lover and where there's a concentration of seafood, the smell makes me hold my breath or breathe solely through my mouth. Some stalls selling hot meals, such as curries, have long queues. Having last night broken the hotel's tacky corkscrew on just one bottle, I find a more robust one for five euros. Whereas most Aussie wineries now use screw-tops, the Europeans continue to use corks. I inquire about the price at a stall selling chic hats, but quickly conclude that I look a bit ridiculous wearing one.

The cheese sellers are unsurprisingly impressive, with the kind of variety I'd only seen previously in the Harrods produce section in

London, but without the sky-high price tags. The varieties of cheese cater for the tastes and pallets of knowledgeable Parisian cheese connoisseurs. Given that I eat only blue vein, stilton, brie and camembert back home, I'm a real amateur in comparison; but, as an Australian on holiday, I'd like to try something different, but "not too different if you know what I mean". I walk away with a package of some kind of soft and smelly cheese having already forgotten its name.

I continue in this mode for the rest of the market's length, purchasing some *saucisson* along the way. This will end up in the fridge back in my room. I plan on buying fresh baguettes each day for the cheese and sausage, to be washed down with Bordeaux red, opened with my new corkscrew. I'm sure it will prove a handy investment in the weeks ahead.

The rest of the afternoon is spent window shopping among the fashionable retailers of the Galeries Lafayette area. There are plenty of boutique items to browse, but it's really just browsing for browsing's sake. Just because you're on a diet doesn't mean you can't look at the menu. That's the philosophy anyway.

Also in evidence are many beautiful French women. More so than London, mainland European women seem unfamiliar and exotic. It could be any number of things that create this impression: their style of dress, skin usually unblemished by the sun, accents and sophistication, unfamiliar hairstyles.

In the evening, I head outside into the twilight for the five-minute walk to Rue Montorgueil, with its plentiful restaurants. It may be 8.30 pm, but if I'd come two hours earlier many of these restaurants would have been empty. It takes no time at all to find a menu and ambience that I like. The restaurant opens out onto the pavement in typical Parisian style, and I take a table very conducive to people-watching, offering both views into the restaurant and out onto the street. I order the familiar "steak-frites" with salad and bearnaise sauce and a glass of Bordeaux red.

There are groups of young locals enjoying good food, wine and company, as one does in Paris. It's a really pleasant scene, but at one point I sense some emotional turbulence only metres away. There's a man and woman, husband and wife, having a very heated discussion in French-accented English for some reason. I begin to eavesdrop and it's soon obvious that he has been a naughty boy – unfaithful for a while, perhaps?

The furious wife berates and peppers him with very direct questions, as if she is cross-examining him on a witness stand. Her pitch and tone are strong and loud enough for any English speakers in the vicinity to decipher her accusations. "How long has this been going on?" "Would you have told me if I hadn't found out?" "Who were these women?" "Where did you meet them?" "And the lies, the cover ups!" "Did any of our friends know?" "What about me and the kids?" He is speechless. "How can you sit there and say absolutely nothing?" She pretty much knows everything and he's ready to raise the white flag.

His staring at the ground only heightens her temper. The small dog at the next table begins to bark, even this little canine sensing trouble is afoot. People look at the couple and at one another as she stands up yelling, "Don't call me! You've broken my heart!" He looks wimpish and a little pathetic. They haven't yet had a meal, and there are just two glasses of wine on the table. The adulterer pays the waiter, who is clearly aware of what has just transpired. The man then walks off awkwardly into the night, with his tail between his legs.

Frenchmen have an amorous reputation. In the last month, I've read an article about a French study that revealed that more than fifty per cent of French men are unfaithful; however, one in three French women also cheat on their spouses. It also found that although infidelity is on the rise, the French are champions of forgiveness.

My meal arrives, the steak cooked to perfection, the French fries thin and fresh and the béarnaise sauce rich and creamy. It's pretty standard fare but tastes damn good with a glass of Bordeaux. I feel a sense of empathy for the couple, but it has been another intriguing Parisian experience of the kind they don't mention in the guidebooks. I wonder if this restaurant is a break-up hotspot? Anyway, the waiters were friendly, the price was right, and I'll be coming back.

With my market purchases stored in the minibar fridge, breakfast becomes a daily routine of fresh baguette with cheese and sausage along with instant coffee. Not very healthy, but it's convenient and cheap. The humble French stick, or baguette, has an interesting little history of its own evolution to tell. The bread, made of four key ingredients – flour, water, yeast and salt – has been a French staple in various forms for hundreds of years. Long, wide baguettes were made from the time of Louis XIV, becoming thinner by the mid-eighteenth century. In the 1800s, some baguettes were up to 2 metres long.

During the time of Louis XVI, sourdough – bread made with a "starter yeast" consisting of yeast and bacteria growing inside a flour-and-water paste – became the bread of choice (as it is for many people today). This was, however, too expensive for the average citizen, and baguettes remained the staple bread for commoners due to their far lower cost. And the rest, as they say, is history.

Today almost all bread produced and consumed in Paris is baked fresh each morning. To the French, bread-making is a highly respected, traditional business, and the very best bakers have a similar status to top winemakers. There is even a movement within the country to have the French baguette listed as UNESCO Intangible Cultural Heritage. It is hoped that this would protect the quality of the traditional baguette against increasing competition from supermarkets and convenience stories, which the National Confederation of French Bakers claims endangers the preservation of the know-how and skills of traditional bakers, or *boulangeries*.

I'd already seen Paris's world-renowned Louvre on my previous visit, making a beeline for the Mona Lisa like many other tourists. This time around I plan to visit a number of the other world-famous galleries in this centre of the art universe. On Monday morning I exit the metro back to street level at Rambuteau station and walk the short distance to the Centre Pompidou, one of Paris's most iconic modern buildings.

Opened in 1977, the Centre Pompidou is the official national collection of twentieth-century French art. It was boldly built "inside out" – in other words, with many of its internal structures and services, such as escalators and plumbing pipes, showing on the outside of the building – and initially opened to very mixed reactions. However, over the following decades it gradually gained a reputation as a high-tech icon, one that helped transform museums from elite monuments into hubs of social and cultural exchange.

The odd building is very photogenic from all different angles, with the external escalators rising floor by floor diagonally up the side of the building. Like a moth to the flame, I absent-mindedly take the external elevator upwards, hoping to enter the gallery on the top floor. However, I soon learn that entrance to the museum's permanent collection is only possible back at ground level.

Entering the ground floor five minutes later, I begin the gallery tour from the bottom up. The extensive collection is divided into various modern art movements. There are computer-generated and cut pieces of furniture, optical illusions, abstract art statements about the twentieth century, strange and nonsensical brass sculptures, beautiful still-life nudes and many Picasso paintings, complemented by works of artists influenced by the Spanish genius. In today's world, where there can be a tendency for disposable ideas to be considered modern art, this collection is wall-to-wall brilliance, and I'm overwhelmingly impressed.

I continuously take photos with the flash turned off while exploring the paintings and sculptures, and they are so impressive that I know many will make the final cut of my travel album. I try my best to zoom in on the artworks so that they fill the picture frame, thereby creating my own art collection on the iPad.

The top floor has a temporary exhibition by an Irish artist I've never heard of. Upon reading the brochure, my feeling is that the exhibition isn't up to the standard of the works in the permanent collection. The Centre Pompidou is only 600 metres, as the crow flies, from Notre Dame and the view of Paris's cathedral from the rooftop is uninhibited and quite splendid, and instantly decides me on my next destination.

Soon I'm wandering through Notre Dame's dark interior as I did six years earlier, again enjoying its gothic beauty, the highlight being the famous giant stained-glass windows which serenely radiate a spring sunlight from the heavens above.

My previous visit to the Eiffel tower was partly disappointing, as the top level, at 276 metres, had been closed due to windy conditions.

Today, however, the sun is shining and there is only a slight breeze. I walk the long and picturesque open green space of the Champ de Mars towards the tower. I love the different angles and views that appear the closer one gets to this iconic structure. At the tower's wide base, I get the same sense of awe as last time looking up at the extensive 7,300 tons of wrought iron above.

Paris's most popular tourist destination receives 6.7 million visitors each year. It was erected for the 1889 World's Fair and named after its architect, Gustave Eiffel, whose company designed and built it. When first erected, the tower attracted criticism from Parisians, especially those in artistic circles. The original plan was for the tower to stand for only twenty years, at which point it would be dismantled. But with technological advances in communication, the tower proved invaluable as a powerful radio transmitter.

One guarantee with the Eiffel tower is that there will be long queues. However, they move deceptively fast and it's not long before we're packed into enormous lifts that ascend the wide bases of the tower – simultaneously upwards and sidewards due to the tower's unconventional shape – to the first floor. The next lift goes straight up to the second-floor viewing platform, at 115 metres. For fitness freaks or other crazies, there are 360 steps to the first floor and another 360 steps to the second.

Having previously experienced this view, I jump straight in the queue to rocket to the very top platform, well over twice the height of the second. I get chatting to a couple of friendly middle-aged women from Philadelphia, one of whom has a fear of heights but has been conned by her friend into taking the lift to the very top.

On a clear day the view from 276 metres up – panoramic, sweeping and detailed – can extend to 60 kilometres, well beyond the city limits. Today is one such perfect day as a result of the lovely spring weather Paris has brought out just for me. However, we are so high that the views lose some of the appeal of those across the city from the first floor. A good example of this is the view to Montmartre and the Sacré-Coeur basilica. From the second floor it's more attractive, as the white church and dome stand out above the skyline, whereas from the top platform they are lost among the mass of rooftops.

Even though I have a rough idea of the location of Roland Garros tennis stadium, venue for the French Open, as much as I try it's hard to spot – some binoculars would be very helpful. The home stadium of Paris's largest football club, Paris Saint-Germain, can be made out in the sports precinct on the opposite side of the Seine, along with a large racecourse. It makes sense that the 47,929-capacity Parc des Princes stadium is not located in the mythological Saint Germain area of Paris, a favourite with lovers of literature, antique collectors and fashionistas, with its chic boutiques and exquisite window displays. The area some of the historic greats of writing have called home is too central, without the space for a ground to house the club's large fan base.

The top viewing platform's extra height does have its advantages, however, providing a great view down towards the Arc de Triomphe, with its thirteen wheel-spoke-like streets, the Louvre and further to the Centre Pompidou – perfect for zooming in with the camera. On the direct opposite river bank is the Palais de Chaillot, from where, famously, photos of Hitler with the Eiffel Tower behind him were taken after the Nazis' successful invasion.

A popular thing to do on the top floor of the Eiffel Tower is celebrate with a glass of champagne. Though it's quite expensive at fifteen euros per glass, the hole-in-the-wall bar is doing a roaring trade with romantic customers. There are a number of photographs of the small apartment Gustave Eiffel made for himself here – a truly great pad! Gustave furnished it with soft chintzes, wooden cabinets and even a grand piano, and here he would entertain the science elite. The private apartment made Eiffel the object of great envy among Parisians during his lifetime. Eiffel also made use of his apartment to carry out meteorological observations, and also used the tower to perform experiments on the action of air resistance on falling bodies.

Eiffel was highly influential and I've seen other buildings designed by him on my travels, notably the General Post Office in Ho Chi Minh City, which he designed, and the Statue of Liberty, to which he contributed.

I say g'day to the lady from Philadelphia, who is more relaxed now and enjoying the view. I feel on top of the world at this lofty height and, only two weeks into my two-month adventure, that the world is my oyster. It beats working anyway! With the sun setting, I'd love to stay for another hour but need to return to the hotel and rest up before the late Moulin Rouge show tonight, to get into which I expect I'll need to join a long and competitive queue.

After a reviving kip, a bite of dinner and a rare Red Bull for that extra edge (These "energy drinks" are the Devil's work and only ever used by me as a last resort), I head out into the night, destined for the famous cabaret club. A friend of mine had been to the Moulin Rouge a few months before and raved about the show. It is an absolute must for me this time around.

I take the same Pigalle metro station escalator to street level as I did yesterday morning. Now it's dark, the bright, red neon lights of the giant windmill dominate the dark urban street scene. The windmill "blades" spin gracefully above the traffic as scores of tourists below take snaps, some getting precariously in the way of traffic. I take a few shots with my iPhone – absolutely no flash required – and the windmill that was unremarkable during daylight is now magnificent, displaying the colours of a gorgeous butterfly.

I head to the queue for the real McCoy, the second, late-night show at 11 pm. Having researched on Google, I join the queue at 10 pm, expecting everything to be fine. However, as I jay-walk across the street, my heart sinks a little, as a few hundred people appear to be already in the queue, which extends around the corner. It seems that I'm an hour too late, but I won't die wondering.

The first show started at 8.30 pm. It is usually booked months in advance and, as it includes a sit-down meal, is very expensive. The late show will still set me back €110, with a glass of champagne thrown in. The expense already a given, I join the long queue, unsure if it will be worth it.

Over the course of the next twenty minutes, another few hundred people arrive behind me, in a worse predicament than myself. Most people seem impatient and worried. Up ahead, a group of twenty-something men and women barge their way through the queue to enter an adjacent pub. Their leader is a big rugby-player type wearing a Contiki Tours shirt, and he sounds Australian. Subsequently, I watch these young travellers downing drinks in the bar, as close to a Moulin Rouge experience as they're going to get.

The queue then starts moving and moving and moving, and before long I'm amongst the bright colours of the foyer in the greatest of all cabaret clubs. Being a party of one is advantageous, as I'm moved quickly to a table inside. Looking back behind me are probably only fifty more people who've been fortunate enough to get in to the show. There must be well over a hundred disappointed visitors, many of them changing their plans for tomorrow so that they can get to the queue earlier.

The theatre's interior looks very much like the Baz Luhrmann's movie version, which had Nicole Kidman swinging through the air on a chandelier. At the table I'm met by three friendly American women on holiday together. They've travelled Down Under before and compliment my home country as "a beautiful place". The remaining seat is taken by a Middle-Eastern man, not looking entirely happy with his seat to one side of the stage. Upon asking the waiter if he can be moved closer, he's quickly rebutted. My guess is that he wants to be more front and centre for the nudity that will follow. After a long wait, the complimentary champagne is very welcome.

The lights dim as the audience clap to the sound of the opening soundtrack, a mixture of disco and circus with great dance beats and rhythm. It's unapologetically tacky, Las Vegas-like glamour, yet idiosyncratically Parisian.

The opening number is exciting, with athletic women strutting out onto the stage in blooming and exaggerated costumes, which shout colour and bling. They move with grace and precision, but also with a veneer of effortlessness. Amid the extraordinary costumes, the ladies' bare chests are merely a part of a grander palette. Many of the outfits feature elaborate adornments resembling the feathers of peacocks.

The ladies are soon complemented by male dancers, prompting a few winks and nods from the American girls at the table. Strong, direct and confident like their female counterparts, the men's presence on the stage is the perfect yin to the ladies' yang.

The number closes with confident kicks from the ladies, as many are hoisted into the air like dolls by the men. The crowd burst into excited applause and there's not an unhappy person in the house, except maybe the waiters. The Moulin Rouge is buzzing as the queue and price become distant memories. I've enjoyed plenty of live music, musicals and theatre throughout my life, but the cabaret is a genre unto itself, a Parisian invention and institution that showcases the best of the country's strong and distinctive culture.

After a variety of numbers, the show kicks back into full gear with the traditional can-can dance, with its red, white and blue costumes, abundant energy and patriotism.

For the final dance, seemingly no costume is left unturned and every breast is exposed. The audience clap the performers to the very end, when the whole cast gets a standing ovation. It has been a unique entertainment and I feel quite privileged to have seen it. It may be well after midnight but there's still great energy in the Moulin Rouge.

When I leave the theatre and head away from the giant red windmill's gaze, Pigalle becomes a little seedy. I quickly navigate the 2 kilometres or so back to the hotel and when my head hits the pillow hard at 2 am I'm exhausted. In retrospect, the Red Bull was a good idea and has got me this far, but the caffeine and sugar are now definitely wearing off and I soon fall into a deep sleep.

After such a late night, I enjoy a lazy sleep-in. Then at 11.30 am, I get on an overground train at Musée d'Orsay station for the thirty-minute journey to the town of Versailles. It is Tuesday morning, yet the train is so full of tourists I have to stand for the entire trip. It's a lot busier than I expected, a common occurrence on the European tourist circuit. Studying the Lonely Planet *Paris* guide to prep for the day, the first fact I learn is that the Palace of Versailles is not open on Mondays, making Tuesday the worst day for crowds. With the spring weather still shining magnificently, the ticket office will make an absolute killing today.

Arriving at Versailles station, I've little idea where to find the UNESCO World Heritage Listed palace that supposedly dominates the town. However, it is simply another case of joining the flock. Through the magnificent, gold-plated front gates the queue waves back and forth for hundreds of metres, growing at an exponential rate. Accepting reality, I join the line and wait patiently.

However, after eavesdropping on English speaking tourists I realise the queue is for those who already have tickets! In a dreadful panic I begin running the 500 metres back to the ticket office which I failed to notice fifteen minutes ago. The run is punishing work – Doc Martens are made for walking but definitely not running. By the time I get back to the queue, it has grown by another 500 metres.

The Lonely Planet guide gives a quick and concise summary of Versailles by numbers: 700 rooms, 2,100 windows, 800 hectares of gardens and parks, 200,000 trees, 6,300 paintings, 2,100 statues and sculptures, and 5.3 million visitors per year. The palace's decadence is a reminder of the incredible excesses of Louis XVI and his queen, Marie Antoinette, which in part led to the French Revolution of the late eighteenth century. Its expansion began when Louis XVI's ancestor Louis XIV completely flattened his father's humble hunting lodge to make way for a palace vast enough to house six thousand courtiers. While their royal subjects starved from poverty in Paris, Louis XVI and Marie Antoinette lived an unprecedented life of luxury, completely out of touch with the poor masses. Needless to say, the decadence ended on a sour note with the royal couple losing their heads under the guillotine in the Place de la Concorde. The indignant French referred to Marie as the "Austrian bitch". However, historians speculate as to whether the "bitch" ever actually said, as is routinely claimed, "If they're hungry, let them eat cake."

Luckily the queue moves in quick fashion and soon I walk in to the marble courtyard. From the courtyard, an entranceway leads up some side stairs into the palace in all its glory and splendour. Among the famous rooms inside are the Royal Chapel, the Diana Drawing Room, the Council Chamber and the standout Hall of Mirrors, or Galerie des Glaces.

King Louis XIV initiated construction of the Hall of Mirrors in 1678. Architect Jules Hardouin-Mansart had to appropriate three rooms each from two of the existing palace apartments at the time, as well as the terrace that separated the apartments, to create the vast hall. Along the its 73-metre length, seventeen mirror-clad arches reflect the seventeen arcaded windows that overlook the palace gardens. Each arch contains twenty-one separate mirrors, giving a total of 357 along the entire length of the hall. The arches themselves are fixed between marble pilasters whose capitals depict the symbols of France, including the Gallic cockerel and fleur-de-lis motif.

When the hall was built in the seventeenth century, mirrors were among the most expensive household objects, due to the Venetian Republic holding a monopoly on their manufacture. In order to maintain the principles of the French rulers of the time, which required that items used in the palace be made in France, several mirror workers were enticed from Venice by French politician Jean-Baptiste Colbert. Legend has it that the Venetian government responded by ordering the assassination of the treacherous artisans, to keep the knowledge of how to make mirrors a secret.

With the long hall now filled with more than two hundred people, I'm regretting my sleep-in. It really would be better to admire this extraordinary place when it is comparatively empty, not with hundreds of others; it's also the kind of place where a professional tour guide would come in very handy.

Taking a good photo is almost impossible – there are just too many people. Further complicating things, a couple of large Chinese tour groups barge up behind me, showing little spatial awareness and forcing me to keep moving. With dogged patience and hawkish timing, I do, however, manage to get a few decent pictures of the hall with its elegantly painted curved ceiling and grand chandeliers.

The line of tourists then shuffles its way through to the separate Queen's and King's bedchambers. Marie Antoinette's enormous bed is surrounded by family portraits. No doubt they were deliberately flattering, but Marie looks like a beautiful woman, in the prime of her life, her face impeccably white under heavy make-up.

In the King's chamber I reminisce and chuckle about a strange scene from Sophia Coppola's film *Marie Antoinette*, in which the ladies-in-waiting and other hangers-on wait to observe the newlywed couple's attempts to make love and thereby consummate the marriage.

After spending a couple of hours inside the palace, I exit to enjoy its magnificent outdoor counterpart, the gardens of Versailles. I take a panoramic photo of the palace behind the large and elegant main fountain. Beyond this is a gentle downward slope with 300 metres of steps leading to a rectangular, 3-kilometre-long lake. With a dense covering of trees either side protecting it from wind, the water is like glass. The lake is entirely artificial and was built by Louis XIV after he flattened the landscape.

The keen rower in me sees a perfect, flat and protected rowing course. I picture myself rowing a single scull up its length, the boat gliding along between crisp strokes of the rowing blades, which are lifted just inches above the crystal-clear water on each recovery. What a beautiful scene to behold as you power the oars along.

At the bottom of the slope, before the lake, is another grand fountain, adorned with four majestic lions, water sprinkling from their mouths. The gardens on either side beneath the Palace are an eclectic mix, with a diversity of themes and landscapes. As I go in search of the famous "orchestral fountain", the trees seemingly play their own classical music – the speakers are so well hidden that the music and trees seem one and the same. It reminds me of the talking trees in *The Lord of the Rings*.

At the orchestral fountain, little is happening as groups of people sit around its exterior. Then, all of a sudden, the music begins. As it builds up, the fountains come to life and begin rising and falling in time to the notes of the soundtrack. It is very impressive, even if it is just Louis XIV still showing off. The performance is over in ten minutes, after which the audience all get up to leave and are quickly replaced with fresh tourists for the next show.

After admiring another couple of beautiful and different gardens, I stroll back to the lake. Keen for some exercise, I decide to walk to its far end on the distant horizon. On the water, romantic couples row tiny boats, and there are even a couple of gentlemen serenading their ladies. There are also half a dozen racing rowboats, filled with teenage boys and girls.

The walking is hard going and I soon give up the struggle while watching more sensible folk ride pushbikes past me. A major problem is that although the lake is just 3 kilometres long, at the halfway point it widens on either side by about 700 metres, thereby adding another kilometre and a half each way.

A few groups of tourists on Segways cruise by, having marvellous fun. Segways have only very recently been legalised in Brisbane. We're a somewhat conservative nanny state when it comes to this type of thing. Australia may present an image of laid-back locals and free spirits surfing, drinking, beach-bumming, roaming the outback and watching sport, but we're actually highly legislated to keep us in check.

For a six-euro fee, I hire a bike for an hour, a good investment as I make quick progress to the far end of the lake. I haven't ridden a bike for probably a decade, and it is terrific fun. These are ordinary, old fashioned, all-purpose bicycles, very comfortable and importantly don't leave me with a sore butt.

People are scarce at the far end of the lake and it's a perfectly quiet spot for enjoying the view all the way back to the graceful palace, without any crowds around. Flanked by the continuous cover of trees on either side, the lake and palace are in perfect symmetry with each other.

After getting some excellent photos, I take it easy on the ride back, staying relaxed and in my own headspace while Segways and pushbikes overtake. After visiting a couple more gardens and feeling thoroughly satisfied, I exit the palace mid-afternoon, observing that the queue is still at least 100 metres long.

After enjoying a few tunes through my earphones, I arrive back by train at the Musée D'Orsay station in central Paris's Seventh District. With plenty of sunlight left, I make my way through Place de la Concorde to the always impressive Champs-Élysées, home to some of the priciest real estate in the world.

Like London's Oxford Street, the Champs-Élysées is also a famous shopping destination; but because it's a wide boulevard, the experience is not as stressful. The dominating Arc de Triomphe sits grandly on the horizon, forming a perfect backdrop. It has to be my favourite view in Paris, just so iconic.

Shops of all the top brands are interspersed with expensive restaurants. There is a long queue of consumers waiting to get into the flagship store of Abercrombie and Finch. As I'm not personally a fan of this brand, this seems a little strange to me.

Cool French street performers are playing for the crowds, notably a modern male dance group of hip, young and athletic dancers, who are grabbing plenty of attention. They move with dynamism to the bass-heavy sound of a boom-box ghetto blaster straight from the 1980s. Their routine is very interactive and skilful, and performed with loads of charisma.

After all the buskers and window shopping, I find myself at the world's busiest roundabout, the Arc de Triomphe. After purchasing a ticket, it is three hundred steps to the top of this behemoth monument. Commissioned by Napoleon, it was built between 1806 and 1836 to honour those who fought and died in the French Revolutionary and Napoleonic wars.

The view from the top down the Champs-Élysées is truly something to behold. From the Arc roads extend out wide in all directions, but the Champs-Élysées is the most impressive by far. It would be amazing to be up at this lofty viewpoint as the cyclists finish the last leg of the annual Tour de France.

Among the really appealing things about Paris are its wide and straight boulevards. The city did not look like this until Napoleon III commissioned the Prefect of the Seine, Georges-Eugène Haussmann, to redesign it. Haussmann's massive renovation of Paris occurred between 1853 and 1870 and included the demolition of medieval neighbourhoods that were deemed overcrowded and unhealthy by officials at the time. Wide avenues and new parks and squares were built, as well as new sewers, fountains and aqueducts. Napoleon III's ambition was to turn Paris into the jewel of Europe and it is an amazing legacy.

Looking east, one gets a fine view of the Sacré-Coeur rising above a small hill on the horizon. The Arc provides another, rather intimate view of the Eiffel Tower. A debate starts in my mind: what's the better view of the tower – up close from the Arc or from afar at Montmartre? The winner, I conclude, is Montmartre, due to the more complete panoramic view of Paris. But looking straight down from the Arc in any direction is a magnificent experience.

That evening I look at the highly pixelated photos of the elongated view down the Champs-Élysées and realise that my understanding of the geographical relationships between some of the major Parisian landmarks is completely wrong. The glass exterior roof of the Grand Palais actually runs parallel to the Champs-Élysées and Place de la Concorde. The Grand Palais is a large exhibition hall and museum complex, an icon of the Paris skyline, which was built for the Universal Exposition of 1900, a world's fair held in Paris to celebrate the achievements of the past century.

The traffic stops at the Place de la Concorde's roundabout, giving way to the public gardens of Jardin des Tuileries. In the commercial CBD area of Paris, somewhat removed from tourist central, one can imagine there are many business executives with corner offices that have prized views over Paris and would be great venues for office parties on Bastille Day.

That evening I watch Sofia Coppola's film *Marie Antoinette* on iTunes, mainly to enjoy the famous setting of Versailles. There was some controversy in France upon the film's release in 2006 for its seemingly empathetic portrayal of the "Austrian bitch". It's definitely not on the level of some of her father Francis Ford Coppola's masterpieces, but the scenes filmed at Versailles are enjoyable, as is the fantastic soundtrack featuring some of my favourite bands. The film won the Oscar for costume and design, especially for Marie's famously elaborate fashions.

Next morning, based on some good recommendations from back home, I head off to see the Musée d'Orsay, an art gallery housed in an old, renovated train station. Located on the south bank of the Seine, the station become obsolete in the early twentieth century due to increasing electrification of the European railway network. By 1939, its platforms were considered too short for the longer mainland trains, and soon after all train services to the station ceased.

The building then fulfilled a number of roles before being converted into a museum in 1986. After it was completed, it took six months to install the two thousand or so paintings, six hundred sculptures, and other works. The building was so immaculately renovated that it is now considered an Art Nouveau showpiece in its own right.

As you enter the gallery's main hall, the view along the full length of its interior is radiant with light pouring in through its curved glass ceiling and glistening on the sculptures below. The gallery's staff are very strict about prohibiting photography, so I have to take a quick and sneaky shot of the long interior. The layout is unusual, with sculptures along the length of an open floor area where the train platforms once stood and paintings on either side spread over a number of floors and mezzanines.

The collections are grouped by various movements, including Impressionism, Post-Impressionism and Art Nouveau. On either side of the ground floor are more traditional oil paintings, some of them absolutely huge – up to 10 metres wide by 5 metres tall. What's more impressive is the high attention to detail on the massive canvasses. Each one must have been a real labour of love. I try to imagine the ambitious artists working on detailed brushwork while keeping a constant eye on the bigger picture.

The layout of the exhibits is quite complex, with small mezzanine areas hidden cleverly between floors. It's the very top floor, with its paintings by Monet, Renoir, Degas and Manet that I'm most excited to see. After Picasso, my next favourite artist would be Monet, painter of colourful natural landscapes and pictures of everyday life, including the famous waterlilies and other paintings from his home in Giverny on the outskirts of Paris. Giverny is a tourist attraction in its own right, often visited on day tours to the Palace of Versailles. While I enjoy the many Monets here, I am also very taken by the Renoir paintings – colourful and vivid pictures of everyday family life, many of which display his famous talent for capturing feminine beauty and sensuality.

The Musée D'Orsay has lived up to expectations. Outside is a pleasant public square by the Seine, brilliant in the sunshine and perfect for a bite of lunch. I share the space with tour groups and plenty of students. The area around the gallery is dominated by imposing government and administrative buildings separated by streets and alleys.

Another must-see for me on this visit is the city's famous Catacombs. Due to hygiene problems in the late eighteenth century, the bones in the city's overflowing cemeteries were exhumed and transferred to underground tunnels, part of a network of stone mines that lay under the city (and which were, interestingly, used as the headquarters of the Resistance during World War II). The Catacombs hold the remains of more than six million people and provide a rather macabre perspective on the city's history, with their skull-and-bone-lined tunnels. But it also sounds unique and like something that will take me out of my comfort zone. Another strong motivation is that I'd passed up an opportunity to visit the Catacombs of Rome six years prior.

They Catacombs are supposed to be open until 5 pm, but after crossing the road from the metro to the entrance I'm disheartened to see that final entry was actually at 4.30 pm – I'm five minutes late! Oh bugger. What to do next? Taking a seat in a nearby cafe, I flick through the guidebook. Paris's famous river cruises are only a ten-minute metro trip away and run to as late as 11 pm. There's plenty of spring sunlight left, so the decision is an absolute no-brainer.

The cruises depart from the Right Bank of the Seine, not far from Place de la Concorde. Just ten minutes later, I exit the metro station only 50 metres from the Bateaux-Mouches cruise terminal. The cruises are very popular with tourist groups, and several large tour buses are parked alongside. With only five minutes until the next cruise, I buy a ticket then grab a good seat on the boat's upper deck.

On days like today, with the sun shining, operating these Bateaux-Mouches must be like a licence to print money. I share the deck with a hundred or so people and only two vacant seats are left by the time the vessel's engines power up. I'm quite excited to see Paris's landmarks from the Seine, as years of rowing have helped me appreciate the unique perspective you gain on a city from its river.

The engines are simultaneously powerful and quiet. The sights are announced in four different languages, in a rehearsed and efficient manner. First on the Right Bank is the almost kilometre-long exterior of the world's largest museum, the Louvre – the sheer length of this building is astounding. We pass under bridges – only a few metres above our heads – as the mighty Louvre continues.

Now on the Left Bank is the Musée d'Orsay from this morning; a number of important government buildings are pointed out too. Another couple of bridges later, Paris's spiritual centre, the island of Notre Dame, splits the Seine in two.

Notre Dame looks best and most complete from the river – awe-inspiring and gothic. At the pointy end of the island, the "Île de la Cité", young Parisians in couples and groups relax by the river bank, enjoying the sudden onset of spring.

The cathedral's famous "flying buttresses", which reinforce the thin walls of the nave, extend out like giant spider-legs. Notre Dame was among the first buildings in the world to incorporate flying buttresses. They weren't part of the original design but became necessary as the walls grew taller and thinner and then stress fractures appeared as the walls pushed outwards.

The cruise boat circles the island before retracing its journey back towards the Eiffel Tower. Above the Seine appears the signature glass roof of the Grand Palais, which can be seen in its entirety from the river, before the journey concludes with another fresh perspective on the Eiffel Tower. In just over an hour we have covered quite some distance.

Four

In Bruges

Awakening next morning, I realise that today is the day I christen my Eurail pass. At the Gare du Nord station, I "activate" the pass while making a reservation for the high-speed train north to Bruges, via Brussels. At this point I discover that reservations for high-speed trains will be more expensive than I originally thought, and almost instantly I remember reading in a travel blog a few months earlier that this is one potential drawback of the all-encompassing pass.

The train isn't until early afternoon, but it's only two and a half hours to Bruges – a comparatively short trip for most Australians. I go to buy a souvenir painting from the shops around the Sacré-Coeur, taking a quick metro ride to Pigalle station again. I could walk there in twenty minutes, but I feel a sense of urgency on my last morning in Paris.

Flicking through scores of paintings, I find a blue-coloured oil painting of the Eiffel tower seen from a narrow street, featuring locals dressed in early-twentieth-century fashions. Costing a mere twenty euros, it'll make an excellent addition to my apartment back home once framed.

Hidden amongst the small streets beneath the Sacré-Coeur is the famous cafe from the film *Amelie*, which I loved when it was released, particularly its fetching leading lady, Audrey Tautou. Walking the quiet streets, I hope to be led there by other fans of *Amelie* on the same pilgrimage. Unsure where to go, I pop my head into a random cafe to ask for directions and behind the counter is the gleaming and mischievous smile of Amelie on the memorable movie poster. This is it, this quiet little cafe – who would have known? I order a coffee, but it's not much of a tourist attraction and, disappointingly, the cigarette counter from the film is no more.

It dawns on me I've taken the seat of the obsessively jealous ex-boyfriend of the cigarette-counter lady, from where he stalked her every move or glance at other men. Also I can see the kitchen door of the cafe, behind which this same girl made passionate love to her fellow employee after Amelie had cleverly played matchmaker. A very funny scene indeed!

I pay with a good tip before some quick photos, none of which turn out well, unfortunately, and am soon walking back down to Pigalle's Boulevard de Clichy. With spare time to fill, I walk back to the hotel, taking the occasional detour. I find a busy street with very obvious red-light brothels and see they're open for business at 11 am on a weekday. It seems a bit early! Of course, as a single male I stand out, so I quicken my pace to move away. But I have been spotted, and lingerie-clad hookers flaunt themselves at me in broad daylight. "Only in Paris," I think to myself. I walk back to the River Seine for a last look and some window shopping, then before long I enter the Sentier metro station one last time with my bags, en route to the Gare du Nord.

The bullet train escapes Paris on its journey north, rapidly accelerating to a top speed of 320 kilometres per hour. Very impressed with my first ever high-speed train, I quickly forget the annoyingly high price of my reserved seat. Soon the train crosses the northern French border into Belgium before arriving at Brussels' Midi station for my transfer to Bruges. Bruges is a big favourite with day-trippers and seats are on a first-come first-serve basis, no reservations required. The train is relatively aged and slow compared to the bullet train. After missing out on a seat, I stand near the doors, keeping an eye on my luggage.

Bruges feels disorientating when I disembark, with a large open area at the station exit. I'm initially confused by the bus ticket vending machine but eventually manage to buy a ticket to the central town square. Tired and stressed, I lose my footing upon entering the bus, actually falling over under the weight of my luggage. I haven't the foggiest idea how to validate the ticket and simply drag my bags up to the rear. Meanwhile, the female bus driver prints a ticket and yells at me from up front. I yell back while showing her the ticket I've purchased in my hand, which somehow resolves the misunderstanding.

There's no mistaking the famous central square, the Markt, which is very crowded when we arrive. As I disembark, I feel that people must notice my backpack and bulging carry-on bag and am conscious that I resemble a pregnant lady carrying twins. A couple of people are probably having a quick laugh at me over their draft Belgian beers.

I know I'm in Belgium when I see the streets are lined with chocolate shops. Their wares are neatly presented and look absolutely delicious as I peer through shop windows at the endless varieties. Willy Wonka, eat your heart out! There's one particularly memorable box in a window, which has chocolate breasts and a penis with balls all contained inside it.

I then follow a picturesque canal, one of many, to reach my hotel, in a small, old-fashioned building next to a bridge. The inside is old but stylishly renovated and well maintained. Entering my room, I figure it has to be below water level. The Eurail pass has survived its first test and it's a relief to arrive and finally dump the weight of my luggage on the bed.

After making myself at home in the comfortable room, I head down the street to a supermarket only 100 metres from reception. After grabbing some chips and snacks, I seek out the beer fridge with its wide array of Belgian beers, including many I've never heard of. Belgium, of course, is famous for three things in particular: beer, chocolates and waffles. I intend to indulge the taste buds, so plenty of walking and exploring must be factored in to avoid a calorie blowout.

Back in Brisbane, the premium Belgian beer at pubs would have to be Hoegaarden. When you order the beer on tap back home, its Belgian flavours seem exotic and it's usually served with a slice of lemon and an exorbitant price tag. Here in the supermarket, compared with all of the different brews on show, Hoegaarden is actually one of the cheapest.

I think back to the mid-1980s in Australia, my formative drinking years, when the German beer Lowenbrau was seen as the premium beer in bottle shops, thanks to all the associated marketing. With the wide variety of premium and craft beers now available back home, Lowenbrau has fallen to staple beer status, one to drink at home for a cheap night around the barbecue. I purchase an array of different beers for the hotel fridge, but no Hoegaarden, of course.

With its cobblestone lanes, dreamy canals and soaring spires crowning its medieval skyline, Bruges is considered one of Europe's most picturesque historic cities. It was Europe's most prosperous city for a good 200 years, during its "golden age" from the twelfth to fifteenth centuries, but then became a backwater due to changing political circumstances and for five hundred years, while other cities were transformed, it remained undeveloped. As a result, it is now an almost impossibly pretty place, with a unique old-world charm. It has a small population of around one hundred thousand, but it becomes packed with visitors on weekends drawn to its beautiful mediaeval centre.

The Hotel Ter Reien is ideally located, and it takes me only five minutes to walk through charmingly narrow streets back to the Markt, which is dominated by its famous belfry tower, the Belfort. On my way, to my initial bewilderment, I spot a four-sided public urinal, or *pissoir*, where at any one time up to four men may stand to relieve themselves, seemingly unembarrassed by any passers-by. It's definitely not something I'm used to back home.

Bruges first came to my attention when I watched the excellent 2008 crime-comedy *In Bruges*. Many of its scenes are set in the Markt. Upon entering the square, it seems far lovelier in reality than on film. Struggling through the square earlier with my luggage, I had barely noticed this visual splendidness.

The large open area is flanked by picture-perfect fairy-tale buildings, with the Neo-Gothic post office generally considered the loveliest. It's now late on a Friday afternoon and overcast, and the square is quiet and almost empty compared to what I expect it will be like when the weekend tourists arrive. Though it's lined with cafes and restaurants, business looks slow and the menus expensive.

On one corner though is a tiny chip shop selling French fries with a selection of fifteen sauces. It's popular and lively, so I snack on fritz while taking in the square's atmosphere. I love how Europeans eat their fries with mayonnaise and other condiments, which seem to complement the staple potato far better than the overwhelming taste of tomato sauce Down Under.

As the late afternoon cools down, I wander aimlessly around corners and along quaint streets and canals. Absolutely beautiful, Bruges strikes me as a hybrid of Amsterdam and Venice. After five days in busy Paris, I'm now in love with this impossibly pretty town. I revisit the street lined with chocolate shops, where they cater to both chocolate connoisseurs and tourists like me who struggle to choose from the endless varieties. A solution is to purchase one of the generic but beautifully designed little boxes containing a dozen or so chocolates selected by the store owner.

Within 20 metres of my hotel is a welcoming pub with a beer garden overlooking a beautiful canal. I enjoy dinner and a couple of Belgian beers under the setting sun, then I am back in my room within minutes. I open the box of Belgian chocolates for a taste test and soon there are only four left. Damn, these are good! I don't normally much have such a sweet tooth, but these are in a different league to Cadbury. I drink three different Belgian brews, which put me to sleep.

Next morning, the first port of call is the Belfort, with its 366 claustrophobic steps to the top of the clock tower. The weather is awful, however, raining heavily, and I'm already cold and wet before I find an umbrella for sale in the Markt.

By the time I reach the last dozen steps of the Belfry tower my thighs are aching as my broad shoulders bang against the walls on the way up. The view from the top over the city skyline of spires is stunning, and only slightly upstaged by the medieval square below. As a result of the pounding rain and gale-force wind, the clock tower is precariously wet inside. I try to take some photos without waterlogging my Canon. The Markt square is empty of tourists and horses with carriages are being sheltered away under buildings on the sides of the square to avoid the downpour.

There are quite a few sights to see today and the blue skies on the horizon leave me feeling more optimistic. Five minutes' walk away is my next destination, the Basilica of the Holy Blood and its venerated phial. Brought to the city in the twelfth century, it is said to contain a cloth stained by the blood of Jesus Christ. Entry is only two euros and, once inside, worshippers wait in pews for their turn to view the phial. On reaching it, some place their hands on the glass above it while praying. I'm a little sceptical as to how genuine the relic could be, but inside this tiny room, with these true believers, the basilica does indeed feel spiritual and peaceful.

After some time reflecting in the pews of the basilica's chapel, I walk the fifteen minutes to what is said to be the most romantic spot in Bruges, the Minnewater or "Lake of Love". With the rain now replaced by clear blue skies, the lake looks beautiful and romantic, with fifty or so swans paddling on either side of one of Bruges' many classic bridges. On the edge of the lake are some local horses, their mouths stuffed in buckets of chaff, having a well-deserved break from carting tourists around.

In the same part of town is a famous Flemish art gallery, the Groeningemuseum, containing what is supposed to be an impressive collection from the fourteenth to twentieth centuries. The gallery's minimal white interior is quite empty of people and easy to roam. However, I soon realise that Flemish art is not really my cup of tea, though it's hard not to be impressed by the artworks' detail and classic colourful style.

Heading back to the Markt, I enter a large thirteenth-century church, the Onze-Lieve-Vrouwekerk, or Church of Our Lady, best known for housing an early sixteenth century Madonna and child statue by Michelangelo. The statue of mother and child is serene, but it's disappointing that the nave of the church is under scaffolding for renovation.

After lunch, with the sun now shining, tourist numbers skyrocket in the streets around the Markt and soon people are shoulder to shoulder on the footpaths. I walk through a lovely little canal-side market selling antiques. Another couple of bridges further down is the main docking spot for popular boat canal tours. With the fine weather, the idea of a cruise is appealing, so I purchase a ticket and a hot chocolate, then take my place in the queue for the next cruise.

Packed to the brim, the boat rocks heavily as some larger people hop on, including me! The cruise then spends a delightful half hour viewing many old Bruges homes from the water. The driver does an excellent multilingual job, informing the mix of international tourists about many points of interest and history. Though he also talks in French, German, Italian and Spanish, I'm grateful that his first explanation is usually in English. There are many advantages to speaking the planet's lingua franca!

After the cruise I continue to explore for a couple more hours before happening upon a cosy little restaurant with a fireplace, overlooking a canal. I make a booking before heading back to the hotel for a break. That evening, the restaurant's food and service turn out to be excellent, and I wash my meal down with some delicious new Belgian brews.

I sleep in the next morning, then check out after asking to leave my luggage at reception. Two hundred metres from the hotel is a bike hire shop and hostel. I've always regretted not hiring a bike while in Amsterdam a few years before, so this looks like an opportunity to make up for that. My first destination on the bike is the train station, to make a booking for the afternoon.

Riding down the main street to the station, I feel as if everyone is trying to ride into me! A policewoman blows her whistle and, in a matter of fact manner, informs me I'm riding the wrong way down a one-way street and could incur a one-hundred-euro on-the-spot fine. With necessary humility, I apologise and, needless to say, find the going much easier on the street parallel.

Booking made, I head back to the Markt, where I notice some policemen standing outside a restaurant/bar, with police tape and a couple of journalists with cameras. There's been an incident the night before, though I can't quite suss out what, but the owner is aggressive and heavy-handed with the journalists, like some kind of local Mafioso. I'm not keen to hang around in case a violent fist fight breaks out, so I take off.

I'm enjoying the bike ride, and an unexpected delight comes in the form of a marching band of proud locals, making loud big band processional music through the Markt and on to Town Hall as I follow. Late morning, I return the bike to the hire place.

Right across from the bike hire shop is a small and intimate square. They're a dime a dozen in places like Bruges, but this one is occupied by several upper-middle class English gents. Obviously still on a bender that started the night before, they're toasting Harry or George or Charles, whichever one is getting married after the bucks' party weekend. They seem like stereotypical toffs, and I feel they could at any moment start singing "Jerusalem", "God Save the Queen", "Rule Britannia" or the like.

This is merely the first of many English bucks' and hens' weekends I will encounter over the next couple of months. No mainland European town is spared the scourge of English pre-wedding celebrations these days.

Five

A Taste of Brussels

After grabbing my luggage, it's only a forty-five-minute train journey back to Brussels. This gives me just the right amount of time to read up on what to see and do during my three-night stay in the city. The guidebook speaks highly of the EU Capital, but a couple of doubters back home reckon three nights is one or, maybe even two, too many. I begin studying the train's approach to the terminal, referenced against Google maps, in the hope that I can more quickly and directly exit the platform in the direction of the hotel.

The area around Brussels Midi station gives an initial impression of being quite ugly and gritty. I cross a main street, heading towards my hotel, which is only 200 metres from the station. I picked it mostly for its location and good value, and happily the foyer feels like an oasis as I escape the grungy scene outside, the front desk service is friendly and my room turns out to be comfortable and spacious.

There's a good supermarket back at the station, where I get some snacks and half a dozen new Belgian beers to sample, and, of course, a chocolate shop where I buy some more chocolates. With plenty of time to take things easy in Brussels, I have an early night.

Next day is Saturday. I exit the hotel and walk straight across the road to a crowded market I'd spotted from my tenth-floor room. It offers the usual fare of souvenirs, clothing and second-hand goods.

There are also some excellent food stands and I feast on a breakfast of some kind of Belgium sausage, with the mandatory double espresso to perk me up for the day ahead.

From the market, it is approximately one and a half kilometres to central Brussels, with its famously beautiful square, the Grand Place, considered one of the most beautiful squares in Europe. There are two official languages in Brussels, French and Dutch, and, as I soon notice, all street names appear in both languages.

Close to my destination, I see a large group of tourists gathered on a corner down a street to my right. They're surrounding the Mannekin Pis statue, a much photographed and famous bronze sculpture of a young boy urinating into the fountain below. Today he is smartly attired in a double-breasted royal blue suit, with a boater hat and large bushy moustache – it's a tradition for the statue to be dressed in costumes, several times each week, according to a schedule that is posted on the railings of the fountain. This little man peeing in public is supposed to embody the sense of humour of the people of Brussels and their independence of mind; there's a less well-known statue of his squatting sister, the Jeanneke Pis, which is a ten-minute walk away, north of the Grand Place. Since being first created in 1619, he has been repeatedly stolen, and the statue on show currently dates from 1965.

The 61-centimetre-tall man is a very well-known tourist attraction but not overly impressive. Over the next couple of days there will be a constant crowd around it, often Asian tourist groups straight off the bus. Next to the statue is a Belgian chocolate shop, its sales booming in this prime location. My accountant-self wonders about the premium rent of this business, given its perfect locale.

I know that the Grand Place is just 50 metres up the lane from the statue. However, I'm distracted by a shop selling delicious-looking Belgian waffles, with cream, dark and white chocolate, and fruit too, if you like. My inner sweet tooth surfaces again, and the calorie-fuelled waffle proves absolutely delicious. Just as I did with the Belgian chocolates, I indulge in the sweet treat while getting as messy as a child would do.

I finally reach the Grand Place and its characterful medieval buildings are captivating to see for real, rather than on a computer screen.

The UNESCO World Heritage Site is surrounded by grand buildings including opulent guildhalls, Brussels Town Hall, and its standout structure, the Hotel De Ville, with its towering gothic spires. The square is Brussels' top drawcard and doesn't cost a cent to visit and admire. There are plenty of outdoor cafes where you can enjoy a latte while soaking up the atmosphere, and they are full of tourists doing just that – enjoying a coffee with a view. Understandably, the Hotel De Ville was the main target of a bombardment by the French in 1695. Lucky for future generations of admirers, they missed.

Every second year in August, an enormous "flower carpet" occupies the Grand Place for a few days. An astonishing one million begonias are arranged in colourful patterns, covering an area of 1,800 square metres, 24 metres by 77 metres to be precise. Given how mind-blowing the carpet of flowers is, it's no wonder that, despite the monumental effort involved, the festival has been held biennially since its 1971 debut.

After the latte I spend the next few hours exploring the streets in the vicinity of the square. There are supposed to be some excellent art galleries but, after London and Paris, I've become art-weary and the prospect of more Flemish art doesn't appeal. Naturally, I buy more chocolates and browse some fashionable clothing stores, which all appear to have high price tags. There are plenty of charming little lanes, famous for their fish restaurants; however, my guidebook has forewarned me that these can be notorious tourist traps, so I try not to be distracted by the salesmen out front.

Also near the square is what is supposed to have been Europe's first proper shopping arcade, the Galeries St-Hubert. Built in the mid-nineteenth century, and similar to the large arcades it preceded in European cities like Milan and St Petersburg, it consists of twin rectangular facades built over long, narrow, street-like courtyards. They were designed by a young architect named Jean-Pierre Cluysenaar, who was determined to sweep away the existing ill-lit alleyways and replace a once sordid space, where the bourgeoisie scarcely ventured, with an upmarket covered shopping arcade. Although conceived in 1836, his idea wasn't authorised until 1845 due to a drawn-out process of disentangling various property rights in this area of town.

Along the arcades stand elegant glass arcaded shopfronts, separated by pilasters. Both arcades have an upper floor in the Italian style and etched glass-pane roofs with an intricate iron framework.

Each of the two separate sections is more than 100 metres in length. I crouch and tilt my camera up at the ceiling, taking long uniform shots of the sunlit glass, then shoot a few more of the symmetrical cafes and shops lining the narrow courtyard. A problem with the first arcade is that there are so many people walking its tiled stone floors. Luckily, the second arcade has far fewer people, allowing better photo opportunities. This venue for elite shopping is definitely more stylish than what would be Australia's equivalent, the Queen Victoria Building in Sydney.

Having sussed out the restaurant touts, I find one establishment I like without the hard sell, planning to dine there tonight after time back at the hotel. After a kip, I take an early evening stroll back to the Grand Place and enjoy a steak-frites dinner – a favourite after Paris – washed down by more fine Belgian beer.

It is then a ten-minute walk to Place St-Gery, a popular nightlife area well known for its hip and characterful bars. Jutting out on a corner is just my kind of bar, heaving with activity, called the Roi des Belges. It's a lively place and I'm immediately taken by the female bartenders having fun working together while throwing bottles around like Brian Brown and Tom Cruise in the movie *Cocktail* – though perhaps not quite so skilfully.

Searching for the bathroom, I move through a labyrinth of stairs, rooms and then more stairs, eventually descending to the basement. On the way back to the bar, a spritely American girl asks me how to find the ladies'. Ten minutes later she's back and, spotting me sitting at the bar by myself, kindly invites me to join her group of friends, college students on holidays. They're a switched-on, interesting group and we hit it off over rounds of beer.

The drinks flow with a few laughs and travel stories for the next couple of hours. They've got an early start in the morning, so we part ways, but with tentative plans to meet again tomorrow night in the same spot. Quite drunk now, I stagger back to the hotel, the night street scene still a bit gritty. There are plenty of Turkish-style and halal restaurants, so I eat the requisite kebab to end a boozy night.

On Sunday morning in the Grand Place I'm surprised by how few shops are actually open – pretty much none! It's very different from Sunday trading hours back home. I walk away from the square to find yet more tourist groups photographing the Manneken Pis statue, still dressed in his blue suit from yesterday. The Belgian chocolate shop next to the fountain is open, so I buy another box. After days indulging in chocolates, waffles and beer – and with few attractions open – today will be devoted to a long, calorie-burning walk.

After a few hundred metres, I come across a four-storey painted mural of Tintin, his dog, Snowy, and Captain Haddock. The painting is tall and narrow, cleverly depicting the three of them walking down a fire escape on the side wall of the building. When I was between about nine and twelve, Tintin and Asterix comics were a very big deal for me and my school mates. The Adventures of Tintin were famously written by the Belgian cartoonist Georges Remi more than eighty years ago.

I then begin my ambitious journey east to the Parc du Cinquantenaire, site of the Arc du Cinquantenaire, Brussels' equivalent of the "Arc de Triomphe". I soon pass through the Brussels Park, or Warandepark, the largest public park in the city centre, which today has a relaxed Sunday atmosphere, with chilled-out locals enjoying picnics and numerous random football games being played by teenage boys. The park's wide, sandy, stone-coloured paths are just like those in Paris's Tuileries Gardens and the Palace of Versailles.

Along one side of the park is the large façade of the Royal Palace of Brussels, whose construction began in 1783 and was only fully completed in 1934. The impressive building is not actually used as a royal residence, as the king and his family live in the Royal Palace of Laeken, on the outskirts of Brussels. However, the central palace is where the king performs his duties as head of state and grants audiences.

After another kilometre or so is a well-known antique market, beneath the flamboyantly Gothic Notre-Dame du Sablon church. There's a wide range of antiques on sale, plenty to satisfy the most curious shopper and the appropriately high prices reflect their good quality.

A classic old record player catches my attention, priced at two hundred euros. I absolutely adore it and imagine it would be a neat addition to my bachelor pad back home. With vinyl records making a comeback, most of my favourite albums are now available as LPs. I make some tentative inquiries and find out that the price is non-negotiable. It's still too early in my trip to spend that much money, and there's no way I could cart it around with me anyway – both good reasons to not commit to the purchase. That said, I could actually buy it right now and arrange to have it posted home during the ample time I still have left in Brussels. I walk on, pondering this option.

After the quiet and quaint Sablon area, I come to a major road that runs direct and straight the last couple of kilometres to the Parc du Cinquantenaire. Along the way I pass a loud protest march, consisting of a few hundred people, seemingly voicing their anger at Eurozone austerity measures. As Brussels is the capital city of the EU, I expected to see some protests – was actually looking forward to a good, proper protest, to be completely honest.

Standing in the crowd and surrounded by police, it's difficult to fathom the specific gripe of these protesters. The female speaker (and chief stirrer) is speaking in Spanish, making it difficult for me to decipher what it's all about. I wonder if I should join in the clapping and cheering. That evening I'll have a look online for any news of the event, but to no avail. Similar protests must be routine in Brussels.

A little tired and sweaty, I arrive at the Parc de Cinquantenaire, with its massive horseshoe-shaped centrepiece arch dominating the skyline, a real statement of a building. In the dictionary, under the word "dominant", they could elaborate on the word's definition by simply adding a photo of this behemoth. Originally planned for the National Exhibition of 1880, to commemorate fiftieth anniversary of the Belgian independence, the arch was finally completed in 1905. It is made from iron, glass and stone, which were meant to symbolise the economic and industrial power of Belgium.

The Parc de Cinquantenaire was a long and arduous construction project, with progress hindered by a continuous battle between King Leopold II and the Belgian government, who viewed the construction price as too excessive. Also not helping matters, the original Belgian architect who spent twenty years on the project died and was replaced by a French architect who, in turn, stamped his own significant changes on the design. Through private funding, the monument was finally completed, just in time for the seventy-fifth anniversary of Belgian independence – only 25 years overdue!

The horseshoe shape is perfect for a panoramic photo. A few shots later I take a seat in the park below to enjoy the blue skies, some people-watching and a sandwich for lunch. The scene is very relaxed. I watch some local boys playing a game of football and I'm tempted to join the game, but fear my rugby-playing background would leave me embarrassingly exposed, most likely tripping or rolling an ankle while being outplayed, or ungracefully falling flat on my face.

A pleasant surprise, after the Arc de Triomphe's steps, is a lift that takes visitors to the top of the central arch. Jutting out from on high are some huge bronze horses, similar to the chariot drawn by four horses I'd seen atop of Berlin's Brandenburg Gate years ago. Up close, I appreciate the detail in the giant bronzes and can see how they have aged and change colour over time. They bring to mind the Statue of Liberty and its famous green patina, which was originally a dull copper colour before oxidisation set in.

Beneath and behind the arch is the Royal Military Museum, which was opened in 1880. I take a brief look inside, but it pales in comparison with the War Museum in the Mitte area of Berlin I'd previously visited.

Feeling rested, I begin my walk back to the hotel via a different route. I soon encounter the official buildings of the EU, which aren't all that interesting. Nevertheless, a few tourists are lining up to go inside the parliament. I take just a quick shot of the Eurozone countries' national flags all lined up in front of the familiar Euro flag with its twelve gold stars on its blue background.

There is one more notable Brussels landmark I'm interested in seeing, the Palais de Justice (Law Courts), a neoclassical colossus of a building, larger than St Peter's Basilica in Rome, with impressive dimensions of 160 metres by 150 metres. The 104-metre-high dome weighs 24,000 metric tonnes while the building has eight courtyards, twenty-seven large court rooms and more than two hundred smaller rooms. Unfortunately for me, when I arrive the building is covered in scaffolding as part of an ongoing renovation (and a huge and impressive scaffolding it is).

Still, from outside this colossal building, you can enjoy panoramic views over the city back to the centre of Brussels and beyond. I can see I've covered quite some distance so far to get to this point. On the other side of Brussels, I spot the iconic Atomium building, originally constructed for the 1958 World's Fair (Expo 58). I try to zoom my camera lens onto the 100-metre-tall structure near the horizon. It consists of nine stainless steel spheres, each one 18 metres in diameter, all interconnected to form the basic structure of an iron crystal, magnified 165 billion times.

I'd like to have seen this construction up close, but it is actually 8 kilometres north of the Grand Place and there is nothing else of note to visit in its vicinity. Unfortunately, it proves nigh on impossible to take a blur-free photo with the zoom on my camera maxed out, but after about twenty or so attempts I hope to have a satisfactorily clear image for the travel album's final cut.

After wandering through the multicultural neighbourhood of Saint-Gilles, I'm soon back amongst the familiar grunge of the streets near Midi station. I enter the oasis of the hotel lobby and the peace and solitude of my room with a view. Looking at Google Maps, I figure I've walked a half marathon today and I feel healthier for it.

I sleep in the next morning, not looking forward to the long and logistically difficult train journey tomorrow to Zurich. Visiting the Eurail website, I try to plan ahead, but whatever way I figure it, it becomes quite complicated, involving at least three separate train journeys. And the hotel's weak Wi-Fi signal makes researching the best route even more frustrating. There has to be a better way.

On my phone, I go to the Apple App Store and search for "Eurail". Fantastic, there exists a "Eurail Rail Planner" app, with good reviews. This will help me no end – brilliant!

I download it and then enter my trip details. Instantly, the most practical options appear in the palm of my hand. I learn that I'll need to make a reservation and head down to Midi station to book my seats.

I'm a little disappointed with Brussels and wonder if it was worth staying three nights, but on my last morning I discover an interesting tourist attraction recommended by TripAdvisor. Less than a kilometre from the hotel is a famous little brewery, the Cantillon. As I have very much enjoyed Belgium's great beers, I go in search of the brewery, which is located in an innocuous part of town. I find the street and, according to my map, the brewhouse should be right in front of me, but all I see is a large, ugly warehouse door. Just as I'm getting a little dejected and ready to leave, a tiny side door then opens, from which emerges a group of Asian tourists. There's no signage at all!

Relieved, I enter and find the inside characterful and unflashy. Founded in 1900 by the Cantillon family, this brewery is famous for being the only one in Belgium to maintain the tradition of lambic beers, which are made from wild yeasts rather than traditional brewer's yeasts. The process has remained much the same since the brewery opened, with only a minor switch to organic ingredients in 1999.

The lambic style of brewing requires that two-thirds malted barley and one-third unmalted wheat are spontaneously fermented in open-topped vats, aged in oak. They are then blended from varying batches and ages, bottled and re-fermented for another year. The brewing process is distinctly different from lagers, with their "bottom-fermenting" yeasts, and ales, which are made with "top-fermenting" yeasts that float on the surface. However, the main difference is that lambic ales are brewed by exposing hot wort (unfermented beer) to the outside air. Often sweetened with fruit flavourings, the resulting beers have unusual names like kriek, faro and gueuze, and are prized around the world. One for the purists!

Exploring the spider-web-filled brewery with its pungent-smelling fermenting vats is a wonder for the beer lover in me. One can imagine any beer drinker would get a lot out of this place. Just like in any typical winery visit, the tour concludes with a tasting. I sample a traditional gueuze beer and a couple of fruit-flavoured beers, the raspberry beer proving to be a taste explosion. It would take a while to acquire a taste for this, though, just as in my younger years it took some time for me to appreciate lagers and ales.

Joining me for the tasting and introducing themselves in an unpretentious manner are a friendly couple from England. We get chatting over a few lambic beers and I find out that the girlfriend, despite her very English accent, is actually from Perth. Having lived in London for six years, I'm very surprised by how English she sounds. He's a soldier in the British army and they've come to Brussels for a long-weekend escape while he takes some leave. They are easy to talk to, and I get on to the topic of AFL with her. Her home team, the West Coast Eagles, are having a poor season, much to her disappointment.

When I elaborate on my itinerary, they tell me about the funky "ruin bars" in Budapest, atmospheric conversions of bombed open-air buildings into trendy nightlife spots. They are a "must-see" they emphasise, and they do sound fantastic! They offer to go sight-seeing with me, but I've already seen enough of Brussels. They tell me they're looking forward to indulging in a classic Brussels dish, *moules-frites*, or mussels and chips. I return the favour by giving them some suggestions for their weekend. Nice people, on my wavelength, I think, as we part company after forty minutes.

At the brewery tour entrance, they are selling some great souvenirs bearing the artsy and minimalist Cantillon Brewery logo. I buy a colourful T-shirt with the logo on its back before departing.

Six

Zurich and Alpine Splendour

The next morning I enjoy a stress-free 100-metre walk to the station to start my first train journey, to Frankfurt. The second leg of my journey will take me from Frankfurt to Basel, on the border of Germany and Switzerland, and the third from Basel to Zurich, hopefully arriving around 6 pm. All up, the trip will take roughly eight hours.

The high-speed train progresses quickly through Brussels' industrial suburbs. Soon it becomes apparent we've crossed the German border – the fields look very German, reflecting that trademark super-efficiency, with every inch of land being farmed to full capacity. Each separate farm is neatly divided and has modern farming equipment. This efficiency is carried into all walks of life. As a keen rower, I've watched and admired German crews race with ruthless efficiency, "catching" the water at the start of every stroke as one, while powering ahead of competitors. I remember that Germany were the outstanding men's eight at the London Olympics, winning gold in the blue-ribbon event.

The train stops at a large platform, but it's not what I expect Frankfurt station to be like. There are very few signs in English and it's not until the train continues that I think, "Oh shit, that was Frankfurt Airport, the transfer!" I feel quite stupid as I knew the transfer was at Frankfurt, but there are actually two main stations, Frankfurt Airport and Frankfurt Central, and I have confused the two. I chastise myself a little and vow to not miss these kinds of details on my train journeys ahead.

In a slightly stressed state, I approach the ticket inspector, who doesn't speak English but manages to comfort me by communicating non-verbally that Frankfurt Central station is next. I learn from my smartphone that while there are more train route options from Frankfurt Airport station, I will still be able to find a direct route to Basel from Frankfurt Central and everything will be alright.

Unfortunately, at Frankfurt Central the next train to Basel has been delayed, meaning that I'll have to wait for a couple of hours. I buy a coffee and a *pain au chocolat* and, with few seats available, park myself at the far end of a long platform, where I look for a Wi-Fi signal. When this fails, I decide to invest in a copy of the London *Times*, at the special, one-time-only price of ten euros. It proves a good read, though, providing a fix of news from the English-speaking world, and I've read it cover to cover by the time my train arrives in Basel.

Though a Swiss city, Basel spills over the border into France and Germany. A couple of middle-aged English ladies are confused as to whether to get off at the first or second Basel station, Basel Badischer Bahnhof or Basel SBB. They make a good point. Checking my you-beaut Eurail app, I inform them that we should all get off at Basel SBB. A funny little observation at the border is that when we cross into Switzerland, there are suddenly very un-German looking vegetable allotments.

The train from Basel to Zurich is right on time and due to arrive at 8 pm. I'm unsure what to expect from Switzerland, though I know the main facts: that it's a wealthy and very civilised little country in the centre of Europe, with mountainous terrain and many glaciers; that it remained neutral throughout the two world wars and other major conflicts, even though it possesses a world-class military bolstered by regular, compulsory military service for all males between nineteen and twenty-six.

As I admire the impossibly lush green fields rolling across the hills at the base of mountains, it seems like a lovely place indeed. The scenery is beautiful, with cows munching on the thick grass and farmhouses and traditional Swiss cottages dotted across fields. It is the polar opposite of the harsh terrain experienced by Australian outback cattle back home, which only make the grade as prime beef by being grain-fed.

From what I've seen on Google Maps, my hotel should be an easy ten-minute walk, being centrally located on the other side of the river from the station. It's still light when I make my way there. The water of the River Limmat, which flows out of nearby Lake Zurich and cuts through the city, is crystal clear. The streets and buildings are very classy; there's money here, and definitely old money, not "nouveau". I start to think about those famously secretive Swiss banks, with their confidential dealings and underground vaults, though perhaps my idea of these is not so much grounded in reality as on my reading of the *Da Vinci Code*. It would be interesting to actually visit one of these banks, to find out how much of this is true and how much was the work of Dan Brown's imagination.

It's a pleasant walk through the Zurich's old town to my hotel and a relief to check-in, knowing my longest day on the trains is over. The hotel has a sophisticated little bar on its ground floor and while my room is small, it is a more than comfortable studio. Hotel rooms come at a premium price in Zurich, but so do most other things I'm soon to discover.

The city centre is even smaller than I anticipated and clearly won't take long to explore. So I'm happy that I've booked a day-long tour into the Swiss Alps for the next day. Looking forward to that and tired after my long day, I quickly drift off to sleep in my studio room.

At 6 am I'm at the bus depot opposite the train station. Originally, I wanted to explore the southern mountains of Switzerland, but that would have been too time-consuming, involving valuable days wasted staying in small towns between short train journeys through mountainous terrain. Given more time, I would have travelled as far south as Lake Como in northern Italy, famous for its picturesque beauty and celebrity residents like George Clooney and Madonna. This day trip seems the best next thing.

The tour group consists of people from all over the world, but I soon strike up a conversation with a fellow Aussie, a young infantryman named Mitchell, on some rest and recreation from deployment in Afghanistan. Hitting it off, we become mates for the day and it's interesting to hear about his experiences in Afghanistan. He seems proud to be a soldier and enjoys the army's valuable work in the field.

The bus travels 90 kilometres south to Lucerne. Like Zurich and Geneva, Lucerne is situated on a beautiful lake beneath picturesque snow-capped mountains. The Swiss watch and chocolate shops are but a mere sideshow to the lake, with its crystal-clear alpine water. Quaint houses and hotels line the shore, but Lucerne is more of a town than city, smaller than Zurich.

The most famous attraction here is the distinct looking Kapellbrücke, or Chapel Bridge. This wooden footbridge runs diagonally across the Reuss River. First built in 1333, it is the world's oldest surviving truss bridge and, uniquely, has a number of seventeenth-century paintings on display inside it. Many of the originals were destroyed in a 1993 fire, but the bridge was subsequently restored and remains the symbol of Lucerne, as well as one of Switzerland's main tourist attractions.

Adjoining the middle of the bridge is a 43-metre-high octagonal water tower, the Wasserturm. It actually predates the bridge by about thirty years and over the centuries has been used as a prison, torture chamber and municipal archive. The bridge's unusual shape leads me to take of a wide variety of photos, looking for different angles and stark contrasts.

Lucerne's other main attraction is the Dying Lion of Lucerne, a giant lion carved into a cliff face, which commemorates the hundreds of Swiss guards who were massacred in 1792 during the French Revolution. When we arrive, dozens of tourists are standing in front of the monument, having their picture taken. The tour guide takes my photo, but it's a bit of a shocker, with me centred in the picture and the lion to my right on a sliding angle. She must have taken the same shot scores of times on her tours – plenty of practice, you would think! Oh well, no big deal, but I'll take all of my *own* photos of the Swiss Alps going forward.

With everybody back on the bus, our guide gets upset when four Indian men start tucking into a curry – eating on the bus is prohibited. Only after the food is hidden away does she retake her seat. The bus continues en route to Mount Titlis via Engleberg and, before long, the Indians have defiantly resumed their lunch. A bit of a cultural difference, but no one really cares (other than the guide).

The views of the ultra-lush green fields in the valley rising up to Mt Titlis are breathtaking and I find it hard to put the camera away. I berate myself, "Enough! Just enjoy the damned scenery!" The valley is a hotspot for para-gliders and I easily spot a dozen or so gliding down from the mountains above. It looks like marvellous fun, but obviously risky at the same time.

At the top of the valley we halt at the base of the mountain. After two chairlifts and a gondola, we climb aboard Mt Titlis's famous spinning "Rotair" gondola. Each of the enormous cabins rotates as it ascends to the snow-covered summit of Mount Titlis, spinning a full 360 degrees over the course of the steep 2-kilometre climb. Snow-covered mountain peaks extend as far as the eye can see, as well as jagged cliffs and deep crevasses.

At the top, we have two and a half hours to explore the magnificent scenery, cross a high-altitude cable-walk bridge, view the inside of a glacier and ride toboggans down the mountain. We are at 3,200 metres, far higher than Mt Kosciuszko back in Australia – where we experience a very hit-and-miss ski season – and the air does feel that little bit thinner.

Mitchell and I head straight for the chairlift down to the toboggan slope. He's not much of a photographer, content to take in the view and chat while I snap away. It's a very happy feeling to be high up in the European Alps, experiencing some proper mountains for the first time in my life.

The toboggan slope is short but fun. However, seeing the snow skiers fly past, I long to boot up and put on some skis. My family used to go skiing regularly when I was growing up, and I also went on a couple of school ski trips. It dawns on me that I haven't actually skied in sixteen years!

We take the chairlift back up then walk across the suspension bridge. There's a long, sheer drop below it, and it provides uninterrupted, panoramic views of the Swiss Alps. The walk inside the glacier cave is interesting in that the ice, which generates a dim turquoise-blue light, is up to 5,000 years old. However, a better bet for a proper glacier experience would be to head over the "ditch" (Tasman Sea) to New Zealand, either to the Franz Josef Glacier or the Fox Glacier.

After lunch at the expensive, captive-market, high-altitude restaurant, I head outside to the open area above the restaurant for some more views while my buddy checks out the souvenirs. The vista is truly inspiring and I take a number of left-to-right videos and panoramic shots. It may not match the experience in southern Switzerland, with its Matterhorn and enormous Aletsch Glacier, but today has been well above expectations and worth the one-hundred-euro fee, and it's definitely worthy of the four-star review I post on TripAdvisor that evening.

On the bus back, Mitchell ruminates in conversation that he finds Switzerland so beautiful that he would move here in a heartbeat. It would be a utopia compared to Afghanistan! "Joining the army has allowed me to see places I'd never have seen had I chosen another career back home," he says. It goes without saying that the Australian army uses that sense of adventure in its recruitment ads back home – a clever marketing tool.

The bus returns to Zurich at 6 pm and I part ways with Mitchell, wishing him well for the rest of his time off. Around my hotel in the old town there are many restaurants. I'm assuming – at least hoping – they're not as expensive as the trendy eateries down by the river-front or on the lake, but when I look at a couple of menus I find that the cheapest mains cost the equivalent of fifty euros. There's no way I want to part with that amount of my hard-earned funds, so I buy some dinner and couple of beers at a kebab shop before heading back to the hotel.

Seven

Salzburg and Mozart

Mid-morning, my train departs from Zurich station on the five-hour journey to Salzburg, Austria. I've enjoyed Switzerland, even though it was really just a pitstop on the way to Salzburg and then Vienna. As the train speeds alongside Lake Zurich, the scenery continues to be quaint and scenic. At the edge of the flat and clear body of water there are plentiful luxurious and expensive-looking residences, in a diverse mixture of modern and traditional styles, probably owned by wealthy Zurich bankers. The views across the lake continue for quite some way – Lake Zurich is actually 40 kilometres long, though only 3 kilometres across at its widest point.

Given the high price of my Eurail Pass, I'd hoped all trains would have free Wi-Fi. As it turns out, different rail companies make up the massive and complicated European train network, and whether or not Wi-Fi is available is a bit of a lucky dip. Fortunately, the train company on this leg is Railjet, which has a fleet of new bullet trains, all with free Wi-Fi.

It's a great opportunity to upload some photos to Facebook, so I look for pictures that will simultaneously impress friends and make them jealous. However, as the train progresses into mountainous terrain, it becomes difficult to concentrate on the task. All of a sudden, the scenery has become spectacular. I continue to peruse social media and so forth, thinking it only a temporary distraction, but as I finally click "Upload photos" I'm aware of the views getting better and better as the train traverses one valley sunk between large mountains.

Having no idea whether or not we've yet crossed the Austrian border, I chill out while listening to music, taking in the views of cattle, country homes, green pastures and jagged peaks. Seeing Europe from the comfort of a train while moving from one exciting or beautiful city to another makes the price of the Eurail Pass more than justifiable. If you were high above in a plane, you'd miss out on all these details. These will be lifelong happy memories, and I feel privileged to be here; I wish some of my less intrepid friends back home could experience this too. The five hours fly by and for once it's not just a cliché: the journey is as good as the destination.

Suddenly I'm in Austria and not Switzerland anymore. The accents have changed, as well as other things. Of course, both countries encompass the incredible beauty of the Alps; however, while Switzerland's alpine lakes are a nature enthusiast's dream, Austria is more affordable and has a stronger focus on art, culture and intellectual discussion. These sudden cultural changes make continental Europe so interesting to a curious soul like me.

Unfortunately, at Salzburg train station it's raining, and it takes a few false starts before I locate my hotel. The reception staff seem emotionally detached, fulfilling one Austrian stereotype, I think, while presenting my passport. Strangely, the lobby is buzzing with fit, athletic-looking men and women of various ages and nationalities. I will discover why soon.

Happy with my new digs, I venture out for an afternoon orientation walk around Salzburg. After a kilometre or so, I cross a bridge over the fast-flowing Salzach River into Salzburg's Old Town, considered one of the best-preserved city centres north of the Alps. It's impeccably clean and well maintained for tourists, with charming little streets between terraced buildings, and a number of open squares with fountains. Boutique stores are abundant, as are tastefully designed restaurants and pubs.

Many of the buildings and churches are in the Austrian Baroque style, characterised by opulent use of colour, large dimensions and pear-shaped domes. I'm immediately in love with all things Baroque. The stroll is good preparation for the next couple of days, giving me a feel for the town's geography. Late afternoon, I return to the hotel with a bottle of a new style of red wine to try.

Now knowing my way around, I return to the UNESCO World Heritage–listed historic centre next morning. Salzburg's most famous site is Hohensalzburg Castle, which overlooks the city, guarding it, like many other famous castles in Europe – Edinburgh Castle comes to mind. Salzburg brings me my first glimpse of Austrian culture.

Salzburg is famously the birthplace of Wolfgang Amadeus Mozart, and the city and surrounding hills were the setting for one of the most popular films ever made, *The Sound of Music*. I've only seen this classic movie once, but once was enough! It's not my kind of film, so I have no interest in visiting the hills above Salzburg, the ones "alive with the sound of music."

Meandering around, I notice some locals proudly sporting traditional Austrian outfits: gentlemen in lederhosen and ladies wearing the dirndl. The dirndl is particularly lovely on some of these women and looks expensive, probably tailored and cut from fine fabrics. I cross the river again into the Old Town, noting the powerful currents swelled by melting snow from the nearby Alps.

My first point of interest is Mozart's birthplace, a museum in a bright yellow townhouse on the Getreidegasse, where Wolfgang Amadeus was born in 1756. The Mozart family lived on the third floor for twenty-six years until 1773. Wolfgang was the youngest of seven children, five of whom died in infancy. In this modest abode, his father, Leopold, a minor composer and teacher, nurtured and moulded his child into a precocious and talented composer. Wolfgang's older sister, Marianne, was a talented musician also, but, given the views of her parents and the norms of society at the time, it became impossible for her to continue her career once she reached a marriageable age.

Meanwhile, her younger brother composed complicated, sophisticated classical music well beyond his youthful age level. The Mozart family travelled to other parts of Europe and word spread of his incredible talents, gaining him attention in Vienna and Paris. In return for writing and playing music for royalty, he received significant financial support. Classical music was at a high point in its history and Mozart went from strength to strength, eventually composing over six hundred works. However, many of the symphonies, concertos and operas that he wrote in his final years in Vienna remained largely unfinished at the time of his early death, aged just thirty-five.

The museum is really just a typical late-eighteenth-century Salzburg apartment. It is worth visiting though for the excellent collection of memorabilia, including the violin Mozart played as a child, some original sheets of handwritten music, his first ever piano and items of his clothing. Taking photographs is strictly forbidden, but I adore his child-size violin and can't resist sneaking up close for a photo without flash.

All around Salzburg are pictures and memorabilia of the city's most famous former inhabitant. While doing a Google search a couple of days prior, I learned that the commonly accepted likeness of Mozart as a child could well be a complete fraud. That image of Mozart as a boy is how many see the genius; however, there's much speculation and doubt as to its authenticity.

In 1924, the International Mozarteum Foundation of Salzburg bought the original portrait of what they thought was Mozart as a child, based on an inscription on the painting. However, recent carbon dating suggests that the inscription was added later and that therefore the portrait may not actually be Mozart at all. Fourteen versions of the image are known to exist in different media, including oil paintings, engravings and medallions, and I see it reproduced on memorabilia all over Salzburg.

From the museum, it's ten minutes' walk to the large, stately square in the heart of Salzburg, the Residenzplatz. It's on arriving there I realise why my hotel foyer was filled with fit athletes from all over the world discussing a big race. There are barriers and a giant inflatable-arch finishing line with digital clock. I read a sign in English informing me that Salzburg's annual marathon is taking place tomorrow, a Sunday. What a picturesque place to put oneself through the 42-kilometre torture test. There are also, apparently, a couple of shorter races for those with less stamina.

In the middle of the Residenzplatz stands a grand fountain, which is surrounded by horse-drawn carriages. At one end of the square is the city's cathedral, as fine an example as any of Baroque architecture. The spiritual centre of the city, it has an imposing façade that dominates the square and, at over 150 metres long and with its distinctive aqua-blue pear-shaped domes standing 40 metres tall, it's an impressive sight.

A cathedral was first built here in the eighth century; it was burned down in 842 after being struck by lightning and then was rebuilt several times during the Middle Ages. In 1598, after it was severely damaged by fire, the Prince-Archbishop of Salzburg, Wolf Dietrich von Raitenau, ordered that it be demolished. Enamoured of the architecture he'd observed in Rome, Raiteneau was a promoter of the Italian Baroque style and he had comprehensive plans for a new cathedral drawn up by Italian architects. Construction was completed under the watch of Wolf Dietrich's successor as Prince-Archbishop, Mark Sittich von Hohenems, in 1628. Building took a mere fifteen years. In more recent history, the central dome was struck by a single bomb during World War II; further restoration was completed in the late 1950s. Inside, the baroque exaggeration of space is impressive, in particular in the enormous marble white nave and ceiling.

When I come back outside after forty-five minutes, a local man is playing an elegant acoustic guitar on the steps of the church entrance and there's been a significant pick-up in activity for the dozen or so horses and carriages that take romantic tourists on scenic routes around Salzburg.

It is then 500 metres walk to the base of a steep hill to Salzburg's most visible icon, the mighty clifftop fortress of Hohensalzburg Castle. Visitors can climb the steep hill or alternatively reach the castle by funicular, which starts just off a small square where some older men are playing chess on a giant outdoor chessboard. It's enjoyable to watch them for ten minutes or so and also browse the nearby stalls selling souvenirs, many of them cashing in on Mozart, some appealing, but many tacky. The funicular is efficient and regular as clockwork and there is only a short queue.

Hohensalzburg Castle is one of the largest and best preserved medieval castles in Europe. Its construction began in 1077, under Archbishop Gebhard von Helfenstein, one of the line of archbishops who ruled Salzburg from 798 AD to 1803, and it was expanded over the next seven centuries by subsequent rulers. The views from the top stretch far and wide, across the domes of the cathedral and over the Salzach River winding its way out of the city. I wonder what route the marathon might follow tomorrow. Back inside the castle walls, I join a couple of tours through staterooms, a former torture chamber and a museum, which are not all that interesting.

Back at the bottom of the funicular, I find the beautiful little Abby Church, which dates back to 700 AD. Its architecture is rich in character and it is surrounded by a cemetery with lovingly tended graves, seemingly arranged at random, with no common theme or style. The view looking back up to the castle from the graveyard is beautifully picturesque. Outside the lower end of the cemetery is a very old traditional bakery, sunk below street level and adjoining a water-driven flour mill.

Strolling back to the river through another open square, I pass a statue of Mozart, a large bronze sculpture, at the base of which people have placed flowers. At this point, I remember fortuitously that the Mozart Museum and Castle ticket also offers a large discount on riverboat cruises. I've timed it perfectly and five minutes after I buy my ticket my boat departs the jetty, three-quarters full.

The Salzach River's currents are more powerful than is usual in spring. A late winter has dumped unseasonably large amounts of snow on the Alps above and, following the sudden onset of spring, the snow has been melting rapidly, fuelling the river's strong flow. Our guide introduces the boat's amiable captain, a Brit with a smiling face and outgoing personality. He informs us that the boat has a high-tech jet system that will propel us upstream, over and above the currents.

Initially we cruise at a snail's pace upstream while cyclists easily overtake us on the river bank. But then the captain then pulls some kind of large lever and the boat suddenly lifts about a foot, like a souped-up, supercharged rapper's car, and we quickly jet upstream, gliding over the turbulent water. Once the cruise coasts past the impressive backdrop of the Old Town, we get a nice look at the natural environment of the Salzach River, as well as the exclusive residential area in the south of the city, where the magnificent Hagen and Tennen mountain ranges rise before us.

It's been a short but pleasant cruise. As the hull nears the jetty once again, the smiling captain informs us that he has one last trick up his sleeve. Over heavy currents he skilfully spins the boat on its axis 540 degrees, or one-and-a-half times, his *pièce de résistance.* As they disembark, most of the guests tip the captain in recognition of this last manoeuvre.

Leaving the historic centre, I cross a popular footbridge decorated by hundreds of padlocks in different colours, designs and sizes, all locked permanently onto the bridge's railing. Written in ink on many are messages, such as "James loves Suzy", "Raphael loves Sophia" and so on. I laugh while thinking to myself that, even as a bachelor, I could add my own padlock: "Angus loves Salzburg". Clusters of padlocks can be found attached to tourist spots all over the world now; I well remember Facebook friends uploading photos of padlock-covered bridges in Paris and Prague, for example.

Back at the hotel, I log onto the free Wi-Fi to listen to samples of some of Mozart's famous symphonies through iTunes. I have the fleeting idea of downloading some of his music to make my long train trips that little bit more ambient. However, I'm soon reminded that his oeuvre is vast, even if most of it is familiar. I decide not to buy any, as I wouldn't know where to start.

In the evening I head back to town for dinner, and to see the historic centre's beautiful streets and lanes again at night.

Eight

Grand Vienna

For my final morning in Salzburg, I take some time to explore other areas. The gardens of the Mirabell Palace are very beautiful, perfectly manicured and dotted with fountains. Their elegance seems very Austrian, and I expect more of this from Vienna in the days to come. The long view of the gardens on a bright morning with the castle up high in the distance is something to behold. A couple of Mozart lookalikes have dressed to impress – with white painted faces, wigs and long, velvet classical composer outfits – in the hope of earning tips.

I also spend some time watching the marathon runners on the home stretch of the big race. They inspire me to think that one day I could complete a half marathon, but that idea's more likely to go the way of so many other resolutions; it's like that famous John Lennon line, "Life is what happens while you are busy making other plans."

During the two-hour train journey to Vienna I watch a new-release movie downloaded from iTunes. The landscape is far less dramatic than the scenery between Zurich and Salzburg, so there are fewer distractions from my in-transit entertainment.

My Vienna hotel is located near the city centre, but a 5-kilometre cab ride from the station. A current-model Mercedes E-class pulls over. I throw my bags in the boot and get into the passenger seat. The driver is a thirty-something man, sincere and slightly serious, like many

Austrians, I suspect. Thanks to his excellent English, I get a quick and informative lesson on how to spend four days in Vienna.

"Is four days too much time for Vienna?" I ask.

Apparently it isn't at all, and that question gets him going straight away. In Australia, this guy would simply be a "good bloke", I think to myself. I tell him of the countless recommendations I've received from friends, including many of Vienna's historical buildings, palaces and world-class art galleries. As it's mid-afternoon, I ask him where to go for a drink while the sun sets.

"Easy. Make your way down to the Danube Canal for Vienna's trendy outdoor bars," he says, "The canal – *not* the river."

Despite the luxury car, the fare is far less than it would be in a Brisbane cab. My hotel is very central, as expected, and the room is large, with very high ceilings. Given that I was staying four nights in Vienna, this excellent hotel came offered at a good discount on hotels.com, and it appears to be quite a bargain as I get comfortable in my new digs.

Within twenty minutes, I'm out on an afternoon stroll through Vienna. After a gentle hill I hit the wide Ringstrasse, or Ring Road, the main road running around Vienna's central Innere Stadt district. The famous road is located where medieval city fortifications once stood and was constructed after the dismantling of the city walls in the mid-nineteenth century. Many buildings were erected along the Ring Road in the following decades in an eclectic style, sometimes called *Ringstrassenstil* ("Ring Road Style").

The area inside the Ringstrasse, the historic centre of Vienna, is a UNESCO World Heritage Site renowned for its cultural heritage and green parks dotted with sculptures and fountains. I soon approach the Hofburg, a grand imperial palace which has housed some of the most powerful people in European history, most significantly the Habsburg monarchs, rulers of the Austro-Hungarian Empire until its collapse during World War I.

The palace was completed in the late thirteenth century and was home to the Habsburgs for the next six hundred years. Its immense size and great architectural diversity are due to the one-upmanship of each successive generation of royals. Over the coming days, I will return and fully explore the palace, including an interesting little museum dedicated to the strange and sad life of "Sisi", the Empress Elisabeth (1837–98), who struggled with the demands of royal life. And there will be several other beautiful royal palaces to visit.

Outside the Hofburg, horse-drawn carts like those I saw in Salzburg trot past, carrying mostly couples around the flat, wide streets of the city. The central shopping street of the Innere Stadt is vibrant, crowded with shoppers and tourists and lined with all of the big-brand shops and fine department stores; dotted around are a few of the coffeehouses for which the city is famous. The pedestrian-only street terminates at a large square, Stephansplatz, named after Vienna's most prominent building, the Stephansdom (St Stephen's Cathedral), which rises high above it. It is nicknamed "Little Stephen", even though it's one of the tallest churches in the world, at over 130 metres in height.

I want to keep on the move, so I just take a quick glimpse inside. Multicoloured rays of light beam down from enormous stained-glass windows and the effect is angelic.

Vowing to come back, I decide it's time to head for a relaxing beer in the hip bars on the Danube Canal. From a bridge overlooking the canal, I can see a temporary beach on the river bank, roughly 100 metres long, where there are hundreds of deckchairs facing the setting sun. The adjacent open-air bar sells beer by the bottle; a small deposit is added to the price to make sure you bring the bottle back. With a beer in hand I find a little patch with a deckchair. Hundreds of people are soaking up the sun and there's a carefree vibe, with clusters of trendy Viennese engage in relaxed conversation. Among them are plenty of children, adding a family-friendly flavour to the mix. It's a laugh watching both kids and intoxicated adults attempt to walk an 8-metre tightrope, half a metre above the sand at one end of the beach. The thought of twisting an ankle at this stage of my trip dissuades me from attempting this slightly risky pursuit.

Europe has always set trends and I think of how this bar could be replicated back Down Under, with just a little creative twist on your typical Aussie pub and beer garden. Melbourne and Sydney have world-class bars, but Brisbane is not really there yet. Actually, Paris has had the similar Paris-Plages scheme since 2002, which creates artificial beaches along the River Seine each summer. It was initiated in response to the annual exodus of city-dwellers trying to avoid the hot, humid weather, especially in August.

The beer is smooth and quenching and before long I return to collect my deposit. Another couple of beers later, darkness descends. I would love to "beam up" (à la *Star Trek*) some of my antipodean friends to enjoy this bar with me, and maybe meet a few local girls.

Leaving the beach bar a bit tipsy, I continue along the canal past some more enterprising outdoor bars. A 60-metre-long ship is docked in the canal and its top deck hosts a couple of hundred drinkers along its entire length. All very casual, the deck is split into distinct zones, with a couple of beer gardens and dance floors, a pool and a smoking area at the stern.

Tired and hungry, I grab a hot dog from one of many street vendors before catching the metro back to the hotel. Vienna's metro is simple and easy to comprehend, having only a small number of lines. Geographically, it is a straightforward city in general. It's also noticeable that drivers seem patient and considerate towards others sharing the roads.

I take the same route next morning to the Hofburg to see the palace's Imperial Apartments and the Sisi Museum, with camera in tow this time. In the Imperial Apartments visitors can immerse themselves in the daily lives of the monarchs. Emperor Franz Joseph and his famously beautiful wife, Elisabeth, lived in the palace in the second half of the nineteenth century with their children and royal household. It's from here that they ran the empire and directed its politics. On show are the large audience hall and conference rooms, where all the important meetings took place. More intimate, though, are the emperor's office, living room, numerous salons and bathrooms, and the bedroom of Sisi, as the empress was affectionately known.

These apartments are less showy than the lavish rooms of Versailles, but they are tastefully decorated with intricate tapestries, crystal chandeliers and antique furniture. Particularly interesting is the emperor's office, where he, a workaholic who kept himself heavily involved in all facets of the empire, worked many long days. I wonder whether his work ethic exacerbated the melancholia of his wife and made her yet more disillusioned with trappings of an imperial existence.

Beyond the apartments is the Sisi Museum, devoted to the life of the beauty-obsessed empress. A close relative of Marie Antoinette, she was born into the Bavarian House of Wittelsbach, becoming Her Royal Highness Duchess Elisabeth Amalie Eugenie. As a young adult, she was considered one of the most beautiful women in Europe, noted for her long hair, which reached down to her calves. Her looks caught the eye of the young Franz Joseph at a time when his family had arranged for him to marry another blue-blooded woman, one with whom he never felt at ease. Instantly infatuated with Sisi, Franz Joseph defied his mother, informing her that if he couldn't marry Elisabeth, he would not marry at all. His engagement to Sisi was announced five days after the ultimatum, and the couple married eight months later in Vienna.

But Sisi was naturally informal and unsophisticated, and she quickly found the conventions and protocols of Habsburg court life stifling. Early on she displayed health problems, and these were a sign of things to come, as she suffered severe depression for most of her life. When she initially failed to produce a male heir, she felt even more uneasy in the palace. She was quoted as saying that marriage is an impractical arrangement, making little sense except to unite powerful families.

Sisi was obsessive about her appearance, and this physical sense of self-worth was a big motivation in her life. She would starve to keep her hallmark "wasp waist" and undertake rigorous and disciplined exercise regimes. Gymnasiums were installed in every castle she lived in and lengthy daily grooming routines maintained her immaculate hair. Over time, however, she increasingly withdrew from many public engagements, spending long spells away from her family while attempting to allay her own physical and mental problems.

In the meantime, she did, however, give birth to a son which at least increased her influence at court. Unfortunately, though, her son and heir, Rudolph, had his own demons, and as he grew older he became mentally unstable. At the age of thirty, he killed himself as part of a suicide pact with his mistress. Sisi was devastated by the death of her son, which haunted her for the rest of her life.

And Sisi's own life ended tragically when she was assassinated by an Italian anarchist while travelling incognito to Geneva, despite being forewarned of possible assassination attempts. Her assassin, Luigi Lucheni, had originally planned to kill the Duke of Orléans, claimant to the throne of France, but he had left Geneva earlier to travel east to the Canton of Valais. Failing to find him, Lucheni targeted Sisi when a Geneva newspaper revealed that the elegant woman travelling under the pseudonym of "the Countess of Hohenembs" was the Empress Elisabeth of Austria.

The museum is sombre and sad but also presents an absorbing account of a troubled life. In some ways, Sisi was an intellectual ahead of her time, someone who did not conform. One could call her the Princess Diana of the nineteenth century – depending on your opinion of Lady Di.

While many would easily write Sisi off as a spoiled little rich girl, I try to think of her as an emotionally complex person and of her story as a life lesson on dysfunctional royal families, also applicable to the present. Interestingly, Elisabeth's melancholy and eccentricity were considered a given characteristic of her Wittelsbach royal family lineage. The best-known member of the family was her favourite cousin, the eccentric "Mad King" Ludwig II of Bavaria.

After exiting the palace, I find my way back to the Ringstrasse. The classical architecture, open green spaces and bronze statues continue through central Vienna. I find a couple of rose gardens in bloom, one with a statue of Mozart. This statue is a younger-looking version of the one I'd seen in Salzburg.

Just past the Albertina art gallery is a Wi-Fi hotspot, one of many dotted around Vienna. Luckily, I have my iPhone with map apps, as I am quite lost by now and looking for the quickest route to the Little Stephen cathedral. After finding my way back to Vienna's main shopping drag, I seek out a coffeehouse recommended by my guidebook, down a quiet side lane. I take a seat at a table and look around while waiting for table service. The guide recommended the cafe for its atmosphere and character, but I'm not impressed. A random cafe I visited near the Hofburg the day before felt more charming and atmospheric. The male waiter who comes to take my order has a gruff and unwelcoming manner, but the Viennese-style coffee and piece of cheesecake are enjoyable.

Soon I'm looking up at Little Stephen again, but with my camera this time. Outside are a dozen or so men dressed as Mozart, approaching tourists in the hope of taking them on a cathedral tour. I decide I'll spend some quality time inside on my final day and today just focus on taking photographs of the exterior. I peer up at the massive south tower, the highest point and the most recognisable feature on the Vienna skyline. The cathedral's 111-metre-long roof is covered with 230,000 glazed tiles. These green, yellow, brown, white and grey tiles form elegant zigzag patterns along its mighty length. As with the beams of light I saw coming through the windows, the roof has its own distinct look, completely different from any other church I've ever seen.

I then descend into the St Stephen metro station and make the short journey to Prater station to see Vienna's famous amusement park. The Prater is home to an iconic Wiener Riesenrad Ferris wheel, seen in the films *The Third Man* and *Before Sunrise*. Built in 1897, it's smaller than modern wheels such as the London Eye, but the red square-shaped carriages on its frame are far more characterful than the slick new pods.

On the metro journey, I reminisce about the 1995 film *Before Sunrise*. I remember that ever since seeing this film for the first time, I've had a romantic notion of visiting Vienna. I re-watched the film just before my trip, and it's in one of these red carriages that the two lead characters, played by Ethan Hawke and Julie Delpy, share their first romantic kiss.

The Prater is quite large, but the Ferris wheel is right at the entrance next to the metro. Have I only come here because I'm a movie buff? Maybe, but there are far more visitors sharing my carriage than there were in the Singapore Flyer a month ago. The views over Vienna are sweeping, with Little Stephen jutting triumphantly out from the skyline.

From the wheel's 65-metre-high apex, I can see the towering Praterturm StarFlyer. Built in 2010, this swing ride whirls fun-loving passengers around its 117-metre-high old-fashioned clock tower.

After a full spin of the Ferris wheel, I can't wait to give the Praterturm a try. Although afraid of heights, I'm sure it will be safe and it just looks so enjoyable. Riders are paired together in seats. Sitting next to me is an attractive blonde lady who drew the short straw in her group of three. The height doesn't bother me one iota and it really is child-like fun. After dismounting back at ground level, my travel companion and her friends get straight back in the queue for a repeat experience.

Walking around the park, I watch with curiosity as teenagers get their adrenaline fixes on various gravity-defying rides. There are no bungy jumps, but plenty of variants on the New Zealand invention, from which shrieks and screams emanate. I think of a theory I read about how teenagers love rollercoasters because they're at an age where their sense of fear is not yet fully developed. These rides provide a chance to put this to the test. The confidence and, sometimes, arrogance of youth, I think.

There are a couple of shooting galleries where young men are trying to win prizes by sinking duck targets. I think back to my teenage years when'd visit Brisbane's Royal Show (the "Ekka"). My friends and I knew that the gun barrels were bent to dampen the prospects of gullible customers; we thought we were pretty cool anyway, not participating while watching others miss their targets. And it's a guilty pleasure here too, watching a couple of men fail to hit their targets, then look dismayed. There are also dodgem cars, a haunted house and pony rides for little kids. After a beer while people-watching, I walk the 5 kilometres back to the hotel for exercise.

The next day is all about Vienna's impressive palaces. Taking the metro and a transfer to the U-Bahn, I make the trip out of central Vienna to discover the Schönbrunn Palace, the former summer residence of the Habsburg royal family. Where I exit the U-Bahn station, the urban area is very plain indeed – most unlike the beautiful city centre. Buying a coffee at a modest little cafe, I ask the lady for directions to the palace. She points to a long and underwhelming yellow building, informing me that it is the palace. Hmm, it must be very well disguised, I think.

I walk along its length for 600 metres then come upon the entrance, which is overwhelmed with tourist buses. I purchase a ticket and proceed through a lovely courtyard to the entrance. Then, after walking under the palace, I ascend to the glorious and picture-perfect complex I was expecting.

The Schönbrunn is one of Europe's most iconic palaces. I've seen countless pictures in travel brochures of this 1441-room UNESCO World Heritage Site, with its gardens and the iconic Gloriette building atop the hill opposite.

Throughout my time in mainland Europe, CNN has been advertising and doing stories on the upcoming summer concerts at the Schönbrunn, which feature orchestras playing Mozart symphonies to thousands of people seated outdoors in the gardens at twilight. These shows are a proud Viennese tradition, and CNN has been interviewing the conductors, who look like they've died and gone to heaven to be given such a prestigious gig.

The area around the palace was originally a flood plain. After purchasing the land in 1569, Holy Royal Emperor Maximilian II ordered that the area be fenced off and game such as pheasants, ducks, deer and boar be let loose to provide the court with a recreational hunting ground. Exotic birds like turkeys and peacocks were isolated in their own separate part of the grounds. The name "Schönbrunn", meaning "beautiful spring", derives from the artesian well that provided water to the court.

For the next century the area fulfilled its intended purpose as a hunting and recreation ground. Over time the royals spent more and more time here and the palace was built between 1638 and 1643. Following the downfall of the monarchy in 1918, the newly founded republic became owner of Schönbrunn Palace and decided to preserve the rooms and chambers as a museum. After World War II, the palace was requisitioned to provide offices for the post-war British delegation to the Allied Commission for Austria. It went on to become an important venue for major international summits, such as the meeting between John F. Kennedy and Nikita Khrushchev in 1961.

As I pass through the entrance to the complex, the stately golden-yellow palace is behind me, while ahead its perfectly designed and manicured French garden extends for about 400 metres. At the garden's end is the Neptune Fountain, itself at the base of a long sloping hill that leads up to the Gloriette. It's a similar arrangement to Versailles, but not quite as large and slightly less extravagant. While Versailles screams "Look at me!", the Schönbrunn says "Less is more." We're talking relative terms here, though: the palace complex is still vast, but more understated.

It's hard to take photos of the palace from close up; its scale can only really be appreciated from a distance. As at Versailles, the gardens consist of open and impeccably manicured spaces separated by lines of sculptures and neatly trimmed hedges from closed-off, maze-like gardens on either side.

A small army of gardeners is at work, keeping everything well maintained. Watching them work, I can only imagine that the task of maintaining the gardens would be never-ending. At one point, on the left-hand side as I walk towards the Neptune Fountain, two 7-metre-high hedges reach over a path, forming a giant archway leading into the side gardens – more a work of sculpture than a simple hedge.

The grand Neptune Fountain incorporates white statues of men and horses and sprays water into a pool below. The view of the fountain, with the Gloriette on the hill behind it, is stunning. And when I turn around, I can finally appreciate and capture the full majesty of the palace. Deciding to take a rest, I sit with scores of others around the fountain to soak up the scene for a while, before continuing along a right-to-left-to-right winding path up to the Gloriette.

The Gloriette is a familiar building I've seen scores of times in pictures and I was aware that it was a European icon, but I didn't know its name or exactly where it was. Completed in 1775, it was the last building to be constructed in the gardens. It was designed to glorify Habsburg power and also dedicated as a "monument to Just War". Just War is a doctrine of military ethics, whereby war can be declared morally justifiable if it is shown, based on a series of criteria, to be necessary and likely to lead to peace.

Internal steps climb 20 metres to the top. The view is priceless – well, actually it costs five euros, to be precise – and is the pièce de résistance of the palace visit. Laid out directly in front of me is the hill leading down to the fountain, which in turn opens up to the wide gardens and the grand but understated palace. Beyond the palace the view extends to the city. It's an enjoyable exercise to use the camera to zoom in on the well-proportioned gardens below and snap a variety of shots.

At a cafe beneath the Gloriette, I have an espresso break before heading back to fully explore the maze-like gardens, which looked especially enticing from above. The gardens prove to be peaceful and quiet, the walkways wide, and a number of small trains cart elderly tourists around. There are also a few rowdy school excursions, which I do my best to avoid.

The Schönbrunn has been one of the highlights of my trip so far. I exit via a side garden and I'm soon back on the U-Bahn. When I get to central Vienna and ascend to street level, dark, threatening clouds are approaching. As part of my "palace day", I'm heading next to the Belvedere, another palace complex.

I grab lunch at a hotdog stand and have to eat on the run. I'm expecting rain to bucket down within minutes and when I'm about a kilometre from the Belvedere it hits, hard. Even though I saw the forecast for the day, I stupidly didn't pack an umbrella.

The Belvedere is another enormous palace, but here too it's hard to find the entrance, which is frustrating in the torrential downpour. I start to panic but then, with relief, stumble upon the ticket booth, now absolutely drenched. Other, more sensible tourists have used umbrellas and they look at me with genuine sympathy as I retreat to the toilets to freshen and dry up, as a homeless man would.

The Belvedere is divided into the Lower Belvedere, the gardens and the Upper Belvedere. There are two types of tickets on sale, one for just the Lower Belvedere and one for the Lower and Upper Belvedere and the gardens in between. The lower building has a small art collection. Of greater significance are the gardens and the Upper Belvedere, which has more impressive Baroque artworks.

After buying the combined ticket, I walk through the Lower Belvedere. However, I'm instantly distracted by the impressive gardens visible through the large glass windows. Looking up towards the Upper Belvedere, past a fountain at halfway separating gardens above and below, it reminds me of the Taj Mahal. The building may not equal that mighty monument, but the gardens are worlds apart from the understated surrounds of the Indian icon.

Generally, the fountains aren't as impressive as at the Schönbrunn, but as I proceed up the stairs, the Upper Belvedere and gardens reveal their beauty. There are also many exquisite small fountains and well-placed statues, and hedge-like plants being tended to by skilled gardeners.

The construction of the Upper Belvedere began in 1717 and was completed in 1723. That seems efficient in comparison to other overblown and erratic royal architectural projects throughout Europe. Ivory in colour, the Baroque palace has four separate levels of windows, defined further by balustrades on the top two levels. The building's roof is the aqua colour of aged copper, just like the horses and chariot above Brussels' Parc de Cinquantenaire.

The exterior and gardens are worth the entry price alone. However, it is inside the upper building, with its impressive art collection, that the Belvedere is at its most impressive. The same style of Baroque art and architecture that I've admired in Salzburg and Vienna creates an extraordinary sense of exuberance and grandeur, most notably in the Upper Belvedere's grand halls, stately rooms and the impressive ceremonial staircase.

The Upper Belvedere is not just Baroque art though; a number of works by French Impressionists are on display too. Looking through windows at the gardens below, I see that it's pouring with rain again, so I wander thoughtfully through every room, taking my time.

After the rain clears, I walk out of the building's back door to yet more gardens surrounding an enormous flat pond – another iconic image of Vienna. I take photos from different angles of the flat, glassy water before sitting down to absorb the scene, enjoying in particular the sight of the clouds clearing to reveal blue sky.

Exiting the palace grounds, I walk out into the busy streets with their loud cars, knowing that just inside that innocuous-looking wall behind me is a palatial oasis. Walking back to the hotel, I look at the exteriors of a couple of buildings I'll be visiting tomorrow. It's been another long and energy-sapping day, so I turn in for an early sleep.

I've been taking advantage of my four-night stay to do some much-needed clothes washing and my room now resembles a makeshift laundromat, with clotheslines tied between the shower head, towel racks, bedroom lights and oversized wardrobe.

Next morning, I walk half a kilometre back along the Ringstrasse, which I now navigate with ease, to the Kunsthistorisches Museum. I've heard that nothing comes close to this place in Vienna for classic works of art.

Erected over twenty years in the late nineteenth century, the Kunsthistorisches Museum is a rectangular building, topped by a 60-metre-high dome, which houses an extensive range of treasures amassed over the centuries by the Habsburgs. Paintings make up a significant part of it, but there are also entire wings of ornaments, clocks and glassware, and Greek, Roman and Egyptian antiquities.

The building's entrance hall is immediately impressive. The main staircase is considered one of the highlights of Viennese nineteenth-century architecture, with a statue of Theseus slaying the Centaur as its focal point, flanked by two imperial lions. Above the staircase is a large fresco painting: classic, elegant and richly detailed. Continuing on from the staircase on the first floor is the Cupola Hall, decorated with precious metals and large blocks of granite and marble. The hall's large open space contains a restaurant, from where diners enjoy a view over the Ringstrasse below.

Wanting to see something different, I head for the Egyptian and Near-Eastern collections in a side wing. The Egyptian collection could match my favourite part of the British Museum. Following on are Greek and Roman antiquities, with works from as far back as the third millennium BC. The bronzes, statuettes, vases, glass and jewellery are carefully ordered and labelled, helping visitors to understand their importance while also appreciating their arresting designs.

The museum is famous for its unique clock and timepiece collections. Their bright gold, complicated moving parts remind me of the Mousetrap game from my childhood. The exhibition concludes with the glassware collection, which includes rock-crystal vases, detailed and translucent with colour. The Kunsthistorisches is an all-encompassing experience, and becomes an instant favourite.

Thoroughly satisfied, I walk another half kilometre to the Naschmarkt, Vienna's most popular market. It is a sprawling place, lined with more than enough stalls for any enthusiastic foodie. On sale are meats, fruits, vegetables, spices, cheeses and, unfortunately for me, some smelly fish.

I enter a cheese shop behind the stalls. After Paris I still know little about the endless variety of cheeses on offer in Europe. Bewildered by what appears to be over a hundred choices, I no doubt have a confused look on my face. Disappointingly, the shop owner shows real impatience while asking me to make up my mind, and when I tell him I'm still unsure what to buy, he simply snarls at me. I decide to leave and find a cheese deli that will appreciate my tourist dollars. Just outside there are a couple of outdoor stalls selling cheeses, and vying with each other for business, where I buy a couple of varieties from more friendly vendors.

Dotted throughout the market are cafes and restaurants, some definitely more expensive than others. I end up finding a good-value Asian noodle place with typically friendly Asian waiters. Next I take the metro back to St Stephen's Cathedral, where I soak up the afternoon's peace and quiet inside the cathedral, making a small prayer of thanks for my privileged trip and for those back home. Tomorrow I leave for Budapest after a thoroughly enjoyable few days. The many positive reports of Vienna I'd heard from people over the years have been proved correct: it's a beautiful city.

After sleeping in the next morning, I check out at the 11 am cut-off. Today is another travel day, with a three-hour train journey to my most easterly destination, Budapest. As a bit of a footnote and an excuse to go for one last outing, I walk a few kilometres to seek out the Sigmund Freud Museum.

The former home of the "father of psychoanalysis" now houses a small museum featuring some of his personal belongings. It proves to be very low key, really just a time-filler. I'm a bit surprised that people would go looking for this place and stump up the seven-euro entrance fee. Well, I guess my guidebook talked me into coming here. Maybe it's all about the location, as this is where Dr Freud devised theories that would change medicine and society forever.

I am interested to learn that Sigmund's daughter, Anna Freud, was also an important figure in the history of psychiatry. She never married, yet made her own mark on the science while living in London – she was quite a feminist, it would seem. I enjoyed the film *A Dangerous Method* recently and wonder if some of the fascinating meetings of minds between Freud and Dr Carl Jung, who was both a follower and rival, occurred in this humble house.

I return to the hotel and am then driven to the station by a taxi driver who exhibits an uncanny ability to find every possible red traffic light en route to the station. I nearly miss my train as a result.

Nine

Budapest, the Paris of the East

On the way to Budapest, I do some reading about this former Communist city, described widely these days as the "Paris of the East". As with many destinations on this trip, Budapest was highly recommended by friends and family back home. However, while my father found the city beautiful and timeless, his experience also provided a cautionary tale.

About five years ago, as a well-heeled retiree and man of leisure, he decided to tour Eastern Europe on his own. After some time in eastern Hungary, he arrived in the capital only to find that the accommodation he thought he had booked was not available. Pondering what to do next, he sat slumped beside his luggage at a train station. He is normally a clever and astute man, but some local boys managed to distract him with a game of soccer. Then, in what was clearly a pre-planned move, they kicked the ball out of the station's main area and, when Dad went to retrieve it, made off with his luggage.

Gone were his passport, visa, plane tickets, money, driver's licence and credit cards. The next few days proved quite a trial as he dealt with red tape and ineffectual police. My family have lived in Australia for decades, but Dad still has a New Zealand passport. Unluckily for him, New Zealand had no embassy in Hungary, and when he sought assistance from the Australian Embassy they were unhelpful. In the end, he was able to obtain a six-month British passport from the British Embassy, which then represented New Zealand in Hungary.

While all this was going on, he managed to have some money transferred from back home via Western Union. He was then able to find a place to stay while sorting out his predicament, and actually got do some sightseeing as well. Eventually, he found his way to the comfort of Margaret and Hampstead Heath in London, but his tale of woe and misadventure have been on my mind.

Guidebooks warn that there are plenty of scams to look out for in Budapest, but that by taking a few more precautions than in other parts of Europe, sensible travellers should be fine. My money belt will make its only appearance here.

The train pulls in to an old-looking, run-down station, seemingly away from the city centre. My guidebook has instructed me to avoid taxis with either no name on the door or only a removable light on the roof and also to never get into a taxi that does not have a yellow licence plate and an identification badge on the dashboard, both required by law. The taxi must have a table of fares visible on the rear right door. As I exit the station, several cabbies try to grab my luggage and drag it towards their cars, but I hold them off and, after a thorough look, find a match for the guidebook criteria.

Actually, truth be told, I got swindled when arriving tired and late in Rome on a Saturday evening six years ago. The journey in the Mercedes cab ended on a slightly scary note 100 metres from my hotel, as Dr Jekyll turned into Mr Hyde, aggressively demanding the hyper-inflated fair of sixty euros. This pissed me off somewhat, given that the exchange rate at the time was one Australian dollar to fifty Euro cents!

With my safe and professional cab driver at the helm, I soon find myself on the Buda side of the Danube River, where the traffic is hectic. After crossing one of Budapest's impressive bridges, I arrive at my four-star hotel on the tourist-friendly Pest side, only a short walk away from Váci utca (Váci Street), Budapest's tourist central.

Váci utca is a safe and friendly place to explore on my first afternoon in Budapest. Large numbers of restaurants and shops cater primarily to the tourist market. All the fast-food and burger joints are here, as well as big-name retailers such as Zara, H&M, Gap, ESPRIT, Nike and Lacoste, and naturally there's a Hard Rock Cafe. With plans now seeded in my mind for the next few days, Váci utca is the perfect "easy as she goes" start for dinner and a beer or two.

The sun is shining and there isn't a cloud in sight as I leave the hotel next morning, the weather definitely less gloomy than I experienced as I was travelling east through Europe. Based on Google Maps, Budapest looks like an easy city to navigate around from the prime location of my hotel. Today is all about the central sites around the Danube River and its iconic bridges.

After walking a kilometre or so along a main road, I cross the Elizabeth Bridge. I look straight down at the mighty currents of the blue Danube. The Danube is one of the world's most important rivers, like the Mekong and Yangtze rivers in Asia, and the Amazon and the Nile. Just like the Mekong and Yangtze, it is a major trade waterway. It originates in Germany then flows east through a number of countries for 2,872 kilometres to the Black Sea in Romania. In Budapest, the Danube is only halfway along its course, which meanders in different directions but generally flows north to south through Hungary.

In Budapest the river is famous for its suspension bridges, which link Buda in the west with Pest in the east. From the Elizabeth Bridge, the next bridge north is the most famous and iconic of the lot, the Széchenyi Chain Bridge. When first built in 1849, it was considered one of the modern world's engineering wonders and a symbol of advancement in Budapest. Also visible from the Elizabeth Bridge and dominating the skyline on the west bank of Buda is the Royal Palace, while Pest's Gothic-style Parliament Building looms large on the east bank.

On the Buda side, I climb the steep steps up to the Gellért Monument. This resplendent structure is a 12-metre bronze statue of St Gellért, who played a significant role in converting Hungary to Christianity, framed by a Neoclassical semicircular series of columns. The view from up there is to die for. Looking straight down the Danube, all of its suspension bridges are on display, and there are uninterrupted views of the Royal Palace and Parliament. It is also pleasant watching the bustle of the traffic below, especially where it crosses or leaves the Elizabeth Bridge.

Back down at river level, I take a leisurely stroll north along the river bank to the "castle district". Viewing the Széchenyi Chain Bridge close up under blue skies reveals the intricacy of its chains and detailed metalwork. From the river, the climb up the hill to Buda's Royal Palace, bombed and rebuilt at least half a dozen times since becoming a royal residence in the mid-thirteenth century, looks daunting.

With a sense of relief, I see tourists gathered at the base of a workhorse funicular, just like its cousin in Salzburg. At the peak, the funicular drops us off in a wide garden-like area, from where you can look straight down at the Széchenyi Chain Bridge and across to the Parliament Building. I snap away with my camera, zooming in and out and up and down the river, taking countless detailed shots.

After enjoying the view and some people-watching, I decide it's time to explore the Royal Palace. Facing the garden courtyard is the Matthias Fountain. Described as a "Neo-Baroque masterpiece", it's is one of the most photographed landmarks in Budapest. Disappointingly, access to the interior is limited, so I simply wander through another couple of stately courtyards.

At the southern end of the palace complex is the Budapest History Museum. Spread over a number of levels, it's a hit-and-miss affair. However, the display on the first floor, "Budapest in Modern Times", proves fascinating as it chronologically traces the city's history from expulsion of the Turks in the late seventeenth century to the present. Budapest has had a turbulent last three hundred years indeed!

The Ottomans pillaged the Buda side in 1526, finally conquered the city in 1541 and ruled it for the next 140 years plus. They built some of the baths that are still functioning today, five hundred years later. Under Ottoman rule, almost the entire population of Christians was converted to Islam.

In 1686, a "Holy League" army of over seventy-four thousand Christian soldiers, comprised of fighters from all parts of Europe, reconquered Buda. In the next several years, all of the former Hungarian lands were wrestled back off the Turks. By the time of the Treaty of Karlowitz in 1699, which recognised the territorial reordering, the city had been destroyed. Hungary was then incorporated into the Habsburg Empire.

The nineteenth century in Hungary was dominated by the struggle for independence. The Habsburgs were defeated in 1849, giving birth to Austria-Hungary and making Budapest a twin capital with a dual monarchy. The chain bridge linking Buda to Pest was built and the city's Jewish population grew large and prosperous, leading to Budapest being dubbed "Judapest" by some.

World War II was traumatic for the city, especially during the Battle of Budapest, when Soviets and Romanians fought against German and Hungarian troops. Over thirty-eight thousand civilians were killed and the Germans destroyed all of the city's bridges. At the end of the war, Austria-Hungary collapsed and in 1949 Hungary was declared the Communist People's Republic of Hungary.

From the 1960s to the late 1980s "the happiest barrack" in the Eastern Bloc had much of the wartime damage repaired, with new bridges being built, as well as Budapest's metro and many of the UNESCO World Heritage Sites that exist today. The city's population grew to over two million, but Communist rule fell with the rest of the Iron Curtain in 1989.

The city's history is compelling and is part of what makes Budapest such an interesting and unique destination. It seems that Hungary's geo-political location between European superpowers has made it prone to a good scrap, just like other small countries within the former Communist bloc. After Prague six years' prior, Budapest is another small step for me into the former Soviet Union. I have every ambition to visit Moscow and St Petersburg some day, and maybe ride the Trans-Siberian Railway as well.

Next I walk to the northern section of the palace complex. At the changing of the guards, the uniforms of the serious-looking Eastern European soldiers remind me of those worn by the guards at Prague Castle and the soldiers are similarly earnest. From lookouts atop sheer stone walls, the view extends up to the Buda Hills, another place I plan to visit.

North of the palace is the slender and graceful Matthias Church. Although modestly sized, it is imposing, with its tall tower and roof of Hungarian tiles arranged in intricate patterns of light and dark green, orange and brown. According to tradition, the church was originally built in Romanesque style in 1050 AD, but no archaeological remains of this structure have been found. The current building was constructed in the florid Late Gothic style in the fourteenth century and was extensively restored in the late nineteenth century.

Below the church and descending down Buda's Castle Hill to the Danube is the Neo-Gothic terrace of the Fisherman's Bastion, whose seven towers offer the very best views of the city. The bastion reminds me a little of Gaudí's architecture in Barcelona – the distinctive terrace at Parc Güell comes to mind. The bastion was designed and built between 1895 and 1902 and its tall, white, conical towers represent the seven Magyar tribes that settled in the Carpathian Basin in 896 AD; the name comes from the fishermen who were responsible for defending this stretch of the city walls in the Middle Ages.

From the viewing terrace, you look directly across at the Parliament Building on the opposite riverbank; around and below the terrace are many stairs and walking paths. It's an unrivalled vista, and one that appears constantly in travel adverts, especially those for luxury river cruises through Europe. It is widely thought that the Parliament Building's architecture was inspired by London's Houses of Parliament and from up close the similarities are apparent. The view is not quite as good, though, as the ultimate aspect of London's Houses of Parliament from the London Eye. I find a small cafe in the Bastion, and it's the perfect spot for a pleasant and contemplative espresso – with a Parliament view.

As I meander afterwards down the winding streets to river level, a couple of American girls approach me, relieved that I speak English. They ask how to get up to the Royal Palace and I tell them about the funicular "about 200 metres south". Back at the river's edge, I realise my directions were really quite poor. The funicular is actually a 1-kilometre walk from where we were standing. I hope they don't get lost! Feeling a little guilty, I vow to think more before giving directions in the future. I then walk across the Széchenyi Chain Bridge, studying its mighty suspension chains and relishing the different angles and photo opportunities that reveal themselves. I'm so caught up in the detail that I almost forget about the hectic traffic flying past.

Continuing back to the hotel through the tourist nerve centre of Váci utca, I notice the many restaurants catering for tourists and I choose one that looks like an ideal spot for dinner tonight. Then, back at the hotel, I get my swimming gear and head straight out again towards the Elizabeth Bridge and the Gellért Baths.

These indoor baths are reputed to be the most beautiful in the city, and swimming in their waters has been likened to bathing in a cathedral – I've seen many appealing images of people doing just that online. Budapest lies on a geological fault producing more than 30,000 square metres of mineral waters, varying in warmth and bubbling up daily through more than a hundred thermal springs. As a result, there are a number of famous baths in the city, a couple of which I've pencilled in to visit during my stay, both quite different.

Crossing back to the Buda side again, I'm soon approaching the giant rectangular-shaped baths building. I'm not sure what to expect, but I see large numbers of tourists and locals with towels and swimming gear, walking in and out of the main entrance. Inside the main hall, people look very relaxed, putting me immediately at ease. Bathing here is just a part of everyday life in Budapest, and there are no real rules, other than the separation of genders in the changing rooms. Concerned about my valuables, I try half a dozen lockers before finding one that actually locks properly.

Looking for the largest internal spa in the complex, I wander through a bit of a maze before I find it. I then slip into the heated water. It's an unfamiliar feeling, sitting lazily in a large heated pool with forty or so other people not doing much at all, just chatting about everyday life. To them, it's quite normal and natural; I find it new and invigorating, sitting in this spa that is literally like being inside a cathedral, with so much character, and with voices echoing off the walls. There are males and females from all walks of life, of all ages and with all sorts of body shapes. It is refreshing how unselfconscious some of the older people are in their swimsuits, even those with unflattering bodies.

The warm, mineral-rich waters are supposed to heal anything ranging from arthritis, muscle and joint pain to poor blood circulation and post-traumatic stress. All I know is that my aches from many full days of walking feel eased and my thighs begin to feel soft, my knees younger. It may only be a placebo effect, but the whole bathing experience is great fun. The baths are excellent places for light conversation, so it's a pity I can't understand any Hungarian.

After a while I make a move outdoors, hoping to catch a bit of sun. There's a giant wave pool, also heated, and at half-hour intervals a whistle is blown as it begins to fill up with swimmers and artificial waves build and build. For me this experience is too much like home, with our beaches and water parks, so I head up to the outdoor spa with its sunbathers. There are plenty of attractive young ladies, just hanging out and relaxing in bikinis. Sunbeds are a valuable and limited commodity, so I grab one immediately when I have the chance. Lying there is a good opportunity to read more of my guidebook and make plans for the days ahead.

Next I sit and float in the spa for forty-five minutes, with jets of warm water massaging my body, until my skin is like a prune. I then return to the changing rooms, feeling fit and refreshed. My leg muscles are ready for another couple of days of walking. On the way out I take a few photos of the outside and inside baths. This feels slightly voyeuristic, with me clothed and the remaining bathers unaware that they're being caught on film. Still, it's worth it, as these pics will be a cherished memory and, no doubt, a hit on Facebook.

Next morning I'm off to see the Parliament Building. However, en route I seek out St Stephen's Basilica, Hungary's most important Catholic church. It houses Hungary's most revered relic, the mummified right hand of St Stephen, first King of Hungary, who reigned one thousand years ago. The two large belltowers anchoring the façade of the basilica are imposing. The interior of the church is dark and a little gloomy, but golden mosaics inside the dome add some brightness and an air of serenity. After a month or so of travelling Europe, I'm quite over churches, but I enjoy the atmosphere inside this one.

It's an impressive church, but before long I head behind the main altar, curious to see its principal drawcard. The Holy Right Chapel houses the mummified hand, an object of great devotion. St Stephen – Stephen I before he was made a saint – was the last Grand Prince of the Hungarians and first King of Hungary from 1000 AD.

His right hand was coveted because of its alleged miraculous properties and was lost and rediscovered a number of times. During the Turkish occupation, around 1590 AD, it ended up in what is now Dubrovnik, where it was held by Dominican friars. The relic was returned to Hungary after Empress Maria Theresa found out where it was.

In more recent history, the relic was stolen again and hidden in a cave in Salzburg during World War II; it was returned to its rightful owners after being discovered by the US Army. The one-thousand-year-old mummified hand is fascinating, making what could have been just "another bloody church" special. No photos are allowed, unfortunately, but these types of rules are always apt and respectful.

As I head out of the church, it begins to bucket down with rain. I desperately look for the metro station while protecting my head with my large paper map, which soon gets soaked and starts to tear.

It feels very counterintuitive buying tickets, then manually validating each one in a small ticket machine – the polar opposite of London's efficient Oyster card system. On arrival at Kossuth Lajos Square station, I take the escalator back to street level. The other side of the Parliament Building, not visible from across the river, is a large and messy construction site with noisy jackhammers and trucks.

I join the queue for tickets next to the ugly work site. After forty-five minutes, having progressed to inside the ticket office, within metres of the booth, I'm told that no more tickets are available for today. Disappointed, I ask if tickets for tomorrow can be bought in advance. All the staff can tell me is to line up again the next day. It's not that big a deal, as I have ample time, but these types of things seem quite disorganised in Budapest.

They give me the address of a website where tickets can be bought online. As I retrace my steps to the metro station, I see that the queue is still about 40 metres long. People are still waiting patiently because word of the sell-out hasn't filtered back down the line. I can't walk past without at least passing on the news.

My bucket list for Budapest is long and as I'm travelling alone I can make quick decisions. My contingency plan is to walk Budapest's leafy Andrássy út (Andrássy Avenue), often described as the "Champs-Élysées of Budapest". Wide and 2.5 kilometres long, it is a UNESCO World Heritage Site. Walking up this famous street (which I hadn't heard of before reading my guidebook yesterday), I find it very low-key compared to the Champs-Élysées, with its wide paths shaded by trees and dotted with park benches along its entire length.

At the far end of Andrássy út is the real attraction for me, Hósök tere or Heroes Square. In the square's centre is the 36-metre-high Millenary Monument, backed by colonnades to the left and right. It is the largest and most symbolic war memorial in Budapest, dedicated to the many people who gave their lives for the freedom and national independence of the country. The square has played an important part in contemporary Hungarian history and has been host to many political events. The Millenary Monument's construction began in 1896 to commemorate the thousandth anniversary of the Hungarian conquest of the Carpathian Basin and the foundation of the Hungarian state in that year.

I find it touching, with its fourteen different bronze statues of rulers and statesman lining the colonnades. The statues are all distinct and individual, handsome and powerful. It's a fun photographic exercise to take an identical shot of each one, capturing their different themes and striking detail. These will make a great little photo collection and a reminder of their strong impression on me.

The next executive decision for the day is to head for the hills – the Buda Hills, which I had been planning to visit the next day. With a full afternoon free, consistently pleasant weather, and a late sunset up ahead, things seem promising. However, according to my guidebook, finding my way up to the hills will require four different modes of transport. It looks rather complicated but also like getting there will be half the fun.

After taking the metro to the Buda side of the river, I hop on a tram for a short ride, keeping an eye out for my next mode of transport, the cog railway. I'm clueless as to what to it will look like, but soon recognise it and hurriedly ring the bell to stop the tram. The railway is actually designated as tram number sixty. About 130 years old, it climbs for fourteen minutes up 4 kilometres of track. During the ascent, I can look into the backyards and pools of some of Budapest's most expensive homes, at the base of the hills.

It is the final mode of transport, however, that is the quirkiest and most fun. The Children's Railway, with eight stations, was built in 1951 by Socialist scouts and is staffed almost entirely by schoolchildren, ranging from ten to fourteen years old. Understandably, the engineers are, however, adults. It is a great chance for these kids to get some work experience and they look as awkward and innocent as I remember being at that age. There's about a fifty-fifty split of boys and girls, and they stand proud in their uniforms and hats.

Hopping off at the fourth station, I look back to see a young boy doing a grand job of changing the tracks. This station is the highest one in the Buda Hills, and I begin a strenuous hike from here to the hills' very peak. The peace and quiet provide a welcome break from Budapest's hustle and bustle, and this proves to be the most peaceful walk of my entire time in Europe, completely free of large numbers of fellow sightseers.

At the top of the hill is the 23-metre-tall Elizabeth Lookout. I pump my quadriceps, powering up the one hundred or so steps. The viewpoint is well above the treeline and on a clear day you can supposedly see the Tatra Mountains in Slovakia, 300 kilometres away. However, there are a few clouds in the sky this afternoon, making this impossible. I have a good look around the still-impressive vista before descending again.

From the lookout, a 1-kilometre-long chairlift takes me back down. I take this mode of transport, as using the cog railway from earlier would require me to retrace my journey back four stations. With my feet dangling and a breeze to cool the sweat, it's the perfect way to relax after the rigorous exercise. The tree canopy is thick and the chairlift route surrounded by greenery. Looking along the valley ahead, distant views of the Danube and the Parliament Building in the middle of sprawling Budapest are visible – a great photo opportunity.

Back at the bottom, but in a completely different location from the cog railway, there's a bus that I think is heading for the city. But, after the round trip of complicated transport options, I've lost my bearings and the bus ends up taking me way off course, dropping me in unfamiliar residential streets. However, I manage to meander back to the metro while using the hills as a reference point. On the train home I reflect on another interesting day in Budapest and am so glad I made the effort to visit to this eastern city.

After a snack that evening while watching Bloomberg, I decide to head out to investigate the "ruin bars" recommended by the Aussie girl and her boyfriend in Brussels, which, it turns out, are only a few hundred metres from my hotel. Like the funky bars around Vienna's canal area, these watering holes make stylish and creative use of formerly abandoned space.

A twenty-first-century phenomenon, the ruin bars (or ruin pubs, as the name translates exactly from the Hungarian) were an exciting turning point in the nightlife of the city. The first ruin bar in Budapest was the Szimpla Kert. It was established in 2004, after a run-down building in the Jewish District was saved from demolition by a group of entrepreneurs looking to open up a bar and community space. Rather than redeveloping the building, they chose to adapt the ramshackle structure, while adding quirky furniture and decorations, thereby creating a mix-and-match aesthetic and making use of a space otherwise destined for ruin.

The venture proved successful and provided a template for a new generation of bars. The ruin bar was born, and Budapest's Jewish

District became the focal point for this new nightlife trend. Buildings in varying states of decay were rescued, and quirky and unique public spaces were created.

The experience of walking from pub to pub – they're all very different and original – with no preconceptions of what you might find on any particular block, is unique, charming and dreamlike. It actually feels like a kind of adult, nightlife version of Alice in Wonderland, especially after a couple of drinks to mellow perception.

The ruin bars I check out look very architecturally sound, and their creative use of space is charming and impressive. Some of the bars have pool table areas and table hockey. I get into a quick game of table hockey with a few English lads, who are fun and instant company, if only for a short time.

A few streets further on, the relaxed scene changes to more conventional clubs, filled with energetic ravers. There are a few bucks' parties of young Englishmen, with the buck commonly wearing a pink dress or chicken suit. Unlike the ruin bars, these clubs have well-built, scary bouncers outside, monitoring the hordes on a Saturday night. I can imagine things becoming hard to handle in the wee early hours of Sunday morning. Yet, even though these are more conventional nightclubs, there's still plenty of character on show, with remnants from Communist times eclectically blended in with more modern trappings, just as the dance music from different eras is skilfully mixed by the DJs.

The next morning, having made a printout of my booking with the help of hotel reception, I head straight over to the Parliament Building. After seeing the 270-metre-long building from Buda, I'm looking forward to exploring the interior. The Parliament is Hungary's largest building, and it was situated here as a counterbalance to the behemoth Royal Palace on the other side of Danube. The interior contains just short of seven hundred rooms and is an operating government building – the tours are confined to its north wing.

Only limited numbers of people are allowed into the Parliament Building at any one time. This means queuing with about fifty others and being assailed by the noise of pulsating jackhammers coming from the adjacent construction site while we wait for our guide to show up.

After arriving, she first tells us that what was spent on design was not matched in building materials. Unfortunately, or lazily, the structure was surfaced with a porous form of limestone that has trouble resisting pollution. Renovations began just two decades after the building opened in 1904 and are expected to continue into the foreseeable future. Nevertheless, the guide says, Hungarians have a proud love and deep affection for their Parliament.

As we all enter the sumptuously decorated rooms, I'm reminded of the beauty of the Palace of Versailles. We watch a ceremonial changing of the guards, then turn 180 degrees to proceed through a very Versailles-like wide hall, with beautiful, large stained-glass windows, and up the main staircase. This takes us to the giant open space of the domed hexadecagon (sixteen-sided) hall, with its adjoining chambers. The ceiling is breathtaking in scale, colour and design, rising on the inside of the main dome to 70 metres above the ground. From the outside, this is the parliament's largest feature. It houses the crown of St Stephen and a tenth-century Persian-made sceptre with a solid rock-crystal ball decorated with engraved lions. These national jewels have their own guards and we see yet another changing of the guards. It looks as though this coincides with each tour group, thirty minutes apart.

As I'm standing on the fringes of the group, the guide is hard to hear and her thick accent adds to the problem. We walk through the vaulted lobbies as she describes some of the important political meetings that have taken place here, namedropping a few famous leaders who've met in these historic rooms. The lobbies lead to the Congress Hall, supposedly identical to the National Assembly Hall where current parliamentary sessions are held. It's very wide, wooden and circular. On the small viewing area we wait our turn to take a photograph of the Congress Hall, a very panoramic view at that.

Finally, we walk down the building's side hall and back to the entrance, where another group patiently stands outside. The interior of the Parliament Building definitely hasn't disappointed. The wait may have been frustrating, but it was well worth it in the end.

After a bite of lunch, it's straight back to the hotel and, with swimming gear in hand again, I set off to Budapest's other main thermal baths, the Széchenyi Baths. The metro takes me near Heroes Square, which is a short walk away from the baths.

The Széchenyi Baths are mostly open-air, and their highly original design resembles a giant wedding cake from outside. The baths themselves are substantially larger than the Gellért Baths but fewer in number; also, with a temperature of up to 38 degrees Celsius, they're unusually hot. Budapest's most popular thermal baths, the Széchenyi Baths are also famous for their summer night spa parties – *sparties* for short – where bright neon lights turn the place into a giant rave. They look amazing fun, based on some YouTube footage.

As I've now come to expect in Budapest, the staff at the entrance are disorganised and the signage is poor. In another queue of frustrated patrons, I get talking to a young English couple, whom I recognise from the Gellért Baths. They seem quite conservative and not really at home in these exotic pools with their public displays of flesh.

The outdoor pools are enormous, with a bright, clean atmosphere, but there's a coldish nip in the air, so conditions are less than ideal – definitely no sunbaking today! Groups of people seem to gather around the edges. I swim to the centre of a large pool to get my head drenched by hot fountains, like other young men. After the cranium pounding, a couple of young English ladies take my water jet as I leave. They shriek initially at the power of the fountain flow as it messes up their hair. The openness of these baths creates a relaxed, social atmosphere. Feeling a little alone, however, I make a move to the other large outdoor pool of the "wedding cake".

There, too, the atmosphere is easy and unthreatening. In the centre of this pool is a whirlpool, which propels laughing swimmers through the water. Entering the circle, the jet-propelled current almost tears off my board shorts. I tighten the drawstring on my shorts and enjoy the ride. Some new arrivals scream and shriek as they enter the pool, including a couple of women with loose-fitting togs, who seem to panic at the prospect of a nipple or breast popping out for all to see. It's fun going round and round for fifteen minutes, but then the novelty wears off. I rest my back on the edge of the large pool for a while while my legs float on the surface, and I close my eyes to relax.

A couple of hours here are enough, though, so I dry myself off before heading back to Heroes Square. There's supposed to be a market nearby, about which I know little. After searching around for forty-five minutes, I find a market of sorts. But it's really just full of junk, like used electronic goods and old toys, with nothing remotely antique – which might explain why it's not well known. The Aussie girl I met in Brussels talked of an amazing market in Budapest, which I appear to have confused with this minor distraction. I should really have done more research!

I've planned to spend the rest of the day at my hotel, enjoying a quiet evening before my cheap but ridiculously early flight to the French Riviera in the morning. I'm at the furthest point east in my odyssey, and I've now travelled 1,600 kilometres from London to Budapest, as the crow flies. Taking a train back west to the south of France would have been a long and complex journey; much simpler at this point to hop on a plane, even if it means going via Brussels to Nice.

Ten

The French Riviera

It's 4 am when my deep sleep is rudely interrupted by the alarm. I've been having a pleasant dream about Monaco. I jump out of bed, take a quick shower and wolf down a couple of plain croissants and an energy drink. My luggage is prepacked by the door; all I need to do is give the room one last OCD inspection. A pre-booked cab is waiting for "Mr Rich" downstairs, a sedan with yellow numberplates, so everything is kosher. With little traffic on the road, we progress rapidly to Budapest's ageing airport.

I'm in the departure lounge at 7.30 am when the announcement is made of a baggage-handlers' strike at Brussels Airport, something to do with pay and conditions. Brussels is a busy and central airport hub, and I fear the strike could potentially cause problems all over the Eurozone. And I already have a tight transfer window before my second flight to Nice.

Brussels Airport is globally important in the transportation of diamonds to Antwerp, where more than seventy per cent of the world's diamonds are traded. I remember that back in early 2013, US$50 million worth of the most precious of stones was stolen in a masterful heist at the airport. The robbery took a mere five minutes, and initially went completely undetected. However, in May of that year, thirty-one people were arrested in connection with the theft, and some of the diamonds were recovered.

The plane takes off twenty minutes late from Budapest, but I'm reassured that my connecting flight will also be delayed twenty minutes. Flying into Brussels, I see the famous city square of the Grand Place from above – a very different perspective from my ground-level view two weeks earlier. As the plane draws into the gate, many passengers are already standing in the aisle, anxiously holding their hand luggage. Through the plane window the replacement luggage contractors can be seen working – I bloody hope they know what they're doing! The rush out of the plane is actually quite civilised, though, and the transfer turns out to be not as stressful as I anticipated.

Unsurprisingly, there are Belgian chocolates for sale duty-free and when my next plane rises rapidly back above Brussels I'm clutching two dozen chocolates in my hand. It's a fine, clear day as the plane travels south over the snow-covered French Alps. Due to the late-ending winter season, the snow seems to stretch on forever. It's a really beautiful part of the world.

Travelling at 40,000 feet, I spot several private jets flying north and south under us at probably half the altitude – quite surreal. Are these private planes of the rich and famous, flying back and forth between Paris and one of the fashionable resorts of the Côte d'Azur, or French Riviera, such as Monaco, Nice, St-Tropez or Cannes? (The Cannes Film Festival actually kicks off in two days' time, and Baz Luhrmann's contemporary version of *The Great Gatsby*, filmed in Sydney, will make its premiere there.) I wonder if I'll ever fly in a Learjet. My only chance of that would be to add an MBA to my CPA qualification then work my butt off to get into executive management for a multinational. But that seems depressingly unlikely.

The snow-capped peaks continue for another 100 kilometres or so, I estimate. Abruptly, though, the mountain range ends, dropping down to meet the blue Mediterranean Sea. I know that Monaco is roughly 30 kilometres east of Nice Airport and, to my pleasant surprise, the plane flies directly over the principality. From above, it looks tiny and densely populated. I easily make out the famous marina and the Royal Palace presiding over it in the west. A stretch too far is to decipher where the famous casino is. South-west of Monaco is the tiny and exclusive-looking peninsula of Saint-Jean-Cap-Ferrat, which is covered largely by mansions with turquoise swimming pools.

The plane turns west and the long-curving beach of Nice stretches out continuously towards the airport, exactly as I'd pictured it in my mind over the years. Dotted along the shore are the private beaches lined with sunbeds that I've read about in my guidebook, where, for a price, tourists can work on their tans in comfort. The plane descends and lands. There are no passport checks on flights within the Eurozone, making plane travel very convenient.

Standing at the luggage-collection carousel while watching the procession of bags on the conveyor belt for twenty minutes, I feel nervous and start discussing my concerns with other stressed passengers, who are all now looking at each other and starting up conversations. The word is that twenty thousand bags have accumulated at Brussels Airport and the strike shows no signs of abating.

I get chatting with a friendly middle-aged American lady. I assume she is well off, as she tells me she lives permanently on Lake Como in Italy, and it's reassuring to hear her say that over many years of constant travelling, this kind of thing happens quite often. Jokingly, I tell her it's also happened to me quite a few times, but all in the last month! We keep chatting while we wander over to the lost-luggage desk.

A couple of young American girls in the next line lose their patience and leave, chatting between themselves about an impatient driver who'll be waiting for them outside. I look ahead to see which queue is the shortest and decide I'm in what looks like the best line. However, up ahead is an attractive but objectionable French luggage claim officer: she's loud, rude and a little bit scary. Immediately, I draw comparisons with the Soup Nazi from *Seinfeld*. She's the "Luggage Nazi" and I'm standing in line like a quivering George Costanza. At least the Soup Nazi made amazing soup!

She shows scant regard for worried travellers and churns through them with an aura of contempt, as if they have simply inconvenienced her. When I reach the head of the queue, she thrusts a form towards me. I am a slow and messy writer at the best of times, and it takes a minute or so to find the address of my Nice hotel. I've scarcely finished filling in the form when she yanks it back off me. Then, in response to my understandable concerns, she simply says the strike is beyond her control. Really, it's just beyond her care factor. Finally, she gives me a stare as if to say, "Why are you still there?"

"Can you please give me an idea as to how I might get information on my luggage?"

"Call this number ... Next!"

"Luggage Nazi, you're full of crap," I think to myself. "Au revoir" would have been an apt thing to say, given that I'll almost certainly be back, with my luggage inconveniently stuck in the Twilight Zone. What a welcome to the Côte d'Azur.

The shuttle bus into Nice takes a scenic route, along the beach and through the main tourist area. Meanwhile I'm thinking about ratbags back in Brussels trying to break my padlock while looking for valuables. After pondering this, for a while, though, I feel safe in the knowledge that they'll be sorely disappointed with old underwear, running shoes and some dirty washing. Everything I need and all my valuables are in my carry-on luggage: iPad, mobile phone, credit cards, passport, guidebook, hotel booking print-outs and Eurail Pass.

From the bus stop by the sea I walk through a square buzzing with people watching high-adrenaline buskers playing to a good crowd in the fine weather. I'm pleasantly surprised to find that my hotel is very centrally located, amongst restaurants and department stores and only 400 metres from the beach. While checking in at the hotel reception, I inform the two female employees of my luggage predicament. I need to get a couple of shirts and underwear, so I ask them where I might buy some cheaply – placing the emphasis on *cheap*!

They tell me there's an H&M store and a Nice outlet of the Paris department store Galeries Lafayette only a few hundred metres away. However, there's also a large shopping mall a little further down. Looking for a bargain, I walk straight past the brand-name stores to the shopping mall, where I find what seems to be Europe's equivalent of

Kmart, C&A. I buy some bare essentials: a couple of five-euro T-shirts and fresh underwear and socks.

With few concrete plans, I return to the hotel for a replenishing shower before heading out to have a look around Nice. I take a seat on a park bench to eat a sandwich and look out at the Mediterranean Sea. The weather is lovely and runners, walkers, roller-bladers and skateboarders are all enjoying some late-afternoon exercise. Observing the waveless ocean and the fat pebbles on the beach, I reflect on how lucky I am back home to have the great beaches of the Gold and Sunshine Coasts only an hour's drive away from my home. We are truly blessed in this regard Down Under. Here, the seawater is so calm that surf activities are very limited. There are a few people swimming freestyle parallel to the beach, making good use of the calm conditions.

Walking south amongst afternoon joggers, I lament that my sneakers are stuck in Brussels, as a run along this path straight down to the airport would have been enjoyable. I watch a couple on roller-blades, doing what best resembles figure skating on cement. They move like free spirits, as if they've been doing it for years. To express one's enjoyment of skating this way, in a kind of public art performed by a man and a woman, seems quintessentially French.

Continuing along the seafront, I recognise the façade of the Casino Ruhl, Nice's most famous casino. I walk through its front door and flash my passport to security before moving to the casino floor. Straight away I notice a young lady from today's luggage claim queue, and we smile at one another, as if to say we appreciate each other's predicament luggage-wise. After watching a few games and tables – twenty-one, blackjack, roulette – I buy twenty euros worth of chips. I'm not much of a gambler and have little idea how to play the card games. Roulette seems more straightforward, so I join a table, where my chips soon return fifty per cent, taking me up to thirty euros. Superstitiously, I move to another table; but, as quickly as I was up, I'm back down and soon watching my last five-euro chip disappear on the spin of a wheel. The house always wins in the end, so they say. Even though I'm visiting Monte Carlo tomorrow, I'm done as far as gambling is concerned.

Once again I notice the girl from the luggage claim as she makes a couple of trips back and forth between the ATM and tables. I hope she doesn't get too carried away. I've never really understood the attraction of gambling and, even though I worked as an accountant at one of Australia's largest gambling companies, my only regular flutter is the annual "race that stops the nation", the Melbourne Cup. When wandering around some of the popular gambling floors back home, usually dragged there by mates after watching rugby games, I find the psychology of gamblers quite curious, however, as they sit glued to their chairs like addicts.

I emerge from the casino and walk back to the hotel while twilight falls over the Mediterranean Sea. As I expected, my bags have not yet caught up with me. After some web browsing and watching cable TV, it is still early, but I'm exhausted after a long day. I'm excited about visiting Monte Carlo tomorrow, the main reason I came to Nice, but soon I fall into a deep sleep.

The train arrives at Monte Carlo station after a twenty-minute journey east from Nice. As expected, there are hordes of day tourists like me who'd never be able to afford a hotel in Monte Carlo. There are also a few local commuters and businessmen, with briefcases and smartphones, on their way to conduct business with Monte Carlo's elite. The train station is huge, like a massive underground bunker, built into the hill above the city.

It proves easy to follow other tourists through the narrow streets that meander down the hill from the station, shadowed by multistorey residential buildings. Most of the apartments look tiny in size, and the price per square foot of real estate in Monte Carlo is the highest in the world. As a keen sports fan, I'm constantly learning that so-and-so was born in somewhere like Russia but now resides in Monaco. Notable residents include tennis players such as Novac Djokovic and Victoria Azarenka, Formula One drivers Jenson Button and Lewis Hamilton, and many famous entertainers and businessmen to boot. The best known of all tax havens, Monaco attracts the rich and famous and offers astute advice from its tax accountants and lawyers. The beautiful weather and the location on the Mediterranean Sea are also attractive selling points.

BMW, Mercedes-Benz and Audi cars drive around the winding streets, which are way too built-up in my opinion, with little evident greenery. Monaco covers a mere 2 square kilometres for its thirty-five thousand residents. It also has the highest number of millionaires and billionaires per capita. It is unsurprising then that Monaco's GDP per capita is also the world's highest, at US$170,000. In comparison, Switzerland, another wealthy European state, has a per-capita GDP of US$80,000. Australia earns US$54,000 per capita, and we are an affluent country, with our almost inexhaustible mineral wealth.

Monaco's official unemployment rate is zero per cent, and it has the world's lowest poverty rate. Tourism is a large source of income for Monaco, with many foreigners attracted to its famous casino, which the principality ironically prohibits its own citizens from using. Monaco is also a major banking and investment centre.

As I near sea level, I see that a large, modern cruise liner is in port. A similar-sized one is out to sea, en route to another port of call. Throughout my trip I've been consistently surprised at how many times I meet couples or families from Down Under enjoying the cruise experience in Europe.

Strolling past fancy jewellers and car dealerships lined with Ferraris, Maseratis, Lamborghinis, Bentleys and Rolls Royces, I have a good look through each window. Very apparent on the streets are the barricades up everywhere: Monaco's largest sporting event, the annual Grand Prix, is only four days away. Temporary stands overlook a few tight corners on the race course and down by the marina is the largest stand of them all. A pit-lane is also being built. It would be awesome to see these high-tech cars fly down the home straight at 350 kilometres per hour. If I'd actually learnt of this in advance, I would have timed my visit better, to be in sync with this weekend's big event.

High up, on the opposite side of the marina, is the Royal Palace of Albert II, Sovereign Prince of Monaco and Head of State, and son of Hollywood superstar turned princess Grace Kelly. In the marina are hundreds of boats, some really quite average, with similarly modest moorings; however, there are just as many multimillion-dollar superyachts on elite moorings.

Walking along the waterline I get a closer look at these beautiful, plush sea machines. Most are moored and empty, a few are attended by a sole maintenance person, but half dozen or so have attractive, wealthy-looking people on board, relaxing in the sun. I've noticed that the French Riviera sun doesn't burn like the sun back home. Apparently it's all to do with the ozone layer, or lack of it where I come from. I'm definitely not a bronzed Aussie, and if I stayed here for a week I'd probably tan properly for the first time in my life.

On my way back up the hill to the casino, I notice many sophisticated and clearly affluent female shoppers. Prince Albert's sisters, Stephanie and Caroline, are the image I carry in my mind of Monaco's high-society women, appearing svelte and tanned in countless glossy magazines over the years.

The casino opens up for tourists at 2 pm. I'm fortunate to find a seat at the front of the well-known Cafe de Paris. It looks straight across the small park of Place du Casino to the iconic casino entrance, where eager crowds line up to be first through the door. Parked out front of the casino are a number of Ferraris, Porsches and Lamborghinis. Fathers and sons stand by each other next to the supercars, as wives and partners take photos of these boys with toys. When the queue shrinks a little, I make my way across to the casino. Soon I have to plug in my headphones to drown out the complaints of a loud American woman in front of me, who is unhappy with having to wait.

Three or four tunes later, I enter the main floor. There are a number of tables, with different versions of poker, none of which I understand, and roulette wheels. Having lost twenty euros last night at the casino in Nice, I decide just to observe other, mainly male, gamblers playing at the tables. I actually spot the girl from the Nice casino and baggage reclaim. She's doing some more gambling but, judging by the colour of her chips, it's not of the high-stakes variety. I notice a couple of men moving from table to table and appearing to blow about a thousand euros at each one. I'd guess that one of them, who looks Chinese, has gambled away around five thousand euros in twenty minutes. Maybe he believes his luck will soon change for the better.

The casino's interior is beautiful and stylish, just as it appears in some James Bond films, with subtle lighting and impressively detailed features. There are attractive murals on the high walls, which are also adorned with wood panelling below and ivory-painted upper walls. Ivory-coloured archways lead high rollers from the main floor through to "private" rooms.

The casino was conceived in the mid-nineteenth century, as a way of earning revenue to help save the principality's royal family. Their financial problems had become especially acute after the loss of tax revenue from two breakaway towns, Menton and Roquebrune, which had declared independence in 1848 and thereafter refused to pay the taxes on olive oil and fruit imposed by the Monaco royals.

Unfortunately, photos are banned inside the casino. So, with no desire to gamble, aside from dropping a few coins into a couple of slot machines, and not much else to do, I walk back out to the Place du Casino with its lovely fountain then head back up the hill towards the train station again. I'm in need of a new T-shirt, and not just because I've lost my luggage: when packing for Europe I didn't expect this springtime sunshine and warmth, especially as winter was lingering before I left home. So, on my walk up I buy an official memorabilia T-shirt of this weekend's Monaco Grand Prix – a much-needed garment and a souvenir in one.

The platform at the station is overcrowded and the trains taking businessmen and tourists back to Nice are running ridiculously late. The announcements are in French only, leaving tourists who don't speak the language puzzled. After one such announcement, half of the passengers change platform; the rest of us tag along after we decipher that the train is now leaving from the opposite platform. People migrate in a similar fashion back to the original platform after a second announcement, and then once again to the opposite platform before the next train arrives, half an hour late.

Several times on my travels in France, I've noticed that services, such as transport, don't seem to work efficiently. The country's economy is in recession and its Triple-A credit rating has been downgraded, and I wonder if austerity measures have led to poorer public services here, and in other European countries.

Back at the hotel I phone the baggage-reclaim hotline for the fifth time today. Still getting the same pre-recorded message, I'm now sure that all calls simply go directly to voice mail, never to be answered by a real person. I'm getting very cheesed off and think I will definitely have to make my way out there tomorrow to get to the bottom of this, which will be a real inconvenience. Meanwhile the hotel gives me a voucher for a meal, so I head out into the lovely evening weather and enjoy a fine dinner and a glass of Bordeaux at a local restaurant.

Next day, I check out of the hotel and, to fill in time before my short train journey to Marseille, head for the path up the cliff at the northern end of Nice's main beach to reach the Parc du Château, which offers the best view of Nice's world-famous seafront. My guidebook recommends stopping on the way at the market at Cours Saleya. It's supposedly "one of France's most vibrant food markets", but the vendors are only just setting up for the day, which is possibly why it underwhelms. The walk up the hill is lung-busting, and I'm slightly disheartened as very fit and athletic men and women fly past me.

Fortunately, I realise as I catch my breath at the top, the view over the 8-kilometre stretch of beach south towards the airport is well worth the climb, providing the perfect postcard vista. Between the beach and red-roofed buildings of Nice is the wide Promenade des Anglais. From the park's northern end, one can look down to the upmarket little Port de Nice and its square-shaped marina.

Next I catch the bus out to the airport while thinking about a strategy for the "Luggage Nazi". I decide to play it cool and stick to the facts. I don't want to get into an argument with this arrogant woman, and I'm actually just poor at arguing in general. I would never have been able to make a living as a lawyer.

At the baggage reclaim are the same three staff from two days ago. It looks as though the strike has yet to be settled and there's still a long queue. I tell a few people waiting that the phone hotline is bogus and that they'll only ever get a message bank.

When I get my chance to talk to the objectionable attendant from two days prior, she informs me that my luggage has yet to arrive.

"I've called over a dozen times and only ever get a message," I say. "You don't even answer your hotline. Why do you tell people to call it?"

"I never tell people to call it", she quips.

"You told me to call it, you tell everybody to call it."

"Okay, well, we're always too busy here at the desk."

"Then why give people the number in the first place?"

She concedes, "You're right, sorry."

That's a better attitude!

"Anyway, here's my baggage claim number," I say. Can you please look at your computer for its status?"

She tells me that the luggage is still at Brussels Airport with thirty thousand other bags. I tell her I'm leaving for Marseille in one hour for two nights and give her my hotel's address. I then begin to list the rest of my itinerary to her in a monotone voice: "Two days at Avignon on at this address, one day in Barcelona at this address, two nights here in Madrid." Smugly, I say, "You just never know, do you? Okay, two nights at this address in Granada, two nights at this address in Córdoba. Here's my mobile phone number for your computer system. Have we covered everything?"

"Yes, sir, I think we have."

"Thank you for your help," I say with sincerity, feeling good to have gotten my point across in a straightforward and calm manner. It's been a good lesson in dealing with difficult people. Travel is always a great way to gain more self-awareness and confidence. No "angry Angus" today. The negotiation with the Luggage Nazi has gone well, I think, as I hop back on the bus to the town centre.

Eleven

The Port City of Marseille

The train journey from Nice to Marseille is only two-and-a-half hours. A young lady in a smart royal-blue business suit sits opposite me in the seat of four, her laptop in a stylish case. She's attractive, with brown hair and a nice figure, but doesn't look like she sunbakes on the Riviera. She's more like an accountant, in a good way – learned and intelligent. After giving me a pleasant smile, she opens the laptop and begins working.

Only 30 kilometres west of Nice, the Cannes Film Festival has now begun. The appealing Côte d'Azur scenery continues as the train approaches Cannes station. Marseille can wait – what if I were to jump off now to look for the famous red carpet lined with celebrities? It's a very fleeting idea.

Further west is the town of St-Tropez. Once a small and unassuming fishing village, during the twentieth century it became a popular holiday spot for famous figures from the fashion world, like Coco Chanel, as well as members of the French New Wave cinema movement. It's supposed to have some of Europe's most celebrated nightspots and was where the Rolling Stones famously fled to forty years ago to write and record the album *Exile on Main Street*, considered one of their best. I'm quite a big fan of the Stones. Unfortunately, there is not much to be seen from St-Tropez train station, so the place remains left to my imagination.

An hour later we arrive in Marseille and I realise I've no idea how to get to the hotel. It's down near the marina, so finding that is my first priority. The only reference point I have is that trains are travelling south-west when they arrive. The marina is supposed to be south-west of the station and, hopefully, not too far. I vow not to get a taxi and to try to work out my way through this famously gritty town.

I don't know much about Marseille except that it's looked down upon by Parisians. It may be France's second city, but it has a bad reputation for crime. Throughout history, it has been a magnet for immigrants, many of whom hail from North Africa, and this has created the hotchpot of cultures found here today. Being France's main seaport, it's a major centre of trade and industry. A couple of people back home had recommended it as an interesting, edgy place, worth checking out on my way along the Mediterranean coastline.

As I walk down the sloping main street from the station, there are a few drifters about and a variety of languages and dialects can be heard. There are almost no upscale shops or restaurants, and it's very unlike the sophistication of Paris. Lost and now wandering aimlessly, I ask a twenty-something girl how to get to the marina. Paris it most definitely isn't, but the girl is refreshingly friendly and eager to help. She points to a set of traffic lights 200 metres away, telling me to turn right there for the harbour. I thank her for taking the time to explain and she wishes me an enjoyable stay in Marseille. Along the way, I notice a few homeless people on the main streets. The city has a large Muslim population and plenty of stores are selling halal meat.

Eventually I reach my hotel, a four-star Mercure. The reception clerks are poor at English but do their politest best. When I try to ask if they've received my luggage, a colleague is called from out back to translate; he then takes me to the luggage storage room. After a thorough look, I'm disappointed, but not surprised, that there's no sign of my bags. I wonder if I can trust the Luggage Nazi now she's seen the back of me?

Things may be quite chaotic on the street, but my room proves large and comfortable, a great deal. As I channel-surf on the TV, I realise it has everything – new release movies, sport, the lot!

Outside the window, rain is fast approaching, so I head out quickly to purchase a pair of much-needed new, fresh jeans before the rain begins to bucket down. It continues heavily for quite some time, so I stay in the room and channel-surf and browse the internet, and by the time I head out for takeaway and a bottle of vino it's dark. Not much is open, but I find a very Muslim halal restaurant, cheap and basic. While waiting for the order, I feel, self-consciously, that I stick out like a sore thumb.

After breakfast in the morning, I head straight down to the famous Old Port of Marseille. Rectangular in shape and about a kilometre long, it hosts hundreds of yachts, all of similar size. There are none of the luxury super-yachts I saw in Monaco. The keen rower in me spots a couple of tall men rowing single sculls up and down the length of the sheltered water.

Standing out above the city of Marseille south of the port is its most famous landmark, the resplendent Catholic basilica of Notre-Dame de la Garde. It presides over the city's skyline, and the citizens see it as the guardian and protector of the city, commonly referring to it as *la bonne mère*, "the good mother".

It's a long way up to the top of the cathedral's steep hill and the only sane option is bus number sixty from the port. But the signage at the bus stop is poor and I don't know which side of the road to wait on. I hop on the very first number sixty bus I spot. When it proceeds in the wrong direction, I check with the driver, disembark and return to my starting point. The correct bus winds up steep streets along a seemingly random route, one to which only the local bus drivers would be privy.

The view from the cathedral is outstanding, encompassing the whole city. Marseille is very old place, founded in 600 BC – in fact it's the oldest city in France. Humans have inhabited the area for almost thirty thousand years and Palaeolithic paintings in nearby underwater caves have been dated back to 27,000 BC.

I take wide panoramic shots extending from the characterful skyline to the rectangular port below and then out to the Mediterranean Sea, where the small island of If stands amongst other, larger islands. Dominating the island is the Château d'If, the Alcatraz-style prison in which Edmund Dantes was imprisoned for six years in the classic novel *The Count of Monte Cristo*. As with Alcatraz, which I visited in San Francisco years ago, there are ferries that run from the mainland to the island, taking tourists to explore the notorious prison.

I look back at the cathedral's exterior, with its stonework layered in contrasting white and green limestone. It reminds me of the iconic Cathedral of Santa Maria del Fiore in Florence, although it's not as large or imposing. Atop the belfry, however, is an impressive 11-metre-high statue of the Madonna and Child, made of copper gilded with gold leaf.

Construction of the basilica began in 1852 and lasted for twenty-one years. It was built on the foundation of an ancient fort on the highest natural peak in Marseille, at 149 metres, and is the most visited site in the city.

Alongside me appreciating the view is a couple from Melbourne and it comes as no surprise that they're on a cruise. When I tell them I hail from Brisbane, their oh-so-predictable response is, "We won't hold that against you."

"Bring on the clichés, you latte-sipping Melburnians," I respond.

We laugh at our shared dry Aussie humour. They've been allocated a few hours to explore Marseille and must be back at the ship at the appointed time. The husband tells me they like Marseille but didn't warm to Parisians. I tell them about my luggage issues and the "Luggage Nazi" in Nice.

Though there are various ferry companies taking tourists out to Château d'If, he's been told they're not sailing due to heavy winds, though I don't know if he has checked out the ferry I'm considering. Though he's the one happily chatting away, it's obvious that his wife wears the pants, and she pulls him away to get on with the sightseeing during their limited time ashore.

The basilica's interior is a continuation of the stone patterns from outside. With its atmosphere of devotion and prayer, it's very peaceful. The inside of the church's famous dome is ornamented with colourful marble murals and mosaics, beautifully restored.

After appreciating the view from outside the cathedral for a while longer, I catch the bus back down to the port. I have only one full day in Marseille and if there is a ferry I don't want to miss it. I share a seat with a typical French elderly lady, dressed with style and understated elegance and looking healthy for her age.

The ferry company recommended by my guidebook is situated at the south-east corner of the marina. The wind is powerful and the seas rough, too rough for a ferry to dock at France's Alcatraz. Instead, in twenty minutes, the next cruise will go direct to Port du Friol, a small port in the same archipelago, the Frioul Islands, 4 kilometres out to sea, offering views of Château d'If en route.

After a frantic lunch I hop on the ferry and head straight up to the rooftop deck. Three twenty-something girls board, one of them, clearly the birthday girl, wearing a hijab. Her two friends are dressed Western-style and have blindfolded her. After tiptoeing across the ferry boarding ramp, they remove the blindfold. I'm unsure how far she's come blinded, but she shrieks in excitement at the prospect of the ferry cruise.

The ferry powers through the port with its forest of masts. The incoming sea breezes feel lovely. As the ferry exits the port, the view of Marseille opens up to reveal more interesting historical buildings, as well as contemporary constructions. Maybe these modern buildings were erected during 2013, when Marseille was designated the European Capital of Culture?

We travel at a high rate of knots. Though there are plenty of spare seats on the top deck, I'm still standing and I start to get thrown around as the boat hits the open sea and large waves pound the bow – it's really quite fun! All of the tourists on the deck can hear the three girls up front, screaming with each rise and fall of the bow.

The ferry travels within 50 metres of the solidly built former prison of Chateau d'If, seamlessly moulded onto the rocky island. The view of the prison changes markedly at different points as we pass by.

Rocky landscapes also flank the entrance to the small port. In the square-shaped harbour, sheltered from ocean winds, are a couple of dozen small sail boats, on which children are learning the basic skills and pleasures of sailing. One can imagine in a city like Marseille that this would be *the* thing to do and a rite of passage for any youngster.

The boat moors and everybody disembarks, walking towards some small shops and restaurants. The ferry is heading back in five minutes, and the next one is not due for another three-quarters of an hour. There's clearly not much of interest on the island, so I get straight back on the boat.

A couple of young local men come aboard, wearing outfits clearly inspired by the *Count of Monte Cristo* story. They must work for some kind of tourist attraction or themed restaurant. The three girls continue screaming hysterically on the return journey, while the two Frenchmen enjoy the show – it's hard to gauge whether they're laughing with the girls or at them.

A large cruise liner powers past us, looking mightily impressive from 70 metres away. The ship blows its horn for its excited passengers, and maybe also for our little ferry, and many passengers wave down from the deck. The three birthday girls wave back excitedly and blow kisses.

After disembarking at the port, I head to Marseille's main shopping street in search of a replacement iPhone charger – it turns out that this was the only useful item I lost with my luggage in Brussels Airport. The main shopping drag has plenty of stores, and I enter a couple of electronic and mobile-phone stores. I talk to various retail assistants, but none of them has the current "lightning" charger. They tell me to go to Marseille's Virgin Megastore, where I soon learn that shop, like the one in Oxford Street in London a month ago, is closing its doors. With the shelves practically empty, a soon-to-be-ex-employee informs me that I'll be able to find the charger in one particular store in the nearby backstreets.

Heading off the shopping strip, I walk through grubby streets lined with stalls, where the air carries the slightly foul smells of meat and other food produce. It looks as though these ramshackle alleys haven't been cleaned in months and the locals are very noisy. I see other tourists who clearly don't know what to think of it either.

Occasionally holding my breath (fishmongers, of course), I eventually find the electronics store. After I interrupt the shop owner's social chat with his friends and use pidgin French and miming to indicate what I want, it turns out that he has the sacred charger! We haggle over the price and I get the necessary receipt for insurance purposes. I then go looking for the quickest route back to the cleaner main street, away from the smells and chaos.

Walking up Marseille's widest street, the Boulevard de la Libération, which terminates at the port near my hotel, I notice a great deal of ethnic diversity among the locals. There are some beggars and plenty of young men lounging around with no obvious gainful employment to go to.

Looking for a bottle of Bordeaux, I find an excellent supermarket. While I'm waiting in the queue to pay, a young couple exiting the storefront are asked to open their coats by a security guard. They do their best to avoid complying, but the guard won't let up; after a minute or so, they sheepishly open their coats and are soon sprung for shoplifting. The two of them are made to wait there, and as I walk past on the way out I wonder what punishment they'll receive when the local cops arrive.

It's been a bit of a mixed day. It was a pleasure to see the cathedral and I enjoyed the ferry trip, but I've found Marseille to be a backward place and a bit of a letdown generally. And that's even though I'd been forewarned to stay in certain parts of town and avoid other, more questionable areas. When I compare Marseille with the French Riviera, the two are like chalk and cheese!

Twelve

Avignon, the City of Popes

It feels refreshing the next morning that my train journey from Marseille to Avignon is only thirty-five minutes. Even better, when I come out of Avignon station, the hotel is literally only 30 metres away! I chose it almost entirely for its location and though it's quite grungy from the outside, the Ibis Avignon is comfortable and homely within, and the hotel reception staff prove very friendly.

From the comfort of my small room on the sixth floor, I can look north towards the historic town centre and its leading tourist attraction, the heavily fortified Palais des Papes (Papal Palace), rising above the other buildings. Avignon is encircled by city walls, 4 kilometres of superbly preserved stone ramparts, which I can see directly below. Now I'm a long way into my hectic trip, a couple of nights in this quiet town should be a pleasant way to complete my time in France. Unfortunately, though, the weather forecast for the next two days is for torrential rain, much like those that caused flash floods back in my river-city home of Brisbane – not promising!

I go for a walk into the town centre, where a small community of twelve thousand residents live within the medieval walls. Often referred to as the "City of Popes", Avignon was home to Popes and Antipopes in the fourteenth and early fifteenth centuries. This important part of Avignon history was the result of a split within the Catholic Church, when the newly elected French pope, Clement V, declined to live in the Vatican. Even though I was brought up a Catholic, I was unaware of this and had always assumed that the Vatican had been the continuous and only home of the popes.

I walk through a gate in the city wall and onto Avignon's main street, the Rue de la République, where I draw some much-needed Euros from an ATM at the local post office. There are tourists everywhere, and many appealing restaurants and stores to cater for them. At the far end of the main drag is the central square of Place de l'Horloge, with its trendy restaurants, bars and boutique fashion shops.

I'm thirsty and hankering for a beer, but the high-end bars here are very expensive according to their menus, so I head back towards my hotel and find a sensibly priced Irish bar. A couple of refreshing Guinness schooners later, Avignon's nightlife begins to pick up as a group of English lads arrive, with one of them dressed in an odd outfit. It seems that Avignon is on the buck's-party circuit too! It's my cue to leave and I pick up some dinner from a pizza place on the way back as the first few drops of two days' torrential rain begin to fall.

Overnight it buckets down non-stop and when I wake the view towards the Papal Palace is very off-putting. I surf Google for any evidence of the rain desisting during the day, but it only looks like getting worse. I read more of my novel, *Cloudstreet*, play Tiger Woods golf on the iPad and watch TV. Boredom forces me out at midday and, having summoned the courage to go sightseeing, I head off in search of an umbrella.

New umbrella in hand, I walk through a couple of alleys lined with boutique shops, heading for the river and Avignon's famous medieval bridge of Pont St-Bénézet. Now a UNESCO World Heritage Site, it was originally built in the twelfth century. Once 900 metres long, the bridge was repaired and rebuilt several times until all but four of its twenty-two spans were washed away in the seventeenth century. It has achieved worldwide fame through the song "Sur le Pont d'Avignon", written in the sixteenth century; in fact the bridge is better known as the Pont d'Avignon. The song is eccentric and quintessentially French:

Sur le Pont d'Avignon	On the bridge of Avignon
L'on y danse, l'on y danse	We all dance there, we all dance there
Sur le Pont d'Avignon	On the bridge of Avignon
L'on y danse tous en rond	We all dance in a ring

Having now hit the river, I push ahead while getting drenched by cars driving through enormous puddles on Avignon's circular road outside the city walls. I look ahead at the four remaining spans of the bridge, which are nigh on impossible to appreciate under the duress of the downpour. The wind is so powerful that it has already broken the new umbrella, which is now a write-off – not such a good investment for ten euros after all.

For a fee, visitors can walk along the bridge, but I decide to climb the steps to the Rocher des Doms park above, from where the bridge can best be viewed. Had the sun been shining, I would have enjoyed walking the bridge, but there's only one courageous sightseer doing that, from what I can see. It's difficult to navigate in the rain, but I eventually find the lookout, along with some other keen but also fully drenched tourists. Maybe the weather is affecting my mood, but the bridge doesn't look overly impressive in its current incarnation. Its status seems to derive from its original and impressive medieval length of two-dozen stone arches and from the timeless popular song.

The park is elevated and exposed, and the wind is gusting out of control. Having deposited the umbrella in a rubbish bin, I descend the other side of the Rocher des Doms towards the Papal Palace. Next to the ticket office there's a welcoming little restaurant with a nice warm fire-place and hot chocolate for sale, so I recover from the drenching there.

Opposite stands the imposing front wall of the palace, built in the thirteenth century after Pope Clement V and his court fled political turmoil in Rome to make a new home in the south of France. Over the next seventy years, vast sums of money were invested in building and decorating the palace.

After passing through the ticket gate, I walk along endless halls, chapels, corridors and staircases, once sumptuously decorated but now nearly completely empty except for a few faded wall paintings.

The emptiness emphasises how absolutely huge the halls are, with their heavily fortified stonework built to last forever. I've visited the Vatican, and the Palais des Papes is another grandiose architectural expression of wealth and power – the largest Gothic palace ever built.

Narrow steps lead up inside a central tower. To continue on to what is considered Avignon's best view, from the magnificent western tower, you have to take an external walkway – today reserved for those with enough courage to brave the elements – then ascend a dozen or so steps. Holding my breath as if I'm underwater, I steel myself before scurrying along the walkway and bravely climbing the steps to the tower. Out on my own now in the torrential downpour, I almost waterlog the camera while trying to photograph the view.

The tower can be seen rising above Avignon's skyline from afar, including from my hotel room, and it is right above the palace's massive front wall, which I saw from the restaurant below. It provides a truly great panorama over the town – almost worth the effort on this occasion.

Soaked through and having had enough, I head down to ground level, ignoring the souvenirs, and back into the town's cobblestone streets. The rain having stopped, I spend the next hour completely lost, walking through a maze of residential streets. Unplanned, the walk evolves into an interesting detour, providing a different perspective on how locals live small-town life. Along the way I pass a couple of old water wheels, originally used to power flour mills, and picture people here making baguettes in centuries past.

One saving grace of Avignon is that once you find its circular wall, it's fairly simple to retrace your steps to the area near the train station, so I'm soon back in my hotel having a hot shower! On reflection, it's been an interesting day and I've enjoyed learning about this "missing link" in Catholic history.

Soon the rain comes back, more powerful than ever. I spend the rest of my day indoors and have dinner at the very ordinary hotel restaurant.

Thirteen

Stopover in Barcelona

My train leaves early in the morning for the 450-kilometre journey to Barcelona. There will be two transfers, one in Perpignan, France, and the second at Portbou, just over the border in Spain. As I take my reserved seat at Perpignan in a slow and aged train, I'm excited about spending my last two weeks in Spain and Portugal, and expecting sunny weather. The train from Portbou to Barcelona is high-speed. In my carriage are a few pension-aged travellers, enthusiastically taking photo upon photo of the speed monitor as we reach the maximum velocity of 320 kilometres per hour.

I have a sense of déjà vu as I exit Barcelona Sants station just as I did on my first visit six years ago, then walk up the very same long, sloping street to the hotel. This time everything is far more familiar, and it turns out my hotel is directly across the road from the one I stayed in on my first visit. Presenting my passport at hotel reception, I get a friendly "Hola, Mr Rich. Do you have your luggage?"

"What do you know about my luggage?" I reply, tired and indifferent, having almost forgotten about the debacle in Brussels, like it was just a dream.

"Your luggage is here for you, señor. It's been waiting for you."

Hallelujah! Praise the Lord! High fives all round! It only took eight days, but in hindsight it was a good strategy to go overboard with the Luggage Nazi in Nice, detailing my lengthy itinerary ahead. Unsurprisingly, some ratbag in Brussels has broken the three digit-coded locks, though nothing seems to be missing.

Barcelona is only a stopover on my journey to Madrid, but it's one Europe's loveliest cities, so I catch the metro down to La Rambla, the famous tree-lined pedestrian street popular with tourists and locals alike. On my previous visit, I spent much of the time taking in many works by the hugely influential architect Antoni Gaudí. The most famous is the gothic cathedral, the Sagrada Familia, with its gravity-defying and organic-looking towers, often described as Gaudí's 'magnum opus'. Another Gaudí highlight was the Park Güell on Carmel Hill, a public park with architectural gems scattered throughout its very walkable gardens. I also enjoyed the old Gothic quarter, Barcelona Football Club's enormous home stadium, Camp Nou, with its full trophy rooms, and the extensive collection of paintings in the Museu Picasso art gallery.

The metro ride to La Rambla is uneventful, with people just minding their own business, until an elderly man with a karaoke music machine and giant speaker comes into the carriage. With the speaker making a bass-heavy, almost *doof-doof* sound, he begins singing the lyrics to the 1970s song "Old Time Rock 'n' Roll" by Bob Seger.

His English has a strong Spanish accent as he sings the lyrics straight off a sheet of paper in the palm of his hand. It's a completely unexpected sight and people don't really know what to think of it. It's also a first taste of the many buskers I'll see as I travel through Spain, all trying to make some cash in this time of high unemployment.

Unfortunately for this guy, the song doesn't quite work – a bit too 1970s, perhaps. He soon stops the karaoke machine while pulling out a fresh set of lyrics. This time it's the more modern and catchy hit "Gangnam-Style". It's bizarre hearing this Spanish version of the hit by the Korean K-pop star Psy, but the audience enjoy the upbeat tune and his gutsy attempt to entertain.

He then walks through the carriage, collecting about twenty euros' worth of tips in his hat for the one and a half songs. Not bad for five minutes' work! Thanking his clapping audience, he exits at the next stop, ready for a repeat performance elsewhere. I assume he has just one train ticket and spends hours in the metro network each day busking. How very industrious.

As I come out of the station onto La Rambla, a familiar scene greets me, still vibrant but a little underwhelming second time around. There are the same street performers as last time, and I wonder if they're the same people impersonating Edward Scissorhands, the Empire State Building and Charlie Chaplin, and painted in gold leaf.

It is enjoyable walking down to Barcelona's beautiful harbour. However, I begin to tire, so I return to the hotel to rest in front of the TV before going on to Madrid. Barcelona is the most football crazy city I've ever visited, so much so that I can watch a Barca training session broadcast live, where thousands of fans are spectating in the vast stands of the Camp Nou stadium. Lionel Messi is easy to spot in his blue and red number ten jersey.

Fourteen

Madrid – the Centre of Spain

Three hours after leaving Barcelona the next morning, my train is speeding through Madrid's outer suburbs towards the city centre. There seems to be an abundance of ugly housing-estate buildings here, with the same drab look as their equivalents in London. We pull into Puerta de Atocha station, one of two main central stations in Madrid, where it appears that security is a high priority. I'm puzzled for a minute or two, then remember Madrid's horrific 2004 terrorist train bombings, which killed 191 people and injured more than two thousand.

Madrid is a large and gritty city, and it makes common sense to cab it to the hotel. The traffic is chaotic, with incessant beeping. My driver occasionally yells at or makes signs towards other taxi drivers. We take a busy road along the length of the Prado Museum (Museo del Prado), Spain's premier art museum and a top tourist attraction in Madrid, then cut across two lanes and drive up a long straight hill and along a few twisting side streets to reach the hotel.

With only the vaguest idea of my location in Madrid, I enter the hotel reception, from which it seems the Prado is only ten minutes' walk away. Even better, Madrid's most famous shopping street, the Gran Vía (literally "great way") is only 200 metres away. I soon exit the lobby for a mid-afternoon stroll.

The Gran Vía is also referred to as "Spain's Broadway" and it has a lively nightlife scene. The "street that never sleeps" also has ornate buildings, upmarket shopping and prominent advertising reminiscent of that in New York's Times Square. A number of five-star hotels and movie theatres inhabit the grand architecture of many of the buildings. The boutique shops and large department stores are pretty fancy, too. The clothing brand Zara has its flagship store here, and I notice plenty of fans of the brand taking photos but not doing much actual shopping. Understaffed, it seems to be just a token flagship store, necessary to keep up appearances on the Gran Vía.

Before long I take a street from the Gran Vía down to Puerta del Sol, a large and popular square in Madrid. It is claimed to be the "official centre" of Spain's road system. In reality, though, the city centre is encircled by a ring road, from which roads and railways lead to all parts of the country.

Wandering in an unassuming manner down a pedestrian-only street, I see many women in bright tops, extra-high heels and short skirts that expose their lingerie. They hover along both sides of the street, singly or in pairs, making brazen sexual offers and catching me by surprise. Madrid has a reputation for having plenty of working girls, but the overt displays of these prostitutes leave little to the imagination. They look like the low-cost variety. I learn later that this pedestrian precinct has the unenviable reputation as probably the sleaziest street in Madrid, frequented by cheap hookers imported from other parts of Europe.

Puerta del Sol is a very happening and vibrant place. One thing that surprises me about Madrid are the high numbers of police officers walking the beat, with females well represented alongside their male counterparts. Their dark blue police uniforms look very smart too.

Off the square, I walk down a wide street, saddened a little to see many beggars, some of them whole families sitting together. There are a couple of interesting shops selling carcasses of cured lamb, along with plenty of other tasty produce and quality wine selections. The Spanish are great foodies, of course, enjoying a wide range of traditional dishes as well as their world famous and influential tapas. With some dinner and cheap wine to take back to my hotel, I call it a night.

Waking well before sunrise, I feel like I've got a hole in my head! There was something off about that cheap wine – maybe too many preservatives? I feel horrendous. My head hurts so much that I can't possibly get back to sleep. I try to see that as a bonus, though, as I plan to visit the Prado Museum today and it's renowned for its large queues each and every morning.

To fortify myself, I have breakfast at the hotel buffet, enjoying bacon, eggs, cheeses, croissants, pastries and plenty of coffee for vitality. Then, worried about running late, I power-walk to the Prado, but on arrival there's no queue whatsoever. Befuddled by my hangover, I've made the mistake of thinking the museum opened at 8 am rather than 9 am. Looking on the bright side, I tell myself I'll at least be at the front of the queue. Meanwhile, I watch museum staff construct multiple queueing barricades, with experienced military precision.

The Prado may have a renowned art collection, but it's an ugly building from the outside. My first impression is that Madrid isn't as attractive a city as Barcelona, the only Spanish city I have hitherto visited. Maybe it's because I see the city as just a stopover on my way to Andalusia, my ultimate destination, in the country's south. Pragmatically, I plan to stay only two nights in Madrid before continuing south. I will, however, return to Madrid on this trip, as I'm flying back to Brisbane from here and will spend my final evening in the popular town of Toledo, half an hour's train journey south of the capital. I've heard people back home speak highly of Toledo.

Inside the Prado, the paintings are impressive in scale and detail but too traditional and conventional for me. Many are of scenes from the Bible; there's also a large collection of Flemish paintings, not very appealing to me since Bruges. However, the many works by Francisco de Goya are impressive and sometimes haunting in their bold and contrasting colours. Perhaps the fact that I'm feeling unwell renders me incapable of fully appreciating the Prado.

On the way back, I find a pharmacy. None of the staff, including the pharmacist, speaks English, which seems surprising in such a large international city, and I have to act out a charade to communicate my symptoms: cough, cough; sniff, sniff; I bang my sore head, miming pain to the pharmacist and probably entertaining the other customers. I walk out the door hoping I've scored some aspirin with codeine or cold and flu tablets, and plan to spend most of the afternoon in bed.

Fifteen

Granada and the Mighty Alhambra

With Barcelona and Madrid behind me, my real journey through Spain begins as the high-speed train departs Atocha train station the next morning. Waiting on the station platform, I contemplate that with a hangover being so unbearable at the ripe age of forty, my decades-long era of enjoying "a few too many" must be coming to an end. I now understand teetotallers completely!

The bland outer suburbs of the big city stretch on, but, as the train accelerates to 300 kilometres per hour, we enter beautiful Spanish countryside and I'm completely taken by it. Under continuous blue skies and sun, the super-train sweeps through arid plateaus broken by river valleys. At this speed, trains on Spain's *ferrocarriles* (literally "iron ways", also abbreviated to FFCC) provide a perfect wide-screen panorama. Crops grow on unirrigated land, relying solely on rainfall as a source of water. Fields filled with olive groves, vineyards and orchards go racing by.

I hop in a cab at Granada station and we head up the city's main street. The driver strikes up occasional conversations with fellow cab drivers stopped at traffic lights, all of whom he seems to know. This is definitely a small town, and a lovely looking one at that. The main street is very clean and tourist friendly.

The driver winds his cab skilfully through narrow backstreets to the secluded hotel. The front entrance is actually on a small square with two or three bars, currently closed for the afternoon siesta. Later I'll discover that a quiet, innocuous street off the square comes to life in the late afternoon and evening, with fantastic little tapas bars, restaurants and guitar-playing buskers.

The hotel reception is staffed by youthful, typical-looking Spanish girls, with olive skin, strong cheekbones, dark brown eyes and long, flowing hair – quite lovely. Just off the reception is a small internal courtyard, a common feature of these small southern hotels. A number of hotel guests are in the courtyard using their laptops and iPads – apparently the Wi-Fi signal is stronger here than in the reception area.

My sunlit room is spacious and quiet, with some stylish pieces of Spanish furniture – I love it. Still feeling unwell, I decide to take some cold and flu tablets and spend the afternoon in the room dozing in front of the TV. Surfing TV channels, I begin watching a live bullfight, something I've never seen before. The macho matador, in his traditional *traje de luces* ("suit of lights") taunts the massive bull with his red cape then, as it tires, clinically inserts spears into the beast's soon-bloody back, the crowd roaring with each blow. It looks as though there are a number of celebrities and glamorous partners of the bullfighters watching in the stands.

It's obvious that the better the bullfighter, the more prolonged and sadistic the killing. With the poor bull almost dead, the "hero" skilfully slides his long sharp sword deep into the beast's back. The crowd roars as the matador bows to the thousands of fans, while the poor victim is dragged across the dirt and out of the arena.

Before long, the next testosterone-heavy alpha male comes out for an exact repeat of the brutal performance. Five minutes later, I switch channels, having had enough of this antiquated and gross brutality. Respect to the Catalonians, who've legislated against this cruel tradition and must be a more sophisticated and civilised bunch.

Tired after a long day on the train, I drift into the deep sleep of someone with the dreaded "man flu". I have a surreal dream about being at a bullfight and leaping out of the crowd before heroically sprinting across the ring and tackling the matador bully, to the scornful sound of booing from the crowd.

Feeling good after my therapeutic nap, I decide to head out for dinner. The quiet street 15 metres from my hotel has come to life in the early evening, with restaurants spilling out onto the cobblestone alley. In close vicinity are a few small, basic tapas bars humming with energy and filled with drinkers sampling the fare. They give me the impression of being genuine local social hangouts.

Also on the streets outside are a number of three-piece bands busking away, playing guitar and singing passionately. Spain's economy is very reliant on tourism and in these tough times such industriousness can be necessary to make a buck.

Still feeling on the tender side, I have only one beer at a tapas bar but plan to come back again when better. I happen upon a small restaurant and am greeted by a smiling local waitress. She tells me straight out that today is her first day on the job. I wonder if she's been struggling to find work, like many young Spaniards – youth unemployment hovers around forty per cent. The Spanish have always had a relaxed attitude to work but, just as in some other countries around Europe, concerns exist that today's young people could become a lost generation. It may be cultural, but it seems like their governments and ruling classes have let them down, and many are now paying the price of belated austerity measures.

The waitress hurries to bring me a menu, asking in advance for feedback about the service she is about to provide. Soon my Diet Coke and tapas plate are quickly followed by my main meal. Granada is jam-packed with tourists from England escaping to the Spanish sun on their annual holidays. I used to wonder why my London work colleagues would just want to lie on beaches in Spain for their holidays, always returning with a tan. I now completely understand, as Spain's weather and relaxed culture are the antithesis of stuffy, rainy, cold England. A married English couple see me sitting at the restaurant enjoying my fairly plain traditional food. It seems to appeal to them, as they sit down at the next table.

The next morning when I'm on my way to breakfast, I check again with the reception girls regarding the bus route up the steep hill of Granada's old Moorish quarter, the Albayzín (or Albaicín). The town of Granada sits at the base of two large hills, themselves below the Sierra Nevada mountain range. On one are the narrow streets of the Albayzín, which look directly across a river valley to the other hillside, the site of Granada's main attraction, the mighty Alhambra palace.

The Moors, a Muslim people from North Africa, invaded what is now Spain in the early eighth century and soon conquered almost the entire Iberian Peninsula, as well as southern France and parts of Italy. For almost eight centuries, until 1492, Granada was an important Moorish city and latterly the capital of the powerful Emirate of Granada. It was one of its rulers, Mohammed ben Al-Ahmar of the Nasrid dynasty, who in the mid-fourteenth century constructed the Alhambra, now considered one of the most graceful architectural achievements of the Muslim world.

The Albayzín was the main Moorish neighbourhood and retains the urban layout and structures first established in the eleventh century, including an intricate network of winding streets. The influence of Islam is still apparent in the buildings, restaurants, tearooms and mosques.

The bus to the Albayzín travels along the main street of Granada, soon filling with tourists, then begins its climb through the narrow, twisting streets. I've read that the best approach is to get off the bus at the highest stop and meander back down to the popular viewpoint at the Church of San Nicolás, from where you can look across the valley to the Alhambra.

A group led by a tour guide exits at what seems to be the right stop. I've no idea where to start, not knowing my north from my south here. A good idea would seem to be to tag about 20 metres behind the group, close enough to hear (if the guide speaks English). The winding lanes rise and fall steeply between old, white, multistorey homes with intricate wrought-iron balconies and tiled roofs. There's always something interesting, unique or different to see around each historic corner and the overall feel is of a hotchpotch of Morocco and North Africa meets Spain and Europe.

I keep moving along, with a vague sense that I'm heading in the right direction; glimpses of the Alhambra can occasionally be seen between the buildings, nestled beneath the distant Sierra Nevada Mountains. Occasionally I get lost when I turn off to explore a side street, and then have to backtrack, but it's a lot of fun, like exploring a giant maze, and good exercise. If I were elderly, like the members of the tour group I followed, a guide would be essential, as the district is a real labyrinth where almost every lane is similar – and worthy of a photo. Around one turn is an interesting, open, souk-like market, selling fresh food and vegetables.

Loving every moment but feeling a little lost, I'm relieved to come upon a direct route uphill to the viewpoint (*mirador*) at the Church of San Nicolás. The view across to the Alhambra is breathtaking. The palace, with its enormous, symmetrical and imposing towers, sits majestically on the lush green hillside beneath the snow-capped mountains of the Sierra Nevada in the background.

It wouldn't be Spain without a few locals peddling souvenirs and crafts. While sitting down with a bottle of chilled water to contemplate the view, I get a shock when an itinerant Spanish man, who appears sound asleep, suddenly jumps to life and starts shrieking something loudly. The makeshift markets on picnic blankets disappear within seconds. All of a sudden, as the local police appear, there are no signs of commerce. The lazing man was, in fact, a lookout, on alert for approaching law officers. It's really quite humorous.

Making a more honest living is a three-man band, singing traditional songs with Spanish guitars for the pleasure of the tourists, with the Alhambra as a backdrop. After capturing some video of the band, I give them a good tip before taking a myriad of photos of the fortress opposite. Looking across the valley at the massive fortified towers, I can see tourists over there under Spanish flags, getting a privileged up-close look at the world-renowned site, which I will visit tomorrow. A few groups and couples then ask me to take their pictures in front of this picturesque background.

From the Church of San Nicolás, a series of long, winding roads slope down to the river valley below. Again, at different spots, the Alhambra can be seen at the end of a lane, framed by tiled roofs on either side. As I descend there are more and more tapas restaurants and Moroccan-style shops with dark interiors selling Andalusian plates, scarves, rugs, candlesticks and so on. I enjoy browsing all of the colours and designs on display, and there's thankfully little of the hard sell usually forced on tourists.

Today has been an interesting introduction to Moorish Andalusia and a taste of the Alhambra for tomorrow. Back at the hotel, I surf the web in the hope of buying advance tickets for my visit, but I have miscalculated badly: it has been booked out for weeks in advance! According to TripAdvisor, I face an early start in the morning for the limited number of last-minute tickets available each day at the main entrance. After glimpsing the Alhambra's magnificence today, I plan purposefully ahead, afraid of missing out. I phone the official ticket hotline and am told with "certainty" that the last-minute tickets available in the morning at the Alhambra's ticket office will be for access to only the Generalife, the palace gardens above the fortress and palace.

Waking at sunrise, I scoff down breakfast and a couple of espressos, exit the hotel and stride up the main street. Climbing the steep, long hill to the Alhambra would be an exhausting and time-consuming exercise, so I plan to take the bus. The number ten leaves every five minutes and, even at dawn, each one usually fills to full capacity. I pay my two-euro fare and the small converted bus begins its steep climb. These buses are specifically engineered to allow them to power up narrow streets and accelerate after short turns. They remind me of the small public buses that drive around the narrow streets of ancient Rome, which are fuelled by electricity to minimise pollution and thereby preserve the precious archaeology and architecture.

Most passengers appear to have pre-purchased their Alhambra tickets and hop off at the first stop at the palace. The few remaining, anxious-looking passengers ask the driver if the next stop is for the Generalife, where the early bird tickets are sold. The queue there is actually quite short when we arrive, and I manage to buy a ticket. A mere ten minutes later, though, things could have been touch and go.

I go through the gate and walk the straight path to the complex's centrepiece, the Nasrid Palaces, for my 9 am group entry. It's a relaxing spot, where I enjoy an espresso from a coffee cart while looking back across the valley towards the Church of San Nicolás in the Albayzín.

Part fortress, palace and water garden, the Alhambra is one of the pinnacles of Moorish art, widely considered one of the most complete and finest of all Islamic buildings, or of any religion for that matter. It was originally constructed in 889 AD as a small fortress on the remains of Roman fortifications. It then went largely ignored until its ruins were renovated and rebuilt, with the complex being completed in the mid-thirteenth century.

The Nasrid rulers who built the Alhambra were the last Muslim emirs in Spain. After they were ousted in 1492, the Alhambra was used by Christian rulers until the early sixteenth century; it then fell into a state of disrepair until extensive restorations were begun in the nineteenth century. Now that the complex is such a key tourist attraction, it is safe to say that it will never be forgotten or neglected again. Over the centuries the palace has also been the inspiration for many songs and stories.

The Alhambra is the most visited tourist attraction in Spain – three million visitors per year come to see what the fuss is about. That speaks volumes when considering the huge range of major tourist sites in Spain, including forty-four UNESCO World Heritage Sites – making it a very close second in Europe to Italy. The Nasrid Palaces are the crème de la crème of the complex, and ticketed entrance is strictly limited to three hundred people per half hour.

The three interconnecting palaces surpass any expectations I may have had. The interaction between architecture and gardens is delightful, as council rooms and royal apartments alternate with courtyards and delicate, flower-shaped fountains. The decoration is mind-boggling, including exquisitely fashioned walls, gardens, fountains and patios as well as an elegant water system, which trickles through the palace, creating an incredibly peaceful aura. Everywhere you look are fascinating details, such as interlocking glazed tiles in deep reds, blacks and greens; lines of the Koran in Arabic script; and creamy plaster reliefs with geometric patterns that seemingly flow in one continuous line.

With groups of keen tourists snapping away in every little corner, patience is a virtue. A young Englishman exhibits the patience of a saint, waiting for everyone to walk through so that he can photograph the exquisite, mirror-like pool reflecting the palace's delicate archways without the intrusion of other visitors. I'm doing my own best to capture the palace, but three hundred people seems about double the right group size for anyone to have a satisfying experience of the place. There must be a magic formula to determine the ideal number of visitors in a group that will satisfy demand while allowing visitors to capture the palace on film.

The palaces are divine, and I feel blessed to have seen them up close, rather than just the pleasant manicured gardens of the Generalife up above on the hill. I'm so very glad to have ignored the poor advice from the hotline last night and made the effort to get up nice and early to queue at the ticket office.

The exit of the Nasrid Palaces leads to intricate outdoor gardens, which also use flowing water to create a sense of tranquillity; this is a common feature of Islamic architecture. Beyond another beautiful fountain and pool another view opens up across to the Church of San Nicolás, from a different angle.

The predominantly Muslim design of the palaces is counterbalanced by the Palace of Charles V, a Renaissance building situated between the Nasrid Palaces and the imposing fortress walls at the Alhambra's most westerly point. The Christian palace was built by Catholic monarchs after the conquest of Granada in 1492 and reflects the Plateresque style in vogue in Spanish architecture at the time. Plateresque was an artistic movement developed in Spain and its territories, which appeared between the late Gothic and early Renaissance, in the late fifteenth century. The style is characterised by ornate decorative façades, which are covered with floral designs, chandeliers, festoons and so on.

The building's 60-metre-long and 17-metre-high exterior walls look conservatively Christian, evoking memories of my Catholic upbringing. Inside is a circular patio on two floors, which appears to be not nearly as popular with visitors as other parts of the Alhambra. The circular interior is reminiscent of a mini Roman colosseum, with a very Italian rustic roof.

A beautiful stairwell curves up to the second level, where a newly married bride and groom are having professional photos taken and looking blissfully happy. The Spanish bride is luminous in her elegant white dress and they make an attractive couple.

After the palaces, I proceed to the fortified walls of the Alcazaba. These are the enormous walls on top of which I saw and photographed people from across the valley at the Church of San Nicolás. *Alcazaba* is the general word used for Moorish fortifications throughout Spain and Portugal. It derives from the Arabic word *al-qasbah*, meaning a walled fortification in a city. These walls date from the eleventh to thirteenth centuries and are the oldest part of the existing Alhambra complex. The towers rise majestically above the complex, their massive scale almost out of balance with the intimacy and details of the Nasrid Palaces.

A number of large flags fly atop the towers and walls, including the EU and Spanish flags. Rising high above the valley below and exposed to the elements, they billow and flap in the wind. To the south-east are the peaks of the Sierra Nevada, while the town of Granada nestles below us to the west, the round-shaped roof of Granada Cathedral marking the city centre. It's now mid-morning, and the square by the Church of San Nicolás is filled with far more people than when I visited yesterday.

From the Alcazaba, I retrace my steps back up the hill, en route to the Generalife, a name that derives from an Arabic phrase meaning "the artist's garden". These gardens filled with trees, flowers and hedges are immaculately set out, the fountains complementing the beautifully maintained flora. It's an excellent place to finish the visit, relax and contemplate the Alhambra from a distance.

At the end of the gardens is the Palacio de Generalife, which houses yet more symmetrical fountains and other water features. The Generalife is lovely but a poor cousin to the splendour of the Nasrid Palaces and the Alcazaba. I take an excellent photo of the palaces and the Alcazaba, with Granada's rooftops in the distance.

After a relaxing downhill walk back to town, it's still early afternoon and it seems an ideal time for a tapas lunch, washed down with a couple of beers. My photos of the Alhambra prove quite a hit on Facebook that evening, with friends posting fond memories of the landmark on their own travels.

After lunch I go looking for Granada Cathedral, the official town centre. From the Alhambra I could easily make out this giant round church atop the city skyline. Unfortunately, at ground level it's not so obvious, as the surrounding buildings are built right up to the cathedral's giant walls and even its impressive clock tower is obscured from below. Still, I manage a satisfactory photo by craning my neck skywards.

An old woman is lying down on a blanket, begging at the cathedral's entrance, while some Roma women try to fleece tourists by placing small palm leaves in their hands, saying a prayer for luck and then asking for money. I don't linger to observe their cunning.

Spain is a very Catholic country, and the interior of the cathedral is a grandiose tribute to God. The walls and columns are absolutely massive and the ceiling above seems to literally reach towards the heavens. The central altar is a large, bold statement, and a series of smaller altars run in a semicircle along the adjacent walls. I'll see this kind of circular layout in many places during my travels through Spain in the next week or so.

After enjoying a slow walk around the church, I find myself at the base of the central altar. People are praying in the pews and lighting candles for loved ones. Still feeling unwell, I enjoy the peace and tranquillity typical of these giant houses of worship. The cool shade and low temperature are the perfect antidote to the fierce Iberian sun outside.

While I'm enjoying this respite, I'm approached by a petite, well-dressed Asian woman, looking not much older than myself. She says, "Don't take this the wrong way, but I saw you in the church and you look like a nice man. I'd like to introduce myself. My name is Wendy and I'm from Germany. I'm a businesswoman, actually, from Hamburg. I'm on a group tour but wanted some time to myself." Her accent, however, is not Germanic in the slightest, but rather an Asian-accented English.

Feeling quite sceptical, I politely introduce myself. After asking if she can use my iPhone, she takes a couple of photos of me, and then tells me I'm handsome.

"Gee, thanks."

She asks me if I'm married or have a girlfriend.

"No, just single. I don't have a girlfriend; travelling on my own."

"Do you like men?"

"No, no," I respond.

To my dread, she asks if I have plans for the evening, to which I answer no. Apparently, she is staying at such and such hotel in Granada. I am then invited to the hotel in the evening, room number twenty-three, if I'd like some female company. I really don't know what to say next, certain that I've just been propositioned in this cathedral by a prostitute!

Just being polite, I say, "Sure, sure. See you at seven?" They are appeasing words only, and I have no intention whatsoever of turning up.

"Are you sure?"

"No worries. See you then." Please just leave me alone right now!

Even though I'm not really religious, more of an agnostic in spite of my Catholic upbringing, this indecent proposal, while funny in an odd way, seems highly inappropriate.

I say, "See you later. Thanks for the photo. Bye."

As she walks away, I stay put, watching her like a hawk as she goes out the side exit. Then I wait another ten minutes before leaving, just to be on the safe side, while kneeling down at a pew and saying a prayer as the coast clears. When I emerge back into the bright Spanish sunlight, the Asian lady is thankfully nowhere to be seen.

The next day is my last in Granada, which proves one more than necessary. It is a good opportunity, however, to recuperate after my gruelling schedule. With only ten days until I fly home, I still have a large surplus of euros. The restaurants have been cheap, beer and wine a pittance, and I've hardly done any shopping for souvenirs.

There are some small backstreet markets selling tacky clothes, crafts and trinkets. However, on the central square near the cathedral, among many restaurants, is a popular souvenir store. They've been doing a roaring trade each time I've walked past over the last two days and I've spotted a great looking multi-coloured Moorish clock, which I now buy for my apartment.

I'm keen to buy a Barcelona football jersey, but, unsurprisingly, the official merchandise is expensive. While meandering through a side-street market, I find a stall with Barcelona supporters' gear. To my disappointment, the owner tells me straight away that he sells only official merchandise. Telling him I can't afford it, I turn to leave the shop.

But then he says, "Psst, señor, don't tell anyone, but I have some gear under the counter for your budget. All my friends and family have this."

He pulls out a full Barcelona kit with the number ten on the back and, above that, "Messi" in large yellow letters. After checking that it fits me, we negotiate a price and make a quick deal.

Sixteen

Historic Cordóba and the Mezquita

Mid-afternoon I catch the two-and-a-half hour train from Granada to Córdoba. I check into my comfortable four-star hotel, only a five-minute cab ride from the station, then head out for dinner at a nearby pub, where I watch the grand final of the UEFA Champions League between two impressive German clubs, on a big screen, with a few beers.

Next morning, I head out again into Córdoba's blue Spanish skies. For an Australian from the "Sunshine State", the blue skies are a blessing after the preceding few weeks. The main drag of Córdoba is dead straight and uncomplicated. After roughly a mile, I find myself amongst fellow tourists in the historic centre.

Walking over cobblestones past some impressive medieval buildings, I head for the river in search of Córdoba's famous and historic Roman Bridge. The city's tourist sites are centred around the city's historic core on the banks of the Guadalquivir River. Approaching the river, I soon spot the wide and imposing bridge, spanning the river banks between east and west.

As with most architecture in Andalusia, the bridge displays a strong Islamic influence. Originally built in the early first century BC, it became an important crossing, connecting Rome to Cádiz, a city and port in south-western Spain that was strategically important to the Roman Empire for its North Atlantic Ocean location. The history of

Córdoba goes back to 169 BC, the time of Julius Caesar, when it was the capital of the Roman province of Hispania Ulterior Baetica. Many famous Romans, including philosophers, orators and poets, came from Roman Córdoba.

In the eighth century the city was conquered by a Muslim army; it was retaken on 29 June 1236 by King Ferdinand III of Castile during the Spanish Reconquista. It's been estimated that by the tenth century Córdoba was the most populous city in the world, and it was a major centre of learning under its Islamic rulers. All in all, Córdoba has a diverse and intriguing history.

An unexpected sight on the river is a rundown but fully intact waterwheel, which would have supplied water to the buildings in Córdoba's historic centre during centuries past. It makes for a good photo op, with the impressive bridge in the background.

The bridge's magnificence is revealed the closer one gets to it: the sixteen enormous arches are firmly built in the strong-flowing river, with solid stone foundations supporting each section, and the structure is 250 metres long and 10 metres wide. It's now pedestrian-only and today is packed with tourists.

Walking its length in a dazed state, my mind wanders while I'm taking in the impressive buildings of Córdoba's historic centre. At one point, my shoulders bump straight into a group of teenage girls with typically Spanish olive skin. They giggle at my English apology, before I continue my walk, now a bit more aware of the tourist hordes.

The bridge is not mentioned much in the tourist guides, but I absolutely love it, preferring it to the tiny bridge in Avignon. This could be subjective, though, as here we have a blue sky as opposed to the storming torrents of rain in Avignon. Another appealing factor is that I've seen this bridge used as a prop in the epic *Game of Thrones* TV series, with some clever computer-generated effects added.

Looking back from the opposite end of the bridge at the historic centre, one gets a clear sense of the geography of central Córdoba. I can see my next destination, the Alcázar de los Reyes Cristianos, and its gardens, which have the reputation for being the most beautiful in Andalusia.

Córdoba is very similar to Granada in terms of its cultural influences, size and Moorish architecture. And as in Granada, there are Roma women near the entrance to the Alcázar, shoving palm leaves into the hands of unsuspecting tourists while attempting to fleece them. Been there, seen that. I ignore them as the Alcázar beckons.

It's the gardens I'm mostly here to see, but first I pass through the former palace and fort of Alfonso X, built in the thirteenth century. The Spanish Inquisition operated from this site between 1490 and 1821. The interior of the palace is nothing overly special but, after some thigh-burning steps up tight passages, the view from the Tower of the Lions is well worth the climb. To the north-east I can see the tower of the world-renowned Mezquita, Córboda's most famous attraction, and directly below me are the Alcázar's lush, green gardens in full bloom. Elegant fountains within the gardens stretch away from the base of the fort.

Separated from the gardens by a thick wall are the Royal Stables of Córdoba. I'm surprised and delighted to be able to see them from the tower, as the stables are quite famous. I study from above, with great interest, a number of male riders practising in traditional outfits, trotting their horses in a dressage-like fashion. One man though is accompanied on a horse by a female, side-saddle passenger sitting behind him, sporting a bright, traditional Andalusian *traje de flamenco* (flamenco dress). The dark-haired woman's flowing dress is strikingly red, curving around her figure and ruffled below the waist. The only problem with the view of the stables is that there are only a limited number of gaps in the fort walls through which one can poke a camera.

On descending to ground level, I enter a lovely isolated courtyard, surrounded squarely by rustic rooftops; the Roman Bridge is visible in the distance. Beyond the courtyard are the gardens, with their long, straight, symmetrical pools and fountains. Bright purple bougainvillea flowers line the edges of the pools and perfectly manicured trees rise on either side. It's an absolute delight to walk along the path to the gardens' far end.

I then retrace my steps back towards the palace, passing large and sculptured rows of hedges, with religious statues scattered about.

Everything seems intensely purple or green, the occasional stone statues being the exception. Next to the palace are some shaded rose gardens, occupied by groups of teenage students making some noise.

The gardens have been stunning, but I soon move on through cobblestoned laneways to the Mezquita. It is just as revered as the Alhambra and given that I was blown away by that majestic palace under the Sierra Nevada Mountains, I have high expectations of the Mezquita.

Originally a Moorish creation, the mosque was converted into a Catholic cathedral in the thirteenth century, and an enormous belltower was added to make it look more Christian. I'd read that the Christian ruler who built the tower regretted its addition once it was completed, saying something along the lines of "Why change something which is already perfect?"

As it turns out, I've made the mistake of visiting on a Sunday and I'm disappointed to learn that it is closed for worship from mid-morning and won't re-open again until the afternoon. The Spanish are certainly very fond of orange-tree-lined courtyards and the Mezquita has a grand one at that. It's a lovely spot to give my legs a break from walking and just sit people-watching at the base of the church's imposing walls.

Situated next to the Mezquita complex, Córdoba's Jewish quarter, or Juderia, is also something of a tourist attraction. I enter its medieval maze of streets. As I look up at whitewashed buildings with flower-filled window boxes, I consider how I have marvelled at the style and industriousness of these Jewish districts throughout my trip. The tiny streets and homes are so well maintained, and I enjoy being a free spirit as I wander around random corners with no particular destination, a great little restaurant or plaza often just a right-angle away. This reinforces my intention to one day visit Tel Aviv, about which I've heard good things over the years from people who've been.

I keep noticing women wearing traditional Andalusian dresses, in many different colours and patterns, in these narrow streets and beyond. They look beautiful and feminine and the dresses are always flattering, no matter how the women may look in more conventional attire. Obviously, there must be some kind of festival going on of which

I am ignorant; I'll have to Google it back at the hotel. I come across a small and inexpensive tapas restaurant, with friendly service and shade from the sun, and enjoy a quick bite of lunch.

Retracing the Juderia's maze of alleys back to the Mezquita doesn't prove easy, thus further time is spent exploring by default. When I finally find the complex, there's a massive queue of ticketholders at the entrance. It's still early in the afternoon, though, and I'm in no rush, so I take a seat again under the shaded side wall, confident that the queue will soon shorten.

It does, and when I enter the Mezquita, the first sensation is of darkness and shade. After my retinas adjust, I marvel at the delicate horseshoe arches dimly illuminated by tiny light globes, giving them a candlelit look. It's unlike the Alhambra but just as beautiful, in a very original and idiosyncratic way. I pull out my camera, but the dim light makes photography difficult. I really should just be taking it all in, not wasting time on an impossible photo that won't do it justice.

As shade gradually turns to light, I see that the interior is vast, with many different styles of architecture. Arches of beautiful orange and cream colours are revealed. These patterns are repeated row upon row, almost like a mosaic, and subtly complemented by black hanging lanterns. A special appeal of the Mezquita is its combination of historic religious architecture, Muslim and Christian, making it unique and a wonder to explore as it reveals its many surprises. The mosque's original layout is understood to be very similar to that of the earliest mosques built, soon after the advent of Islam.

With the light and colours now appearing brighter, I redraw my camera and take some fantastic photos, but with so many fellow tourists around patience is essential. The lines of arches eventually end as I enter a number of side chambers housing gold brought from various parts of the Spanish Empire. I'm not overly captivated by these rooms, as I don't I really like the "bling" of gold, preferring the subtler attributes of precious stones.

After passing back through the curved arches, I find the more recent addition to the Mezquita, the Christian cathedral, dead centre in the giant complex. There is a large and impressive Christian altar with an organ, as well as a choir section made from beautifully preserved mahogany woodwork, with a Baroque ceiling above.

It's fascinating to find two such significant, yet different religions, Christianity and Islam, come face-to-face in this wonderful architectural masterpiece. Seeing the Mezquita and the Alhambra provides some much-appreciated exposure to the beauty of Islam, as opposed to constant the doom and gloom in the news about religious extremists and terrorism. I've read that the mosque's reconversion to a Catholic church helped to preserve it during the turbulence of the Spanish Inquisition.

After some more time, with noticeably fewer tourists, I wander back into the bright sunlight outside. The Alhambra and Mezquita are quite different and each is unique, but they offer equally special experiences.

At the end of a long day, I walk back to the hotel, buying a few San Miguel beers on the way. Later, feeling refreshed, I grab a towel and take the lift up to the rooftop pool. The view from up top is mainly of surrounding hotels and commercial buildings, really quite boring, but the sun is still shining thanks to daylight saving and the pool area has a very relaxed feel. There's a slight nip in the air, though, as I work up the courage to dive into the cold pool. After my swim, I lie under blue skies while listening to a couple of my favourite albums through headphones.

Before bed, I discover from Google that the end of May is the Córdoba Feria or Fair, during which the local women enjoy stepping out in their flamenco dresses while men don the traditional flamenco costumes of their ancestors too.

Seventeen

Exotic Seville

The following day I've booked a high-speed train to Seville in the early afternoon, so I have a few hours to kill after checkout. The travel brochure at hotel reception recommends a popular Spanish garden, as well as Córdoba's largest public square, the Plaza de la Corredera, both located away from the historic centre from yesterday. Walking the couple of miles to the square for exercise, it proves underwhelming upon arrival, not worth going out of my way for.

Another five minutes' walk away is the Palacio de Viana, the "best Spanish garden in Córdoba", according to one brochure. But upon entering the ticket office, they want me fork out fifteen euros to enter. After yesterday's highlights, I'd rather spend money on something more worthwhile.

By midday I'm loaded up with my backpack and carry-on bag. It's a dead straight 2-kilometre walk to the station. With my luggage now on the heavy side, I take it slow and easy.

The high-speed train bullets me at 300 kilometres per hour to the Andalusian capital of Seville and I'm almost there after a couple of rounds of my Tiger Woods golf game. Leaving the platform, I walk to the far corner of the station, from where I spot the rooftop sign of my hotel, the Ayre, only 100 metres away. How perfect and stress-free.

After hearing so many stories of how beautiful Seville is, the area round my hotel looks disappointingly plain. The hotel is large and frenetically busy, but the reception staff are very friendly and professional.

Spain has quickly become my favourite country on this trip. The captivating countryside you see from the trains and the dignified, friendly and proud people are two strong reasons for that. Of course, there are also the many historic tourist sites, not to mention the beautiful weather, but the Spanish people have been a particular pleasure. I had expected that, given their economic problems, they'd be a sad lot, but their way of life doesn't seem to revolve around money and work, certainly not to the extent it does in Australia. However, both Aussie and Spanish cultures share the importance of family – definitely a good thing to have in common.

My room on the twentieth floor looks straight down at a blue pool, where tanned guests are swimming in bright sunlight. I go down and take a refreshing dip then read by the pool. It's mid-afternoon as I begin the 2-kilometre walk to central Seville. All the tourist sites are in close proximity to one another on the eastern side of the Guadalquivir River. The Old Town, with its UNESCO World Heritage sites, is supposed to be a labyrinth of narrow, winding streets, with Seville Cathedral at its centre.

At a random point, I leave the main road and turn into the maze of streets. The map from hotel reception isn't a north–south representation and is completely out of scale, so I totally lose my bearings, along with several other befuddled tourists. I somehow expected the giant cathedral to be a point on the horizon guiding me, but the buildings are tall and the streets narrow, leaving me anxious and confused.

Then I happen upon a small square and its name corresponds to one on the map. Perfect: all I need to find now is a succession of streets with particularly long Spanish names that lead straight to the cathedral. Having become more adept at finding my way through the maze of alleys, minutes later I stand facing the awesome external wall of the cathedral, which towers up to the blue sky. The church is so large that it takes some time to walk around its base. Impressed for now with the cathedral's exterior, I plan on seeing the inside on another visit in the coming days.

Early evening, I decide to have a first look at the famously atmospheric streets of Seville's Jewish quarter, or Juderia, which are situated only five minutes' walk east of the cathedral. Very beautiful from the outset, these quaint and charming alleyways are the Seville that everyone raves about. Having sussed out the Old Town, I head back to the hotel, confident of doing some proper exploring in the coming days.

With three nights in Seville, there's no need to rush, and after a sleep in and brunch, I return to the medieval Juderia in the afternoon. I soon lose myself in this enchanting neighbourhood, passing the hours away exploring its maze of shady cobblestone lanes and plazas. The Juderia of Seville served as the Jewish quarter until the late fifteenth century, when the Jews were expelled from Spain.

Little cafe bars and shops are everywhere. As in other Jewish quarters, there are secluded courtyards and balconies with wrought-iron latticework, draped with vines, flanked here by shimmering white and amber walls. There are a few well-known open plazas, all different and all arresting, with their perfectly maintained flower gardens and hedges.

Hidden away behind high walls are a few high-end hotels. What a beautiful place to escape to. On the down side, though, I see some departing hotel guests dragging hard and heavy suitcases on wheels along cobblestone streets in search of transport. I could definitely stay here for a few nights, though. It would be nice to revisit in the future if my single status changes, with a hotel room for two.

Late afternoon, I walk back to the cathedral. En route, I encounter a tall local man in his twenties, standing outside one of the boutique hotels while spruiking an "authentic" flamenco show for later in the evening. Respectful to passers-by, he's definitely no cheap salesman, so I approach him and learn of a brand-new flamenco show, which opened only a month and a half ago.

Without the hard sell, I enjoy talking to the young man and book a ticket to the evening performance at 8.30 pm, starting "right on the dot", he emphasises. Having decided not to bother with a flamenco show in Madrid, I look forward to this seemingly low-key version, where I should get an up-close view of this legendary form of Andalusian folk music and dance, a tradition going back hundreds of years.

Flamenco draws on various folkloric music traditions of southern Spain, including styles from ancient Greece and Rome and, later, elements from Indian, Moorish and Jewish cultures. Today's flamenco is the dazzling result of centuries of absorbing and sewing together these influences.

With this new plan in mind, I resume my walk back towards the cathedral with extra enthusiasm. From the narrow streets of the Juderia, I take some beautiful shots of the cathedral's 105-metre-high spire protruding above an alley between tiled roofs or above small courtyards. According to local oral tradition, the cathedral's clerics said, "Let us build a church so beautiful and so grand that those who see it finished will take us for mad." It took just over a century to turn this grandiose statement into grandiose reality.

Opposite the cathedral's tourist entrance is a quiet spot to sit with a gelato beneath the impressive Door of the Prince, one of fifteen doorways on the cathedral's façade. With time to kill before the show, I have dinner at another tapas restaurant, washed down with a couple of beers.

Any reservations about the flamenco show are put to rest when I enter the courtyard, where there's a square dancefloor roughly 10 metres long on each side. The show looks fully sold out, just as the young man had promised, with a good mix of people, around fifty in all, sitting on folded-out chairs around the stage, two rows deep. The cast is standard: a singer, a guitar player, a male dancer and a female dancer.

The show kicks off with songs played on the acoustic guitar. Wearing traditional flamenco dress, the beautiful, olive-skinned female dancer smashes her shoes boldly on the floor, her body and facial language declaring her intent. Now this is dancing! As she pounds the floor, it's seriously loud!

The man and woman dance together, in a long wooing ritual, holding nothing back; it's very natural, even primal. I think of how great it would be to express oneself to the opposite sex in such an unabashed and direct way – no games or social conventions, just pure passion. The male is a dashing Spaniard, who clearly appeals to the females in the audience, just as his female counterpart catches the men's attention.

There's plenty of variety throughout the show, including many costume changes, and it builds to a blistering finale. Cameras are banned until the last dance, when everyone can take their photos and videos. It's been an intimate experience, probably much more to my liking than an expensive show in Madrid.

I wake the next morning to more lovely spring weather, definitely a better proposition than the summer temperatures in Seville, which regularly climb into the high thirties. Today is all about the Alcázar complex, originally a Moorish fort but now a royal palace. It is actually the oldest European royal palace still in active use, founded in 913 AD as a Muslim fortress and since added to and rebuilt many times. Catholic monarchs set up court here in the late fifteenth century while preparing their strategy for reconquering Granada. The Alcázar is also famous for its beautiful gardens, which are a more recent addition.

As at the Alhambra and Mezquita, the inside of the palace has exquisitely detailed Moorish architecture, and it holds its own in comparison to those two more famous places. Tourists first enter the large Courtyard of the Maidens, flanked by Moorish walls decorated with intricate Islamic patterns, similar to those in the Nasrid Palaces in the Alhambra. The courtyard's name derives from a legend that the Moors demanded one hundred virgins every year as a tribute from the Christian kingdoms in Iberia. As in the Nasrid Palaces, the walls are beautifully preserved, but unfortunately the Alcázar's walls are far higher, making them more difficult to take in.

Just off the main courtyard is a lower-level side patio, which permits a closer view of the Moorish inscriptions. Behind the patio are a number of lavish reception rooms and another, smaller courtyard with intricate carvings. The courtyard's walls rise up three levels, each with symmetric archways of various sizes – absolutely beautiful Muslim architecture.

At the centre of the palace is a large rectangular reflecting pool, perfectly symmetrical, like those in the Nasrid Palaces. The water feature is long and narrow, with crystal-clear water and sunken gardens on either side. Unsurprisingly, it has been used as a set for movies and the TV phenomenon *Game of Thrones*.

Hidden behind the fortress are the gardens. With their wide range of differently themed areas, their fountains, and a diverse array of hedges and trees, they're one of the most beautiful gardens I've ever seen. They're not as large as, say, London's Kew Gardens or Singapore's Gardens by the Bay, but dense and rich in exquisite details. In the centre of one large pond, where tourists enjoy feeding frenzied goldfish, a statue is sprayed by a fountain extending out from the fortress above.

Such is the beauty and tranquillity of the gardens that I wander around for a couple of hours, occasionally resting on a park bench, with time easily ticking away. I particularly like an enormous bright purple bougainvillea that flows down the side of the fort. The gift shop has an excellent range of souvenirs, and I buy a green Moorish-patterned glasses case to replace my current old and haggard one.

A noticeable sight on leaving the Alcázar is a dozen or so elderly tourists on mobility scooters having a frightful argument, for all and sundry to see. Seville's winding streets must be frustrating for many, let alone the walking impaired. I've been fortunate enough to wander around on my own with ease and no timetable to adhere to, caring little about getting lost. Clearly it's been a long day for this group, and they are at their wits' end with each other as they try to decide where to go next.

Fifteen minutes' walk away lies the Plaza de España, part of a redevelopment of southern Seville that took place after it was selected to host the 1929 World's Fair. This famous and instantly recognisable plaza is a huge 300-metre wide half-circle complex, with government buildings running around its edge. In the plaza's centre is the Vicente Traver Fountain, accessible by numerous bridges representing the four ancient kingdoms of Spain. Floating under these bridges are a few romantic couples in rowing boats. The fountain is named after notable architect Vicente Traver y Tomás, who created his most important works in Seville between 1915 and 1933 and helped design the Plaza de España.

Most interesting are the dozens of mosaic-tiled alcoves at the base of the plaza's walls, each representing a different province of Spain. After walking the semi-circle, I take a seat in the province of Ibiza. A Spanish lady then asks if I could move while she has her photo taken in the alcove, which references her island home.

The plaza is largely used for administrative purposes and not really promoted as a tourist attraction. However, I'd seen it during many Google searches for "Seville" and thought it looked mightily impressive. It doesn't cost a cent to admire and I'm not disappointed. The complex was famously used as a set in the Star Wars prequels and in the classic film *Lawrence of Arabia*.

My final day in Seville is devoted to the cathedral. On its completion in the early sixteenth century, the cathedral became largest in the world – taking the title from the previous holder, Istanbul's Hagia Sophia mosque, which had held it for nearly one thousand years – and a symbol of the city's wealth at the time (it was a major trading centre).

Seville Cathedral is also famous as the burial site of Christopher Columbus, although there has been speculation in the past as to whether or not his body is actually here. This speculation began when a lead box bearing the inscription "Don Christopher Columbus" and containing bone fragments and a bullet was discovered in Santo Domingo in the Dominican Republic in 1877. However, recent DNA testing of fragments of the body in Seville Cathedral were matched to corresponding DNA from Columbus's brother, supporting the idea that both individuals had shared the same mother. This evidence led researchers to conclude that the remains in Seville truly belonged to Christopher Columbus. However, the authorities in Santo Domingo have never allowed the remains there to be exhumed, so it is still not known if any of those remains could be from Columbus's body as well.

I feel humbled upon entering the dark Gothic interior, with the longest nave of any cathedral in Spain, rising to the impressive height of 42 metres. Enormous columns climb up to the Gothic ceiling, which is illuminated by a golden yellow colour to emphasise the contrast with the columns' darkness. At the end of the long nave ceiling are beautifully crafted stained-glass windows, which project light serenely over sculptures of Christ on the Cross. Overawed, I forget about Christopher Columbus, before realising I've already walked over the unremarkable little in-ground tomb beneath the main altar.

Walking out the door on the other side of the nave section, I reach the Patio de los Naranjos, a cool, large, rectangular outdoor area within the cathedral's giant walls. Sixty Sevillian orange trees are evenly distributed over the area. From ground level visitors can look up to the 105-metre-high Giralda tower, topped by a large Baroque belfry.

I re-enter the interior and find the tower entrance on a corner at one end of the main nave. I know there's is no lift and I'm dreading hundreds of steps, so I'm pleasantly surprised that it's actually just one long continuous spiralling ramp, on which people ascend on the left and descend on the right, though there are some claustrophobic steps as the passage narrows in the belfry.

From the top of the tower, the views change markedly depending on which way you look. First I see the dark Gothic roof of the cathedral in close detail, which reveals the curvature and grandness of the church's upper exterior. On another side I look straight down at the orchard of orange trees below and further out to Seville's main bullfighting stadium, which stands out in the city skyline. The next side looks straight down at a popular open area of restaurants around a large statue.

I am wearing an R.M. Williams "Brisbane" T-shirt and, out of the blue, a Spanish-accented Aussie asks me where I bought it. He has a friendly face, so I tell him "Indooroopilly Shoppingtown", thinking he might be a fellow Brisbanite. It turns out he's actually travelling with his family from Sydney and – surprise, surprise – they're on a cruise. He was born in Spain, he tells me, then emigrated to Australia and settled in Sydney, but most of his relatives still live in Spain.

"A bit like me, only all of my relatives are Kiwis and Poms," I reply.

He comes across as a nice bloke while introducing his family. His late-teenage daughter and I get talking about the great exchange rate and how she's bought ten pairs of shoes. I've already witnessed many husbands or boyfriends waiting patiently for their other halves outside stores, perplexed by all the inexpensive and fashionable Spanish shoes on sale.

She also tells me that their ship is an American line with the inconvenient drinking age limit of twenty-one. While she can drink legally at home, being unable to enjoy cocktails on this holiday has made the cruise frustrating and a tad boring for her. After an enjoyable chat, I wish them safe travels before beginning the descent of non-stop right turns.

Tomorrow I'm flying from Seville to Lisbon, my next destination, as there's no direct train service. So I decide to spend more time in the delightful and still largely undiscovered Jewish quarter. Along the intertwined streets, more tapas bars appear out of nowhere. With the sun setting, there's enough time for a quick meal and drink before an easy stroll back to the hotel.

Eighteen

Lisbon's Seven Hills and Fairy Tale Sintra

In the morning, I pack quickly, now used to this regular ritual. My taxi turns up on time then whizzes me out to Seville Airport, a small airport 12 kilometres from the city centre. While passing through security, I get pulled over to the side and into a small room. An official gestures to me (no English) to open my carry-on bag. He points, as if to say, "No, deeper". At the bottom I find my small pocket knife and corkscrew.

"Gracias, señor. Lo siento" – "I'm sorry" – and straight into the bin they go.

For an Anglo news fix, I buy a London *Times* newspaper before boarding. The plane takes off, quickly rising above the fields of Andalusian Spain. It's great to get another perspective on the countryside that I loved looking at so much from the various trains below. Seville has provided me with my last impression of Andalusia and particular colours linger in my mind – the greens and purples of the Alcázar Palace gardens; the red-orange tinge of the Juderia's alleys and plazas, intermingled with white walls; and Seville Cathedral's stained-glass windows and yellow-lit ceilings. I will forever think of Seville as a strikingly colourful place.

My route to Lisbon takes me 900 kilometres north-east to Barcelona before a quick transfer, then 1,200 kilometres west to Lisbon – the distance as the crow flies between Seville and Lisbon is only about

300 kilometres. That's the way Vueling Airlines makes profits for its shareholders: the extra intake of passengers obviously makes the long detour worthwhile.

As we circle over Barcelona before landing, it's easy to spot Gaudí's Sagrada Familia, with its iconic towers jutting out of the flat skyline. They look almost organic, like tall thin versions of the termite mounds I've seen in Australia's outback.

A very popular shop at the terminal is the official Barcelona Football Club outlet, with its endless array of supporter clothing. It's perfectly positioned in the busy transfer lounge and trade is booming. The store is filled with customers and FC Barcelona shopping bags can be spotted throughout the terminal. With surplus funds still in my Euro bank account, I buy a Nike Barcelona cap, which immediately feels like a perfect fit.

Before long, I'm flying through the early evening sky above the "seven hills" of Lisbon, getting a great first glimpse of the small country of Portugal, about which I know little. I'm here for four nights, intending to relax before the reality of the long journey back Down Under hits.

Once again, the EU open-borders policy makes the arrival smooth, with no passport control. I hear locals talking in unfamiliar Portuguese. Fearing my backpack might not turn up, I wait with nervous anticipation for the carousels of the luggage pick-up to start. Spotting a long blue and black bag coming out of the hole in the wall, my eyes focus on its recognisable red travel tag. There's been no news of strikes or delayed flights, but my relief is understandable after Nice.

Outside, the metered taxi rank has a decent-sized queue, but plenty of taxis soon arrive. The drive from Lisbon Airport to the city's central Pombaline Downtown area seems a long way. Maybe it's because of those "seven hills" I've been reading about. We drive along many different streets and main thoroughfares, including quite a few one-way streets, I suspect. Yet even after what seems like half an hour, the cab fare is less than ten euros – excellent. I get out in a darkened side street where the cobblestones look old, worn and characterful, just like the surrounding buildings.

I picked my hotel almost purely for its location in the tourist-friendly neighbourhood of Baixa. It didn't look like a low-budget place on the website and I assumed it was a good deal because of the poor state of the Portuguese economy. But upon passing through the very modest doors into reception, it's immediately obvious that the Pensão Residencial Roma is really just a cheap hotel.

For some strange reason my large room has three single beds, each one tiny. At least with such a spacious room, I can scatter my junk everywhere and hang the "Do not disturb" sign on the door each day. The glow of a bright-red neon light outside the window could be a potential problem given my insomniac ways, but I fortunately still have the Qantas eye mask from the flight over.

The area around the hotel looks interesting, so I soon head out to explore. In under a minute I'm at the cross-section of the cobblestone streets again, where I'm offered hash by a local, who probably spotted me twenty minutes ago leaving the taxi. Looking directly into his eyes, I say, "No, not today, thanks." I've read that you're likely to get offered hash in Lisbon and there will be many more such offers in the days to follow.

Further down the street I enter Praça Dom Pedro IV Square, known locally as Rossio Square, which has been one of Lisbon's main squares since the Middle Ages. Its current name pays homage to Pedro IV, King of Portugal, who reigned over the country in the early nineteenth century.

A variety of charming little restaurants are dotted around Rossio Square. Each one has waiters out front, putting the hard sell on passers-by. The restaurants are very rustic and full of character; it's a great selection for the days ahead. So, on second thought, the hotel might be basic but it's also perfectly located.

Just off Rossio Square I come across a couple of Lisbon's famous port bars. Offering many different varieties of port, they have a very social atmosphere, with people standing out front sipping away, engaged in close conversation. As I head back towards the hotel, I see that the hash entrepreneur has moved on, to be replaced by a couple of policeman on the corner instead. They look quite laid-back, and not about to arrest anyone too soon. As I drift off to sleep, I reflect on how I have enjoyed my first taste of Portugal and look forward to the days ahead but am also aware of the ever-so-slightly depressing reality that my trip's days are now numbered.

The complimentary breakfast is in tune with the room price: very basic. From the hotel, it's almost a kilometre to Martim Moniz Square, where I'll catch Lisbon's famous Tram 28. A must-see in Lisbon, it takes visitors on an idiosyncratic forty-minute journey west, up and down steep, winding hills with amazing views and sights. The delightful *Remodelado* trams date from the 1930s and in any other city would probably be housed in a museum, but in Lisbon they are an integral part of the public transport network. With numerous tight turns and steep gradients, Tram 28's route would be completely unsuitable for modern vehicles.

The tram is really quite inefficient, however, covering only 5 kilometres as people hop on and off along its route through the oldest city in Western Europe. (Actually one of the oldest cities in the world, Lisbon predated other modern European capitals, such as London, Paris and Rome, by centuries.) Whether it's the polished wood panelling or bee-yellow paint job, the conveyance resembles a full-scale version of a collector's model. Old and a little gritty, it buzzes with character, much like the town of Lisbon itself.

The tram is supposed to depart every ten to fifteen minutes. I approach the long queue, made up mainly of tourists – families, couples and singles – with the odd local thrown in. However, the trams arrive intermittently: two or three in quick succession then none for a while.

My eyes light up when one of the distinctive yellow carriages enters the square diagonally opposite. At the front of the queue a few people push in, clearly thinking they are more important than the rest of us. Adopting a herd mentality, the waiting passengers push forward to counter this. As the tram pulls in, though, it's heartening to see the driver consciously cut off the cheats not in the queue proper.

The tram soon fills, with just as many passengers standing as sitting. The windows only extend up to about a metre high, which is less than ideal for those standing. I just miss the queue cut-off, luckily, so I'm now at the very front! Five minutes later another tram arrives, I pay the €2.85 fare and take my choice of seat. Everyone seems to pay cash while boarding, which is distinctly at odds with our modern Oyster card–style transportation. One benefit of being seated is that Tram 28 is notorious for pickpockets.

The tram jerks into motion, beginning its loud, rickety journey, taking passengers back in time to a completely different era. As it powers up and down seemingly random streets over hilly terrain, nothing seems to run in a straight line. Traditional shops and markets fly by the window.

The views tend to be fleeting, so I put away the camera for most of the trip and focus on the journey, watching people and their lives pass by, from the perspective of a guest in their town. On a couple of long, straight hills, though, I take out my camera, and risk leaning out of the tram to attempt a photo looking ahead to the front of the mini-locomotive.

Lisbon feels like a higgledy-piggledy place, where maps and smart phones would struggle to compete against sound local knowledge. I've no idea how far I've travelled, but I suddenly notice a popular tourist spot as we swing around a bend, with some cafes looking out over rustic rooftops to the Atlantic Ocean. It's a beautiful spot, perched high in the hills, and I impulsively decide to get off there.

I sit down for an espresso caffeine fix and reflect on the similarities between these trams and the cable cars I rode in San Francisco in the late 1990s. My memory may be hazy, but Lisbon's version seems a great deal more fun and ramshackle, and there's no need for the kind of tour guide they have in San Fran. Another yellow tram comes around the corner below the lookout and it looks grand taking the bend in all its old-world glory.

Still unsure exactly where I am, I board the next yellow Tram 28 west to its final destination in Campo de Ourique. The interesting views and sights continue and I notice a couple of shopping hotspots just before I disembark. I have a quick look around Campo de Ourique, but there's nothing much of interest to me there, so I buy a ticket back to where it all began at Martim Moniz Square. Full-day and multi-day Lisbon transport tickets are available, but I am not overly fussed about that.

After scanning my large paper map at Martim Moniz Square, I begin a short walk to Rossio Square. A smaller square gets my attention en route, the Praça da Figueira, or Square of the Fig Tree. A large bronze equestrian statue of King John I, which was inaugurated in 1971, juts magnificently out from one corner. The square was built after the destruction of Lisbon's great earthquake of 1755. The large area had been previously occupied by a hospital, before it was destroyed in the quake.

Taking place in the small square is a market selling a variety of interesting foods. The sun is extremely bright (even brighter than in Spain) and the temperature unseasonably warm. According to my watch it's *almost* high noon as I contemplate a stand selling draught beer for the bargain price of one euro. The "Super Bock" proves very refreshing accompanied by a Parma ham and strong cheese focaccia, the cheese literally melting in the sun.

Some charismatic young local men are very successfully selling the focaccias while complimenting or flirting with customers, depending on their gender. The square has a few tables with umbrellas and chairs for today's perfect beer-drinking weather.

At the next table to me, a vigorous discussion is going on. A female tourist is talking about austerity measures with a Portuguese couple, having seemingly been forced into conversation by the limited seating. The three of them seem to agree that the austerity is going too far.

The beer is refreshing and way too easy to drink, so another slips down in quick succession. The broad cross-section of tourists at the market provides anecdotal evidence that supports an article I'd read, which claimed that tourist numbers in Lisbon have picked up strongly in recent years.

A few hundred metres further on, I enter Rossio Square. It is a long, open rectangular square with stunning baroque fountains at each end. The ground surface is an elegant and wavy pattern of black and white mosaic, and the centrepiece column of Pedro IV rises a good

10 metres. Vibrant Rossio Square has been a famous setting throughout its history for popular revolts and celebrations, as well as executions and bullfights. It looks to be a protest hotspot too: an anti-austerity march is happening as I arrive.

A number of long, wide and parallel streets run from Rossio Square to the Tagus River, Lisbon's gateway to the Atlantic Ocean. The Tagus is the longest river on the Iberian Peninsula, flowing for over 1,000 kilometres from its source in Spain, and it enters the sea at Lisbon. Like many significant historical cities, Lisbon owes its importance largely to its strategic geographical position.

All these long streets have beautiful cobblestones underfoot, polished by age. Being so flat and grid-like the streets are also important routes for the city's trams, and perfect for a bit of "tramspotting", which could keep the mind occupied for many hours in Lisbon. The trams are a mix of old and new, in varying colours. None are quite as characterful as Tram 28, being generally more modern and utilitarian. With patience, I try for a perfect photo of multiple trams passing each other at the same time.

Even though I hail from Queensland, the sun in Lisbon seems incredibly bright. Two months in Europe may explain this phenomenon? Rue dos Sapateiros is lined with souvenir stores, where I buy some fake Rayban Wayfarer sunglasses for five euros. The street ends at my ultimate destination, the Praça do Comércio. This square on the river front, where arriving boats have docked throughout the city's history, is considered the "gateway to Lisbon". Like Rossio Square, Praça do Comércio has witnessed countless historic events, including the worst of Lisbon's 1755 earthquake and the fall of the monarchy in 1908. In the middle of the square stands its famous centrepiece, a triumphal statue of King José I, built in the wake of the devastating earthquake. Having seen photos online, I expected it to look magnificent, with the blue waters of the Tagus as a backdrop, but disappointingly it is surrounded by scaffolding and awaiting renovation.

All over the square, tourists are being taught to ride Segways by a local entrepreneur. I previously wondered about trying one on this trip, and this could be my last opportunity. But a tentative inquiry reveals that the deposit, for a single person like me, is roughly half the price of a brand-new Segway. Thinking of the potential for accidents on Lisbon's cobblestones, hills and alleyways, I decide against it.

In a prime position on one corner of the square is a stand selling port. The young man operating it seems knowledgeable and recommends a white port – a novelty to me – for five euros a cup.

Along one side of Praça do Comércio is a shaded area lined with popular cafes and restaurants. A curious sight amongst these eateries is a sign advertising a strange tourist attraction, "the world's sexiest toilet". It's good timing, as I need to go! Inside the small lobby, where there's some kind of toilet museum-thing happening, I say, "I'd like to use your toilet."

"The world's sexiest toilet" is large, clean and colourful, with plenty of posters and pictures on its walls. It's very good, but probably *not* the world's sexiest. Exiting, I tell the young lady at the counter, "Great toilet!" She notices my empty cup of port and informs me that I'd get a whole bottle of similar quality port for five euros at most liquor stores.

I head down to the river front, where an energetic one-man band juggles up to five instruments with military precision while singing. A supremely talented multitasker, he is soon well rewarded with some good tips. The riverside beach is a mere 10-metre strip of sand between a concrete bank and rocks, where a couple of groups of bikini-clad girls are taking the opportunity to sunbake.

In Lisbon's grid-like Baixa neighbourhood, I now walk away from the river up a long street parallel to one I came down an hour earlier. A port store called Manuel Tavares catches my eye, its windows filled with all kinds of varieties. After entering, I get chatting with the shop owners and am given a quick lesson on the different varieties and how to store them. I learn that expensive bottles can sell for thousands of euros. As with a winery tour back home, the lesson ends with a tasting. Afterwards, I exit, satisfied with a fifteen-euro bottle of white port. One negative with the white port, as explained to me, is that it needs to be refrigerated, and my meagre hotel room doesn't have a fridge.

It's now mid-afternoon. On my way back to the hotel, I discover a very popular port bar, where customers are standing outside chatting in groups, some even having a little dance. For some strange reason, it feels like I'm in Havana or Rio de Janeiro, though I've never been to either of those places. It just feels like a leap back in time, to the mid-twentieth century perhaps.

Sitting nearby the port bar, and in other spots around town, are groups of Afro-Portuguese. The Afro-Portuguese make up a small sub-culture of the Portuguese population and are mostly the descendants of people who came here from Portuguese colonies in Africa.

I then walk back to near the hotel, and at the same street corner as last night, I get offered hash again by my local drug dealer. Upon re-entering my room, I learn online that Manuel Tavares is actually a famous store, dating back to 1860 and considered one of Lisbon's top retailers of Portuguese wines. Apparently the branch I visited has a wine cellar downstairs, which is only opened for wealthy port connoisseurs prepared to part with thousands of euros for a bottle. Often in my years of travelling, I've found myself aimlessly wandering around cities without a map and somehow finding a landmark, shop or restaurant not in my guidebook, only to discover later that it's popular with locals and second-time visitors. Maybe I have a sixth sense that I don't know about.

Later I head out for dinner and select a clean-looking restaurant with its fair share of tourists and an Italian menu. Taking my order is a smiling young male waiter. Up high in the corner of the restaurant is a TV, currently showing Rafael Nadal playing live at his home away from home, Roland Garros. It's Rafa's Grand-Slam comeback after injury and the waiter can't help but constantly monitor the screen – obviously he's a fan of the great player. To the young man's credit, his service is friendly and efficient, but there's the occasional small fist pump each time Rafa wins a big point.

The food is great too, and it's a bonus for me, as a major tennis fan, to be able to watch a top-quality match on a big flat-screen TV at the same time. On leaving, I give the waiter a good tip. It's a universal truth, I think to myself, that no matter where you are in this world "boys will be boys".

Before I get back to the hotel, the local dealer offers me hash again, which I politely decline. Do I look like a pot smoker or does this guy just not discriminate?

I strike up a conversation with the learned-looking young man at the hotel reception, asking him how to get up to the famous fortress that overlooks the city, the Castelo de São Jorge. The steep hill does not look inviting.

"Just take a bus from the exact same spot as Tram 28," he says.

I mention to him something he told me this morning, assuming he'll remember. After a quick chuckle, he tells me I must have been talking to his twin. Apparently guests get confused all the time.

His friendly manner and excellent English encourage me to ask him what he thinks of today's big news story that José Mourinho, the self-proclaimed "special one" and famously difficult Portuguese coach, is leaving Real Madrid Football Club and returning to Chelsea in London. I am a little surprised to find that the young man is a big fan of José.

"People think he's arrogant," he says, "but, really, he just knows exactly what he wants and what he's doing as a football manager." He also tells me that José is popular with the Portuguese people in general.

I have to tell him – he'll love this story, I think – about one afternoon while I was living in London during the 2006 football World Cup, when Portugal knocked England out in the quarter-final play-offs. It was an interesting day around the pubs of Camden Town, which were packed with excited but nervy drinkers. Tension was in the air as I walked into a movie at the Camden Odeon, but when I came out of the cinema two hours later, the high street was a ghost town. It was immediately obvious that England had once again lost in a World Cup, disappointing an expectant nation.

The Castelo de São Jorge, Lisbon's magnificent Moorish castle, looks out over the city from a rocky outcrop, reminding me of Edinburgh Castle. It dates back to the eleventh century and the time of the Moors and has endured wars, changes of rulers and a history-defining earthquake, and has also been used to incarcerate convicts.

Boarding the morning bus at Martim Moniz Square, I notice the queue for Tram 28 is longer than yesterday. The small buses that run up to the castle have powerful engines, like those that serviced the Alhambra in Granada. There are plenty of keen walkers, though, their hearts and lungs pumping as they enjoy the challenging climb.

The castle is Lisbon's top tourist attraction, but the ticket line proves short. I am soon walking through the nineteenth-century entrance gate surmounted by Portugal's coat-of-arms and the name of Queen Maria II. Inside are the shaded main square and gardens of Praça d'Armas, with old cannons and a bronze statue of Alfonso Henriques, the Portuguese monarch who took the castle from the Moors.

The castle's gardens are shaded from Lisbon's endless sun by pine trees and provide a wide panorama over the city's rooftops. The uniform, rustic, orange skyline reminds me of the view of Florence I saw seven years back from the top of the Cathedral of Santa Maria del Fiore's iconic dome.

The vista towards the river is magnificent, with Lisbon's famous suspension bridge, the Pont 25 de Abril, looking deceptively familiar – it's often compared to San Francisco's Golden Gate Bridge. Indeed, the long red suspension design is very similar in style, and it was actually built by the American Bridge Company, which constructed San Francisco's Oakland Bay Bridge. However, it's still relatively young, having only been inaugurated in 1966.

The view encompasses all of the city's famous seven hills. Lisbon may be one of the oldest cities in the world but, on one inauspicious November morning in 1755, its past almost completely disintegrated, when an earthquake measuring 8.5–9 on the Richter Scale struck. The disaster killed up to 40,000 people and buildings collapsed like a house of cards. Eighty-five per cent of the city was destroyed and the death toll was devastating, considering the population at the time was in the two-hundred-thousands.

Lisbon's leaders swiftly set about reconstruction, pledging to "bury the dead and heal the living". Working with military engineers and architects, they rebuilt much of the city in what became known as the

Pombaline style, which incorporated early anti-seismic features. Mainly this involved using flexible wooden materials to provide a "shakes but doesn't fall" outcome in the event of another earthquake. Downtown Baixa, the area most affected by the 1755 quake, lay on particularly unstable ground and required special reinforcement – the buildings here sit on a forest of highly flexible buried poles.

The castle gardens are enjoyable, with their morphing views and surrounds, their intriguing ruins and colourful peacocks. They lead to the grandly preserved Tower of Ulysses. One of eleven towers in the castle, it once housed the Royal Treasury. It was nicknamed the Torre do Tombo, or "tumbling tower", as the most valuable treasures in the kingdom seemed to "tumble" into it.

A quaint little stone bridge crosses the remnants of a moat to the tower complex, with its robust stone walls, a great place to explore. The towers are built on a massive scale, much like the walls of the Alhambra's Alcazaba. Stone steps lead up to ramparts on all four sides. At each corner a guard tower provides a unique and unimpeded view of Lisbon. To reach the complex's highest point you have to climb a few narrow stone ladders; in the presence of fellow tourists, this requires patient and careful negotiation. At the summit, a large Portuguese flag waves imposingly in the wind.

Leaving the tower, I continue on to an archaeological dig in a quiet corner of the fortress. The archaeologists are working away, unearthing the remains of the city's first settlement, which dates back to around 800 BC. After watching them closely for a while, I can just make out the remains of Moorish dwellings.

Back towards the castle's main entrance, there's another, smaller garden inhabited by peacocks, as well as the Nucleo Museologico, a museum containing artefacts from throughout the castle's history. I have a quick look inside at the Iron Age pottery, Roman wine vessels, medieval oil lamps and coins.

Enjoying the walk *down* the hill, I search for the tram to my next destination, the UNESCO World Heritage–listed Jerónimos Monastery. This tram couldn't be more different to Tram 28; it's super modern and accelerates rapidly up to 60 kilometres an hour between stops.

After about ten minutes, I reach Lisbon's Belém district and the monastery. Founded in 1501, it is both enormous and ornate. Once populated by monks of the order of St Jerome, it became a school and orphanage after the order was dissolved in 1833.

Fifty metres short of the tourist entrance, the original main entrance is very grand and detailed, at 32 metres high and 12 metres wide and extending up two stories. I take a vertical photo that captures in detail the abundance of gables and pinnacles, with many carved figures standing out under various niches. They surround a statue of Henry the Navigator, standing on a pedestal between the two massive doors.

A different type of distraction near the entrance is a cool little restaurant inside an old tram that looks like it has simply been picked up and dumped outside the monastery. There are tables and chairs outside and overall it looks a bit like a typical American diner. And there are plenty of lunch goers.

The ticketed entrance leads into the main church, where tree-trunk columns run all the way along the nave and reach up to the ceiling. The best aspect is from the upper choir, looking down upon the rows of pews before the altar, flanked by walls adorned with stunning mural paintings. It's hauntingly dark inside and I take various shots of sunlight radiating through the beautiful stained-glass windows. A side chapel is graced with a circular stained-glass window, through which light pours onto Jesus on the cross, as if breathing new life into him before his resurrection.

Next on the tour is the central part of the monastery and its large square cloister. The open two-storey square has delicately sculptured arches and twisting turrets and columns, intertwined with carved leaves and vines. The four bays look out onto an open square, where two perfectly symmetrical, wide paths cross in the middle, with lush green grass covering the rest of the open area. Each bay rests on massive buttresses, and wide cloisters link the four corners on each side. The cloisters' inside walls bear a wealth of intricate motifs, an eclectic mix of different architectural styles.

Off one side are the chapter house and refectory. The large square chapter house room, with its elaborate wall decorations and art, contains the large and lonely tomb of famous Portuguese writer-historian Alexandre Herculano; it stands isolated in the centre of the room and people walk around and contemplate it.

After exploring more of Belém, I catch the superfast tram back to Rossio Square. The protests are still going on there, but it's a Sunday, so there's more of a carnival atmosphere. A popular photo subject for families and singles alike is a line of six life-size cardboard images of world leaders: Barrack Obama, Nicolas Sarkozy, Angela Merkel, Vladimir Putin, IMF CEO Christine Lagarde and a sleazy, smiling Silvio Berlusconi. Obama is the most popular, but Berlusconi is also a hit with a few Italian women, who pose while mimicking a kiss on his cheek. Nicholas Sarkozy is short, looking up like Napoleon at Merkel and Lagarde.

I revisit the smaller market square, where the Portuguese boys continue to flirt and carry on with customers while I buy another moreish ham and cheese panino. Being Sunday, all the shaded seats are taken, so I sit in the sun with my panino and beer, sweating profusely. After a shower and a kip back at the hotel, I go looking for a meal amongst the nearby restaurants, where touts compete for my business, offering free beverages and other such perks. While reading the menu of a tapas restaurant, I get offered a couple of free beers with dinner – a good enough sales pitch for me and my tourist euros this evening, I soon decide.

At 8 am in the morning, my train leaves Lisbon's Rossio station for the fifty-minute journey to Sintra. This small town is located on the edge of Sintra-Cascais Natural Park, which extends to the Atlantic Ocean at Europe's most westerly point of Cabo da Roca.

During my last week at work, I mentioned to a colleague that I was visiting Lisbon. "Make sure you visit Sintra," she quickly responded. On Google I found intriguing photos of unusual, fairy-tale palaces and ruins with incredible views towards the Atlantic. The Lonely Planet guide to Lisbon had Sintra in a page towards the end in its "Worth a Look" section; by today's end, this small reference will seem a travesty.

Another UNESCO World Heritage Site, Sintra is a major tourist attraction visited by many day-trippers from Lisbon and famous for its nineteenth-century romantic architecture. Based on online photos, it appeared to be mountainous with steep walks, and in places rather like the Great Wall of China. Thankfully, though, Sintra station has an excellent tourist centre, explaining exactly what to see and how to get there and fortunately it turns out that I won't have to hike up the "Great Wall of Sintra" after all.

The three must-sees, it seems, are Sintra National Palace, Pena National Palace and the Castelo dos Mouros (Castle of the Moors). It's a pleasant half-kilometre walk with fellow tourists to Sintra National Palace. From there, a bus takes pilgrims up to the castle and then on to Pena National Palace. My work colleague also took the well-worn path west to Cabo da Roca, a romantic spot for watching the sunset, but I decide it's a bit too far out of the way.

The Sintra region was occupied by the Romans from 49 BC and was also held by the Moors until the Reconquista in the ninth century. Sintra evolved into a kingdom in the twelfth century.

The Pena National Palace was built in the nineteenth century, while Sintra National Palace was inhabited more or less continuously from the early fifteenth century to the late nineteenth century. However, the Castle of the Moors dates back to the Moorish occupation of the eighth and ninth centuries, when it was a vital military stronghold. It was eventually re-taken by the Christian forces after the fall of Lisbon in 1147.

As I approach on foot, I can see the two highly distinctive white conical chimneys of Sintra National Palace standing out above the village's other buildings – a memorable feature that I remember looking at on my computer months prior. Dotted along the side of the road are twenty or so quirky sculptures, all very different, seemingly recent additions erected to beautify the walk.

At Sintra National Palace I buy a combined ticket to the palaces and castle. The beautiful main building is the best preserved medieval palace in all of Portugal. I explore its many rooms and courtyards with their interesting and varied Islamic architecture. Amazing azulejos (ceramic tiles) adorn the palace's many rooms, dating from the fourteenth to eighteenth centuries. In the large kitchen, I gaze directly up the 33-metre-high chimneys, which are a yellowish white, and can see bright sun coming in the narrow opening at the top.

From a western-facing balcony, I gaze out to the Atlantic Ocean, which looks like it is within walking distance, then, after exiting the palace, I spy the Castle of the Moors up high on the peaks above.

I board the bus for the castle. As it winds up steep hairpin bends, I'm hoping the engine is well maintained. After ten minutes the bus stops and the driver yells something in Portuguese to the passengers. No one seems sure whether this is the stop for the Castle, so a married couple yell "Castle here?"

"Yes, castle," the driver responds. The road is so steep that exiting at the wrong stop would be inadvisable.

A shop stands at the entrance to the castle walk, which runs between two large stones and then for half a kilometre to the castle proper. I'm soon looking up at the impressive structure.

"I'm gonna have a goddamn heart-attack. I'd rather be sitting around the pool with a beer," an elderly American complains to his wife in a John Wayne-like drawl. I myself am eager to start the climb.

Power-walking to a viewpoint, I easily reach my goal of what looked like the very top in about ten minutes. However, on arrival, I realise there's another peak up high in the distance, reached via an even longer climb. Taking a relaxing breather, I enjoy the spectacular sight of Sintra National Palace below and the perfect backdrop of the Atlantic Ocean behind thick ruined castle walls.

The American man didn't have a cardiac arrest after all, I see, as he and his wife join me at the viewpoint. However, his heart must have skipped a beat on seeing the next climb. They prove a friendly couple as they ask me to take their picture. They take mine as well before I'm off again, primed for the next challenge.

It's easy to see now how the images online looked like the Great Wall. The castle and its ramparts really resemble a miniature version of the famous Chinese structure, and with all sorts of views and perspectives available along the way, photos can be deceptive.

The view from the highest peak is spectacular and I can now see the fortifications in their entirety. In the opposite direction is the Pena National Palace, with its very distinctive and colourful architecture. I overhear someone say that on a clear day it can be seen from Lisbon, high on its hilltop position. I steady my camera for multiple shots of the castle walls with the Atlantic Ocean behind. Looking up, I see a couple of young women, to whom I apologise after getting in the way of their photography.

"No worries mate. You're right," say the clearly Aussie travellers. I could introduce myself but am too shy.

With plenty of time and no need to rush, I take in deep breaths while relaxing at the peak, without a care in the world, before the easy walk back to the shop at the entrance. The bus takes me on to Pena National Palace, where I face another steep climb to reach the palace foundations. A small mini-train supposedly leaves every twenty minutes and costs five euros, but it just sits there devoid of passengers, showing no sign of setting off. I notice a young Asian man with glasses, Japanese I think, say something that probably translates to "Oh, bugger it" as he begins the climb. It's the last of my stops today, so I follow, though not at the same energetic pace.

Up close, I can see that the base of the palace stands on solid rock foundations, *Lord of the Rings*–like, with the steep grey walls accentuating the vibrant colours of the palace above. The largest tower is canary yellow, topped off by a grey slate dome roof. Peering in through the ticket gate, I can see what appear to be other quirky and random towers to examine or climb in the palace. Once through the booth and onto the Queens Terrace, I'm able to admire the palace's overall architecture in all its beauty, detail, eccentricity and varied styles.

I walk through a couple of large rooms on the western, Atlantic-Ocean side. Obstructing potentially uninterrupted views of the ocean from the western terrace is a series of arches. I take photos that frame the arches, the blue ocean and the greenery of Sintra-Cascais Natural Park, which encompasses the 15 kilometres from the palace to Cabo da Roca. A couple of men arrive who take their photography very seriously, looking like real professionals as they set up expensive-looking camera equipment and a tripod. It is interesting to watch them go about their work for a short while.

Through the arches and down the western side of the rocky foundations is a striking pink tower, with an external high walkway curving around to the northern part of the palace. My natural instinct is to follow others around the tower just to see what's there. It's difficult to know what to expect in a quirky place like this!

Around the bend is a ledge that juts out from the palace, supporting a terrace made with thick blocks of stone – and waste-high rock barriers to prevent anyone falling to the depths below. When you walk out onto the ledge, the view opens up to the south and extends further over the Atlantic and to the north, while also encompassing the Moorish castle below.

Sharing the terrace are a couple of American women and their male friend. I take a photo of the two girls and they offer to do the same in return. They suggest I get a photo with a girl on each arm, to show off to mates back home. They are both quite attractive, so of course I agree to this.

Back inside are some of the palace bedrooms and bathrooms, and I imagine how special a place this would have been for its royal inhabitants hundreds of years ago. There are so many pieces of unique antique furniture, and the views through the windows are truly special. Half an hour later, I walk back down the hill to the bus stop. Behind the souvenir shop are a few plastic chairs at a simple bar, a good spot to rest my weary legs and have a couple of beers to take the edge off.

When I get off the bus, a train is leaving in literally twenty seconds. I sprint to get there in time and to avoid waiting half an hour for the next one. Mellowed by the beers, I listen to music through my earphones on the journey home. Sintra has definitely become the highlight of my time in Lisbon.

In the evening, sleeping proves difficult after the long and stimulating day and with the constant bright neon lights outside. Also not helping things, my Qantas eye cover has now broken; I'm surprised it lasted even *this* long. In a last-ditch attempt to knock myself out, I down half a bottle of port.

I sleep in with a hangover in the morning, eventually checking out right on the 11 am deadline. This evening involves a night train all the way back to Madrid. I'm not feeling well, so it's important to take it easy today.

After making the compulsory overnight train reservation at the station, I waste some hours at Starbucks, sipping a couple of coffees while making use of their free Wi-Fi. Unsurprisingly, there are many international visitors doing the same, making Skype calls back home and so on. I spend a couple of hours in the popular shopping area around Rossio Square. There are stores selling great little models of Lisbon trams, but I settle on a slightly tacky Tram 28 fridge magnet.

Now I'm in the twilight of my trip, many of life's everyday stresses are a distant memory. There's a melancholy setting in, though (perhaps exacerbated by my hangover), with the prospect of job hunting on my return, although I look forward to catching up with friends and family too.

At 5.30 pm I pick up my luggage and walk the few hundred metres to the metro, en route to Lisbon's main railway station. Of course, I get offered hash one last time by a new dealer on a different corner.

At the metro, the ticket machine instructions are all in Portuguese. Feeling unwell, I become confused and a little stressed. A ragged-looking man appears alongside me, gently asks my destination, then pushes three or four buttons to obtain the ticket, which I pay for with loose change. He tells me he's homeless and that any small donation would be greatly appreciated. His speech has some dignity about it and his actions have made my life easier, so I tip him two euros.

The overnight train is waiting at the platform and people are boarding to find their sleeper cabins. It's four to a cabin, so I'll be sharing with three others, and, as I open the door, three young Portuguese men greet me. They seem nice enough and, I soon suss out, are about to embark on a European holiday, but they speak absolutely no English. Initial greetings prove hard work and the language barrier almost insurmountable.

Through various methods of communication, I manage to gain a sketchy understanding of their itinerary as they reel off universally recognisable names such as Paris, Rome, Prague and Barcelona. I manage to convey that trains are a great way to travel – "up to 300 kilometres an hour!" We then have a good-hearted laugh at our communications difficulties before they head to the bar. They invite me to join them but, planning to knock myself out with a sleeping pill, I respectfully decline.

Nineteen

The Walled City of Toledo

After an uninterrupted and deep sleep, I wake in the familiar outskirts of Madrid, relieved that, from what I can tell, the boys didn't wake me with any drunken antics. They're still half asleep and hung over when I disembark and go looking for the next train south to Toledo.

Toledo is a hugely popular daytrip, thirty minutes south of Madrid. Having heard good things from people back home, I plan to spend my last night relaxing and sightseeing there, hoping to soak up some small-town Spanish life.

The first train is fully booked with day-trippers, so I miss out. An hour later, I join a queue with hundreds of others on their way to see what is often described as a miniature Rome. I get chatting to two middle-aged couples hailing from San Francisco. They prove quite interesting, as I'd expect from liberal and cultured San Fran, and they've loved their time in Spain. Having spent a while in the north, they tell me about a couple of places well worth a visit there.

I take my reserved seat for a "power nap" on the journey south. Upon arrival, there is heated competition for cabs at Toledo station. At the taxi rank are two rude young men who are pushing in front of an old woman, trying to steal the next taxi. Abruptly, I tell them to get in the queue, while hoping they're not prone to violence. My taxi takes me on a scenic route around the large walls that contain the compact town of Toledo then, once inside, along a few disorienting streets to my secluded hotel.

For my last night I've gone a bit more upmarket, a good decision considering my disappointing digs in Lisbon. The four-star Sercotel Pintor El Greco hotel provides some much-needed emotional comfort, as I'm dreading the long flight home via Dubai. It's a renovated old building, as is the case with many small hotels in Toledo. Inside is a lovely, quiet courtyard, and the staff at the front desk are friendly. My room is modern and spacious, with a small window looking over the medieval town.

After a quick shower I head out to explore. The young man at reception advises me to take a direct left from the hotel, while marking specific points of interest on a tourist map. He says that Toledo has a reputation for people getting easily lost in its labyrinthine streets. The walled city has many beautiful alleys that wind intricately up and down the side of the hill-town. These narrow streets are very much to my liking, and have a compactness reminiscent of the streets in Venice. Although there are many tourists, one redeeming feature for overnight visitors is that Toledo metamorphoses back into a typical small Spanish town after the hordes head back to Madrid on the trains.

Many souvenir shops are selling magnificent traditional medieval swords, and Toledo steel is world renowned. On display are pictures and video footage of *The Lord of the Rings* trilogy. I find a display explaining how the Romans turned Toledo into a major centre of weapons manufacture and metalwork two millennia ago. Known for being unusually hard, Toledo steel first came to the attention of Rome when it was used by Hannibal in the Punic Wars. Thereafter, Toledo became a reliable source of weaponry for Roman legions.

In the modern world, Toledo's fabled swords are bought mostly for decoration, but the manufacturers also supply the film industry with authentic weapons for fantasy epics such as *The Lord of the Rings* and *Game of Thrones*. There's also a plethora of Toledo "steel" jewellery. Retail trade seems very slow, however. I can't imagine it would be easy to import a sword back to your country of origin at the end of a Spanish holiday.

I find a great little shoe store selling typically stylish and colourful casual Spanish shoes. I'm so used to wearing the same styles of shoes constantly back home that a pair of these unusual grey leather shoes with blue soles is appealing. With their soft leather, they prove very comfortable, and there's fifty per cent off! I've got luggage space to spare, so I buy a pair and walk away very pleased with my purchase. Given all the shoe shopping I've seen throughout my time in Spain, one pair of shoes seems quite frugal.

Two main buildings in Toledo dominate the skyline, the Alcázar and Toledo Cathedral. The large church reflects the city's significance as a historic centre of Catholic Spain. The Moorish city was retaken in 1085 by Alfonso VI, the first breakthrough made by the combined kingdom of Leon-Castile during the Reconquista.

The unpredictable and confusing streets wind their way up towards the town's central square. Located just beneath the Alcázar, this open space is peppered with restaurants, cafes and ice-cream vendors.

With the sun beginning to set, I make my way back to the hotel, while looking for a spot to have dinner. Up to this point in my travels I've not yet tried Spain's famous paella dish, always being turned off by restaurant menu photos of a giant prawn stuck smack-bang in the centre of the dish. I soon find a restaurant that serves paella and offers a chicken version as well; there's no way I can turn this down.

While not quite as classic as the seafood variety, it proves very tasty and healthy to boot, with white rice, green vegetables, beans and seasoning. I'm certain that if I'd looked hard enough I would have discovered the chicken variety earlier, but the photo of the crustacean put me off every time. Not wanting to get lost, I retrace my steps along the streets I walked earlier to reach my hotel.

I wake in the morning well aware that my flight home from Madrid leaves this very evening. After an excellent breakfast, I make my way to Toledo's famous cathedral. One of three thirteenth-century High Gothic cathedrals in Spain, it's considered by some authorities to be the "magnum opus" – the country's best example of the Gothic style. Begun in 1226 and eventually finished in 1493 during the time of the Catholic Monarchs, it's as impressive as I expected, but not quite on a par with the unforgettable cathedral in Seville, though I'm sure my impression would be different if I'd visited Toledo before Seville.

One disappointment is that the audio tour is poorly marked out. I continually find myself looking at one feature but learning about a different feature in another part of the cathedral. I have to think outside the box to adapt to the tour and learn about the cathedral. It's like solving a puzzle.

Coming out of the cathedral late morning, I walk to the former Jewish quarter near my hotel. Like every other Spanish town on my trip, Toledo has an interesting Jewish district and, as in other parts of Spain, the bulk of the Jewish population was expelled by Christian rulers in 1492. The city was originally home to eleven synagogues but only one remains, the Synagogue of El Transito, which is extremely well preserved and architecturally impressive – a must-see for visitors. It's famous for its richly decorative stucco walls and its beauty is often compared to that of the Alcázar in Seville or the Nasrid Palaces of the Alhambra. It was originally the private synagogue of a notable and wealthy local family, whose patriarch defied traditional Jewish laws that prescribed that synagogues should be smaller and lower than churches and plain in decoration.

El Transito's walls are huge and ornamental, and covered with Hebrew inscriptions and quotations from the Psalms. There are also multifoil arches and an enormous panelled ceiling with Arabic inscriptions intertwined in its floral patterns. The large, rectangular room is mightily impressive. Visitors can walk outside the synagogue past the main altar and come back inside on the second level, from where the synagogue's detailed walls can be better appreciated.

Sentimentally, I think to myself that this is the last of so many beautiful historic buildings I'll see this time in Europe. It's a bit of a bleak feeling for an Australian, living in a two-hundred-year-old ex-British convict settlement, an architectural backwater in comparison. Nothing seems or feels old in Brisbane. The earliest structure in my home town is the convict-built Old Windmill in the inner-city suburb of Spring Hill, which was constructed in 1828.

Back at the hotel, I pack for the very last time, checking for any pocket knives or corkscrews or any other sharp objects that may have come into my possession since Seville. The pre-booked taxi arrives and I ask my driver to take the scenic route to the train station, crossing the Tagus River beyond the city walls for the ultimate view back towards the town. The vista, encompassing the whole of Toledo – wrapped by its magnificent walls, crowned by the Alcázar and hemmed by the Tagus – isn't done justice by the photos I've seen online. It's a magical note on which to finish, but it would be at its most beautiful at dusk, I imagine.

The taxi then proceeds to Toledo station. The short and relaxing stay here has been a fine way to round off my visit to Spain and my whole two-month adventure. On the train journey back to Madrid I flick through my thousand-plus photos from the last eight weeks, culling many while feeling a fondness for all the destinations, sights and activities I've been privileged to experience: the great Viennese palaces, Swiss mountains, Belgian chocolates and brews, Budapest's public baths, Singapore's Gardens by the Bay, new discoveries in London such as Kew Gardens, Paris's Moulin Rouge and Palace of Versailles, scenic train routes, Austrian Mozart experiences, Monte Carlo's casino, Seville Cathedral and the unexpected flamenco show, the mighty Alhambra and the Mezquita, and Sintra's fairy-tale palaces. Even the Luggage Nazi in Nice gets a dishonourable mention.

I reflect on the appeal of travelling in Continental Europe, where there are so many memorable sights. You never forget the first time you see the Eiffel Tower on the horizon or Rome's Colosseum, Switzerland's mountains or Spain's sun-blessed, vibrant beaches. Even though these places are already familiar to most of us, experiencing them in real life – places you've perhaps long dreamed of – is truly extraordinary.

However, Europe is much more than historic buildings and beautiful scenery. It's an exotic realm of myriad microcultures, languages and accents, with so much diversity in a relatively small area and the constant sense of a long history having been lived and living on. It's so very different to Australia. Seen from our antipodean ex-colonial nation, Europe seems like the centre of the world. Of course, as a visitor sticking to the main tourist areas, I may have been looking at the continent through rose-coloured glasses, steering clear, for example, of the effects of Spain's high unemployment, ignoring the impact of terrorism in France or Belgium.

Any melancholy I feel about all good things coming to an end is, however, replaced by fond memories. Travel can change your life, open your mind, make you more tolerant and appreciative of other cultures, put life back in perspective.

That evening, my Emirates plane will take off on the journey home via Dubai. As I endure the long, boring wait in Madrid Airport, I get to thinking: why not combine my enjoyment of travel with a long-held ambition to give writing a try? I am not the world's most passionate accountant. A career change, to something more creative like travel writing, has definite appeal, or it could just become a new hobby. Travelling in my own company, I have a vivid memory of the last two months. Why not give it a shot? I have nothing to lose here and I ponder this at the airport.

As the weeks pass by back in Brisbane, while waiting in frustration for recruitment consultants to return calls, I power up my laptop and type a thousand or so words at a time. I'm hoping I can build up some kind of discipline and momentum and keep this going. Can I make this fleeting idea a reality?

About the Author

New Zealand-born Angus Rich was raised and educated in Brisbane, Australia. He is a qualified CPA by profession, and has worked in various finance roles for nearly twenty years, including two years in London.

His real passion, however, is for travel and to share his experiences with others by writing about them. He is constantly searching for new discoveries and wonders. *A Man Abroad* is his first published book but if Angus has his way, it won't be his last.

www.ingramcontent.com/pod-product-compliance
Ingram Content Group UK Ltd.
Pitfield, Milton Keynes, MK11 3LW, UK
UKHW020144250726
13967UKWH00002B/847